THE ARCHAEOLOGY OF FOOD

The Archaeology of Food explains how archaeologists reconstruct what people ate, and how such reconstructions reveal ancient political struggles, religious practices, ethnic identities, gender norms, and more. Balancing deep research with accessible writing, Katheryn C. Twiss familiarizes readers with archaeological data, methods, and intellectual approaches as they explore topics ranging from urban commerce to military provisioning to ritual feasting. Along the way, Twiss examines a range of primary evidence, including Roman bars, Aztec statues, Philistine pig remains, Nubian cooking pots, Mississippian squash seeds, and the bones of a medieval king. Her book introduces both archaeologists and non-archaeologists to the study of prehistoric and historic foodways and illuminates how those foodways shaped and were shaped by past cultures.

Katheryn C. Twiss is an archaeologist who studies ancient foodways in order to learn about social structures in the prehistoric and early historic past. Her primary areas of expertise are southwest Asian prehistory, zooarchaeology, animal management and symbolism, and life in early farming communities. She co-headed the team studying animal remains at the well-known Neolithic site of Çatalhöyük in Turkey, and she is currently in charge of analyzing animal bones from the famed Mesopotamian site of Ur. She edited *The Archaeology of Food and Identity* (2007). She has published on topics ranging from feasting in early farming villages to Mesopotamian ceremonialism.

The Archaeology of Food

Identity, Politics, and Ideology in the Prehistoric and Historic Past

KATHERYN C. TWISS

Stony Brook University

CAMBRIDGE
UNIVERSITY PRESS

University Printing House, Cambridge CB2 8BS, United Kingdom

One Liberty Plaza, 20th Floor, New York, NY 10006, USA

477 Williamstown Road, Port Melbourne, VIC 3207, Australia

314–321, 3rd Floor, Plot 3, Splendor Forum, Jasola District Centre, New Delhi – 110025, India

79 Anson Road, #06–04/06, Singapore 079906

Cambridge University Press is part of the University of Cambridge.

It furthers the University's mission by disseminating knowledge in the pursuit of education, learning, and research at the highest international levels of excellence.

www.cambridge.org
Information on this title: www.cambridge.org/9781108474290
DOI: 10.1017/9781108670159

First published 2019

Printed in the United Kingdom by TJ International Ltd. Padstow Cornwall

A catalogue record for this publication is available from the British Library.

Library of Congress Cataloging-in-Publication Data
NAMES: Twiss, Katheryn C., author.
TITLE: The archaeology of food : identity, politics, and ideology in the prehistoric and historic past / Katheryn Twiss.
DESCRIPTION: Cambridge, United Kingdom ; New York, NY : Cambridge University Press, 2019. | Includes bibliographical references and index. | Summary: "The Archaeology of Food explains how archaeologists reconstruct what people ate, and how such reconstructions reveal ancient political struggles, religious practices, ethnic identities, gender norms, and more. Balancing deep research with accessible writing, Katheryn Twiss familiarizes readers with archaeological data, methods, and intellectual approaches as they explore topics ranging from urban commerce to military provisioning to ritual feasting. Along the way, Twiss examines a range of primary evidence, including Roman bars, Aztec statues, Philistine pig remains, Nubian cooking pots, Mississippian squash seeds, and the bones of a medieval king"– Provided by publisher.
IDENTIFIERS: LCCN 2019017863 | ISBN 9781108474290 (hardback : alk. paper) | ISBN 9781108464062 (pbk. : alk. paper)
SUBJECTS: LCSH: Food habits–History. | Food consumption–History. | Food–Social aspects–History. | Social archaeology.
CLASSIFICATION: LCC GN407 .T85 2019 | DDC 394.1/209–dc23
LC record available at https://lccn.loc.gov/2019017863

ISBN 978-1-108-47429-0 Hardback
ISBN 978-1-108-46406-2 Paperback

Contents

Contents

Figures

ix

Tables

Acknowledgments

This book has been immense fun to write. I am indebted to everyone who has helped make it so, from my colleagues at Stony Brook University to my editors at Cambridge University Press to my wonderful friends and family. I have loved spending two years immersed in the writings of my fellow food archaeologists (note to readers: there is far more terrific work out there than I could fit into this book!), and I extend to them my appreciation and admiration.

Several people donated images to the book: Jessica Pearson, Bonnie Clark, Elizabeth Stone, Katherine Kling, and Elvis Rakotomalala, thank you very much! Many more people donated time and energy. Barbara Voss, Amy Bogaard, Stuart Tyson Smith, Naomi Sykes, Kate Grillo, John Shea, Fred Grine, Carrie Wright, Cortni Borgerson, Melina Seabrook, and Jason Ur, your comments enabled me to make meaningful improvements to the text. I am sincerely grateful. Asya Graf and Beatrice Rehl, I appreciate your editorial time and talents. Kate Thompson and Sarah Mincer, your art consistently impresses me. Greta Charles and Eleanor Twiss, thank you for modeling and it was an absolute joy watching you in action. A mega-thank you to Sharon Pochron and Elizabeth T. Newman, for two years of comments and edits on I have no idea how many of my chapter drafts and revisions. It is a luxury to have you as my writing group partners. And thank you very much, Diane Gifford-Gonzalez, Nerissa Russell, and especially Christine Hastorf, for introducing me to the archaeology of food and mentoring me as I learned to love it. I have been and am extraordinarily fortunate in my teachers, my colleagues, my students, and my friends.

Mom, you taught me how to write. Dad, you taught me to make terrible jokes while doing so. Nora, you brighten my world. I love you more than I know how to say. This is for you.

CHAPTER 1

What Is Food, and Why Do Archaeologists Study It?

What do you want to know about the past? Do you wonder about family lives, or about international relations? Are you curious about ancient warfare, or about human sacrifice? Perhaps you're interested in the origins of private property? In prehistoric gender roles? Possibly you're fascinated by how ethnic identities develop, or by how members of a faith vary in religious observance? You will find all of those topics in this book, because you can investigate all of them via food.

As omnivores we human beings face a world full of potential edibles. Our intellectual and physical abilities expand our options still further, allowing us to alter nature's menus by growing, cooking, and combining foods. We thus have choices about what to eat, how to get it, how to prepare it, how to consume it, and how to discard it. The world is dauntingly full of options. Our responses are constrained by the ecologies in which we live, the technologies to which we have access, and the communities in which we live, but choices remain (e.g., Brumberg, 1988:164–188; Bynum, 1987). We make those choices not just in accordance with our economies but also with our politics and our faiths, our heritages and our ambitions. In doing so, we reinforce or challenge existing traditions – and we propel our cultures and civilizations onwards through time. Our foodways reflect our lives.

Our foodways also leave traces in the archaeological record. Plant and animal remains are still scattered throughout ancient neighborhoods and campgrounds. Human remains lie in graves and in dumps, their physical and chemical characteristics shaped by ancient diets and activity patterns. ("We are what we eat," after all.) Ovens, bars, and storage bins stand inside homes, palaces, and bars. Microscopic fat deposits remain in the walls of prehistoric cooking pots, and starches, proteins, and pollen linger in centuries-old dental plaque that no dentist scraped from someone's teeth.

We archaeologists have innumerable data sets with which to reconstruct past foodways – and thus to investigate past social as well as biological lives.

Much of the excitement we feel when studying ancient foodways lies in food's omnipresence, and thus its ability to testify to many different aspects of life. The chapters in this book delve into how archaeologists use food to explore economics, politics, faith, gender, ethnicity, and more. In each of these spheres, food plays an important role: who eats what, who avoids what, where does the food come from and where is it eaten, how does it get to the table, and in which dishes does it sit. Before we get to those explorations, however, I want to emphasize that food isn't just any substance that happens to get tangled up in various aspects of our lives. Food is arguably unique in its power to attract us and to move us, because we experience food physically, intellectually, and emotionally.

Food and the Senses

Gardening, grinding, cooking, dining, and virtually all other food-related activities stimulate multiple senses; eating involves all five simultaneously. Our interactions with food are not remote or coolly intellectual: when we eat our noses are filled with scent, our mouths with flavor, our hands with the warmth or chill of food or utensils, our ears with the sounds of chewing, our eyes with the sight of our meal and our dining companions. Harvesters sniff and feel the fruit to see if it is ripe, trying all the while not to prick themselves on its thorns or snag their clothes on its twigs. Cooks surround themselves and others with a wide variety of sounds, scents – and stinks. They crimp crusts and dye eggs to please the eye, before arranging their dishes on plain or on colorful platters. Eaters savor sweetness and pucker at tartness. Their mouths crunch into the cool crispness of a fresh apple, sip at the velvet smoothness of a cream-filled soup, and gnaw at the stringy chewiness of beef jerky. Heat from cooking fires warms bodies and homes; smoke from the same fires perfumes the air or sends people choking away, blinking to clear their eyes of its sting.

Food's constant stimulation of all five senses makes it deeply powerful. We record our food-related experiences not just in our rational brains, but in our feelings; our memories fill with pleasant and unpleasant sensations and the emotions that accompany them. These memories color our perceptions of current realities and our anticipations of future ones; the present "seems to 'hum' with memories of past words and past times" (Sutton, 2011:472). The taste of commercial macaroni and cheese resonates with laughter at Dad's kitchen table or with loneliness in the dorm room.

The smell of tomatoes in the sunshine summons happy picnic-dates or days of sweaty labor weeding the garden.

Foods thus 'hum' with social experiences and emotional associations. These associations are initially intensified and later called to mind by varied sensations. This is another reason that archaeologists and anthropologists (notably Hamilakis, 2008; Sutton, 2001, 2010) argue that food makes a particularly potent social tool or symbol. When cooks and hosts work to enhance meals' flavors, sounds, and settings, they please their guests – and they heighten the social and emotional impacts of their gatherings (Hamilakis, 2014; Hayden, 2014:12–14).

Time

> *When you ate buckwheat cakes in winter you thought of that hot July Fourth when it had been sown, "wet or dry." You smelled the bee-sweet odor of small white orchid-like flowers upheld on their stout, wine-colored stems and heard the hum of a million wings …*
> *Like God, you looked back upon your work and called it good.*
>   *Della Lutes, 1936: 175*

"[E]ating does not mark time, it creates it" (Hamilakis, 2008:15). "Dinner time" is not a set time of day that we recognize by eating a meal: it is whenever we choose to eat. The same goes for breakfast, lunch, and snack times. The social and cultural experiences that we associate with meal times, from setting the table with one's child through chatting with one's friends to washing the dishes with one's lover, occur when we decide we're going to eat.

When we make that decision, we do not simply punctuate our day and its schedule. Rather, we bring into the day both the past and the future, the memories 'humming' in the food on the table and the framework it provides for meals to come. We note that finishing the jam now leaves none for tomorrow morning; we eat yet another winter potato and dream of the asparagus and spring peas to come.

When we eat, therefore, we reach back into our pasts and project ourselves into our futures. In the present, our meals set the rhythms of our days. Specific foods are in our lives at specific times: oatmeal at breakfast, stew at dinner; water the vegetables at dawn, harvest the herbs after the sun has dried the dew. These foods cycle throughout the course of the year and shift through the generations. Each culture's food patterns maintain and repeat across the days, weeks, months, and years that make up people's experiences (Sutton, 2001).

Unusual eating events such as feasts or ritual meals disrupt our food rhythms, marking our mental calendars with occasions we may long remember and discuss (Hamilakis, 2008:16; Hastorf, 2015). The disruptions make people more aware of the routines from which they're diverging as well as of the highlighted nature of the special occasions.

Those occasions, meanwhile, reflect days and even months or years of planning and preparation (Dietler, 2001; Hastorf, 2016:196). Lavish meals are never isolated events; think of how much planning, shopping, cooking, and cleaning happen ahead of a family Thanksgiving, and how many years later people still remember what happened at that meal. (Roughly thirty-five years ago my grandmother accidentally baked the sink drain in the Thanksgiving turkey. I will still be talking about it thirty-five years from now.) That's one meal, attended by perhaps six to twenty people; imagine the time and saved-up resources required to stage a feast attended by hundreds or even thousands (e.g., O'Connor, 2015:58; Perodie, 2001; Sutton and Hammond, 1984).

More prosaically, food is enormously time-dependent (Halstead, 2014; Logan and Cruz, 2014; Parker Pearson, 2003; Stallibrass and Thomas, 2008b). Wild foods come into and go out of season; domesticated crops and herds require work at specific times of year and, in some cases, at specific ages. All foods take time to grow, and all perish if left uneaten for too long. Hunter-gatherers as well as farmers therefore store food. In prolonging their food's utility, they create deposits that memorialize past activities and assets and also promise future survival and perhaps success (Hendon, 2000:47). Regular withdrawals from these stores keep them, and their symbolic messages, ever-present in people's lives and thoughts (Hastorf, 2016:109).

Establishing the Topics at Hand

Let me now establish what this book is about. Words such as "food" and "feasting" have varying definitions. Obviously, you must know how I'm using them if you are to grasp the intended scope of this book as well as the implications of many of my statements. Please be aware that other authors do not necessarily embrace my preferred definitions.

Food

> . . . the local boys started to poke me and tease me about my obvious reluctance to eat a live bug.
>
> James Skibo (1999:95)

He was a bold man that first ate an oyster.

Jonathan Swift

Tell me what you eat, and I will tell you what you are.

Brillat-Savarin

What is food? For those of us interested in its cultural more than its biological importance, "nutrients" does not suffice. When we think and talk about our dinners, we talk about salad, not fiber and vitamins; sashimi, not proteins and lipids; spaghetti, not carbohydrates topped with antioxidants, vitamins, minerals, and monounsaturated fat. We punctuate our lives with meals and snacks, not with episodes of calorie and protein ingestion. We reject nutrients that our cultures deem unacceptable – no insects, dog meat, or human flesh for us – and we seek out items with no recognizable nutritional value (diet soda being the classic example).

This book focuses on what modern Westerners typically consider food: solid edibles. This is not a definition that all archaeologists use, and for valid reasons (Twiss, 2015). One problem is that the boundaries between "food" and "drink" are fuzzy at best. The same materials are often found in both food or beverages: any bin of wheat can become beer or bread, porridge or whiskey, depending only on how people prepare it (Dietler, 2006, 2007; McGovern, 2017). (Sometimes people bake bread specifically to use as an ingredient for beer. Thirty-eight hundred years ago, Sumerians hymned the beer goddess Ninkasi with "It is you who bake the beerbread in the oven. . ." [Black et al., 1998-].) Ethnographically documented farmers often turn 15 to 20 percent of the grain they raise into alcohol (Dietler, 2001:81). Alcoholic drinks are nutritionally important in some cultures, and many groups consider alcohol to be a form of food (Dietler, 2006). Even within a culture, individuals may disagree about the boundaries of "food": how do you classify a smoothie?

Likewise, in segregating the categories of "food" and "medicine" this book implies a distinction that rarely if ever exists. Across the world and through time people have eaten in order to achieve health aims: slimming down or fattening up, of course, but also clearing skin, easing digestion and excretion, healing pains and aches, and more. Moreover, substances that in one context are easily recognized as "food," in other circumstances are equally easily recognized as "medicines." For example, people sometimes use mustard to add zing to meals, and sometimes they mix it into poultices and plasters to smear on ill people's chests (McGuire, 2016).

This book nonetheless focuses on solid edibles for two reasons. First, there is an extensive and fascinating archaeological literature on drink that only partially overlaps with the archaeological literature on food (see Dietler, 2006; McGovern, 2009, 2017; Smith, 2008 for overviews). Second, a key feature of alcohol is that it can significantly alter the consciousness of its consumers. Because of this, alcohol – by *far* the most prominent subject in the archaeology of drink – is often used and valued differently from other consumables. People think about mind-altering substances in ways that they generally don't think about foods that can fill the belly and excite the tongue but not induce euphoria or suppress inhibitions. This is why other psychoactive drugs (e.g., mushrooms, betel, coca, San Pedro cactus, haoma; see Fitzpatrick, 2018; Guerra-Doce, 2015; O'Connor, 2015:67) are also beyond the scope of this book.

Even if the term is limited to solids, "food" is a culturally specific label. Dogs, horses, cats, and bugs have been or are cheerfully consumed in cultures across the globe, but most Brits and North Americans quail at the idea of even tasting any of these meats (MacClancy, 1993; Skibo, 1999). The same Brits and Americans eat beef, but that appalls Indian Hindus. Such Hindus enjoy tubers and root vegetables, though, which their Jain neighbors reject (MacClancy, 1993). Cultures also often see specific foods or food preparations as appropriate only for certain subsets of the population. Few healthy young American adults would even think of pureed chicken and green beans as a dinner option: such a meal is "baby food," and not for those whose teeth have fully emerged from their gums. Among the Hua, substances' edibility varies not only by age, gender, reproductive status, and ritual status, but also by the relationship between the eater and the person who produced and/or cooked the potential food item (Meigs, 1984). An unmarried youth may not eat white pandanus, for example, but a married man may – as long as it wasn't peeled, cut, tasted, or stepped over by his firstborn child (Meigs, 1984:151, 177).

Furthermore, within a culture the meaning of "food" changes through time. Today the American antipathy to eating horse meat is such that in 1998 Californians voted 59 percent to 41 percent to criminalize its sale for human consumption. (California Proposition 6 made a first offense a misdemeanor, and subsequent sales felonies. Selling horse meat for *dog* food remained entirely legal.) A mere half-century earlier, however, horse meat was accepted enough that the July 9, 1951 issue of the influential news magazine *Time* advised cooks preparing equine pot roasts to "remember that the meat tends to be sweet. More onions should be used and fewer carrots … In broiling horse fillets, spread some butter over the meat because it is lacking in fat." Such changes highlight the need to be cautious about identifying "food" in the archaeological record. Researchers cannot safely assume that the boundaries that they set around "food" are those that past people would also have set. They cannot presume that ancient people saw all non-toxic, digestible, potential nutrient sources as edible. They must remember that nutrient sources that they themselves don't eat – insects, amaranths, extinct herbs, and modern fodder crops – may have been seen as important foods (e.g., Fritz, 2007; Koerper and Kolls, 1999; Nymann, 2015; Sutton, 1995; Valamoti, 2017).

Feasting

A startlingly large proportion of the archaeological literature on food and foodways centers around feasting. Of the 630 food archaeology articles and books in this book's bibliography, 72 (11.4 percent) have "feast" or "feasting" in their titles; many, many more discuss it in-text. Given the obvious archaeological importance of feasting, one might expect that we would all know what feasting is: we'd share a working definition and ideally also a set of criteria for identifying feasting in the archaeological record.

One would be wrong. Not only do we not all agree on how to identify feasting archaeologically, we don't agree on what feasting actually *is*. Consider the work of the two archaeologists who are probably most widely associated with the topic, Professor Michael Dietler of the University of Chicago, and Professor Emeritus Brian Hayden of Simon Fraser University. Together they co-edited *Feasts: Archaeological and Ethnographic Perspectives* (2001), which is cited and beloved by archaeologists across the globe, and individually they have authored many, many other works that you will find in the bibliography of this book. Dietler and Hayden have been the two most prominent voices in the archaeology of feasting, and they have profoundly different perspectives on what feasts are and why they matter.

Dietler defines feasting as "a form of ritual activity centered on the communal consumption of food and drink" (Dietler, 2001:67, 2011: 180). Hayden defines feasting as "any sharing between two or more people of a meal featuring some special foods or unusual quantities of foods (i.e., foods or quantities not generally served at daily meals) hosted for a special purpose or occasion" (Hayden, 2014:8). Hayden[1] says that Dietler's

---

[1] I should note in the interests of full disclosure that Hayden clearly disagrees with my conception of feasting, having referred to "definitions proposed by some other authors" as "counterproductive," while citing only me and an unpublished conference paper. Specifically, Hayden (2014:8) argues that I (Twiss, 2012:8, 23) question the validity of distinguishing

definition has "problems of vagueness" and dislikes Dietler's requirement of ritual activity, arguing that he can't tell whether or not Dietler considers two-person meals feasts and that "for many people, tying consumption to rituals implies that feasting only occurs in religious contexts" (Hayden, 2014:8). Dietler, meanwhile, gently notes Hayden's "eccentric understanding of the nature of ritual" (Dietler, 2011: 180), explaining that rituals are simply activities that in some way are symbolically differentiated from normal, everyday life. (It is the norm in archaeology and anthropology to distinguish between ritual activity and religious belief [Hicks, 2010; Madgwick and Livarda, 2018; Swenson, 2015; see also Chapter 7].)

I wrote (Twiss, 2012:23) that "It is difficult to argue that a term ["feasting"] that covers all of these variants is of significant analytical utility (contra Dietler and Hayden 2001:3–4)." My point was – and is – that these ethnographically based definitions of "feasting" incorporate such a wide range of activities that the term itself isn't helping us understand what people were doing, why they were doing it, or how what they did impacted their lives. What is the analytical value of a word that refers to both a romantic anniversary dinner for two and a political fundraising dinner for two thousand? They have different purposes, different social implications, and different material signatures. All that the term "feast" is telling us is that the meal is "special" in some way (Twiss, 2015).

An additional complication is that "feast" is a word in widespread use, and it has clear meanings and associations for all English-speakers that do not match the definitions that we archaeologists keep trying to give it. The *Oxford English Dictionary* (www.OED.com, accessed May 25, 2018) says that a feast is: "a sumptuous meal or entertainment, given to a number of guests; a banquet, *esp.* of a more or less public nature.[. . . or] an unusually abundant and delicious meal . . ." A lot of food, and multiple guests: scale and luxury are what characterize feasts in lay English.

Scale and luxury are also what commonly characterize the feasts that appear in the archaeological literature (e.g., Hastorf, 2016:195; Mills, 2004; Peres, 2017; Pluckhahn et al., 2006; Potter and Ortman, 2004; Twiss, 2015). We most often identify feasting on the basis of big cooking or serving equipment or large collections of food remains, foods inferred to be

---

feasts from daily meals. As what I wrote (Twiss, 2012:8) is that "feasts are closely related to everyday meals in form as well as in meaning but are also consciously distinguished from those meals . . . the relationship is a complex one, and highly challenging to archaeologists who wish to avoid slighting either the links between domestic consumption and feasts, or the special, set-aside nature of those feasts," I politely reject his overall criticism.

delicacies, prestige goods, and valuable materials (e.g., Ben-Shlomo et al., 2009; Junker and Niziolek, 2010; Peres, 2017: table 2; Turkon, 2004:234). This is because we have to focus on practices that leave perceptible traces in the archaeological record, and large and elaborate events are far more visible (meaning archaeologically distinguishable from quotidian meals) than small, simple ones. On the limited number of occasions when small-scale feasts have been recognized, archaeologists have again cited the presence of ample, valued food remains and/or special vessels (e.g., Pluckhahn et al., 2006; Reinhart, 2015).

We are, I think, fighting an uphill battle when we attempt to redefine "feast" away from its common usage. Anthropologically justifiable as the alternative definitions may be, they match neither the familiar meaning of the word nor what we archaeologists primarily discuss. Using them requires students and laypeople to set aside what they know the word "feast" to mean in order to grasp our work. Using them also distances archaeologists from each other, since we don't agree on a single alternative definition. As multiple alternative definitions are currently in use, however, readers of the archaeological feasting literature must remain alert to each author's concept of his or her subject.

One more important point about "feasting" is that a culture's feasts – whatever they may be – are culinarily, stylistically, and symbolically related to other meals in that culture (Fletcher and Campbell, 2015; Hastorf, 2016; Hastorf and Weismantel, 2007; Joyce and Henderson, 2007; Potter and Ortman, 2004; Twiss, 2007, 2015; Van Keuren, 2004). People do not create wholly separate cuisines, manners, and social norms for feasts. Feast dishes, decorations, and drudgery (dishwashing duty!) may not be the same as those seen at everyday meals, but the two are in conversation with each other. Cultures where the genders habitually dine together don't segregate the men from the women, for example, and bread-centric cultures don't replace their baked goods with manioc or rice... *unless the feast is making a point of that change.* Everyday patterns may be scaled up or elaborated (more courses, more guests, fancier dishes, live music, special settings, special prayers), but they are not fundamentally changed without people recognizing the shifts and focusing on their differences from everyday practice. Whether a feast recapitulates day-in, day-out eating habits or whether it violates them, it is always referring to them.

Everyday meals refer constantly to feasts as well, as conversations are not one-sided. This resonance between different kinds of meals intensifies and extends the social messages each sends (Douglas, 1975). A group of women do the cooking for a religious feast, linking gendered behavior with faith; in cooking her husband his Tuesday lunch one of those women demonstrates her acceptance of the divine order of the world.

At present many archaeologists believe that it's time to increase research into daily food habits, which have received far less archaeological attention than has feasting (e.g., Peres, 2017; Pollock, 2015). These researchers point out, entirely accurately, that feasts represent only a small proportion of the meals people consume. If we archaeologists let unusual events dominate our discussions of ancient foodways, we miss much of the culinary "story," and we do so in a way that biases our understandings of the past. Feasts may make or ruin reputations, showily violate norms or transform local politics (see Chapter 5); many feasts bring people together who wouldn't normally socialize. Ordinary meals seldom do any of these things, and if they change rather than reproduce the status quo they do so gradually, not convulsively. Paying attention to daily meals also helps focus attention on domestic labor (which should loom large in our thinking about past economies) and on gender (Pollock, 2015). Women are consistently prominent in discussions of domestic foodways, but are often relegated to behind-the-scenes cooking or total invisibility in feasting reconstructions. Increasing numbers of archaeologists are answering this call with an explicit focus on daily cuisine.

Should we in fact discard "feasting" as a focus of archaeological research? There are certainly problems inherent in using a dichotomy of Feasts and Not Feasts to discuss past meals, as most of us do. Many societies stop at multiple points along the continuum from simple family meals to over-the-top celebrations attended by hundreds. If rural Greek weekday dinners aren't feasts, and Easter and wedding dinners are, what is the proper classification of Sunday dinners, where a handful of friends and relatives may join a family as they dine on pie or chicken as well as standard fare (e.g., Halstead, 2015)? Are these meals feasts, or not? Researchers (and diners) can reasonably disagree, and subjectivity is unavoidable in the decision-making.

Most archaeologists nonetheless prefer to keep discussing "feasts" and "daily meals" as opposed to variously large and elaborate episodes of food-sharing. Our argument is that feasts are qualitatively, not just quantitatively, distinguished from everyday meals. Symbolically differentiated from normal practices, their contents and social meanings resonate with but are not limited to those of the quotidian table. We may struggle to determine which of the past meals we've identified were feasts, and which were not, but as long as we are open about the criteria and the models that we're using to decide, we are acting justifiably. Interpretive challenges are not reasons to discard ideas.

We have now established that archaeologists use a variety of definitions for both food and feasting. Even more variability exists in how we choose to study these topics: the perspectives we adopt, the assumptions we bring to bear, and the goals we pursue. The following section briefly characterizes what I consider to be the two main schools of thought in the archaeology of food: (a) behavioral ecological perspectives that discuss foods as sources of nutrients evaluated according to the energetic costs of their acquisition and processing, and (b) social perspectives that focus on how food shapes and is shaped by cultures.

Archaeological Approaches to Food

Ancient subsistence practices have long been of interest to archaeologists (e.g., Childe, 1928; Pumpelly, 1908). Dietary research really took off, however, in the middle of the twentieth century, with the rise of palaeo-economic and processual archaeology. Both theoretical and methodo-logical advances enabled the blossoming of dietary studies. A rising focus on human adaptation to the environment brought with it more and more interest in the biological and evolutionary aspects of the human experi-ence – emphatically including how and why people developed the subsist-ence strategies that they did. Tremendous improvements in recovery methods meant that plant and animal remains were regularly available for investigating ancient subsistence practices. The result was many studies in the 1970s and 1980s seeking: (a) to reconstruct which species prehistoric people were eating and how they acquired them; (b) to explain how those dietary choices helped humans adapt to their local environments; and (c) to evaluate the demographic, technological, and political ramifications of those choices (e.g., Dennell, 1979; Earle and Christenson, 1980; Jochim, 1976; Keene, 1985; Wing, 1978; Wing and Brown, 1979). These studies discussed food as a source of nutrients, required by humans (and hominins) for survival, health, and reproduction.

Receiving far less attention at the time was a comparatively small group of archaeologists developing a very different kind of food archaeology. Historical archaeologists never embraced adaptive perspectives as prehistor-ians did. The resistance was particularly pronounced among those who studied relatively recent and/or historically well-documented cultures. Researchers studying eighteenth-century battlefields and nineteenth-century neighborhoods saw little use in working toward cross-cultural generalizations about human adaptation. As archaeological recovery methods improved and food became an increasingly prominent topic of discussion, these scholars discussed how people's diets related to their social and political situations (e.g., Crader, 1984; Ijzereef, 1989; Langenwalter, 1980; Olsen, 1964; Schulz and Gust, 1983).

Archaeological interest in specific cultures and the varied groups that exist therein blossomed during the 1980s. Researchers working in prehistoric as well as historic contexts were talking about gender, about ethnicity, about symbolism and the importance of belief. As the 1980s moved into the 1990s, the archaeology of food tracked these developments. Seminal papers used food data to discuss the effects of Inka rule on women's labor and political participation (Hastorf, 1991), status distinctions between enslaved people at Monticello (Crader, 1990), Aztec labor demands (Brumfiel, 1991), Mississippian politicking (Blitz, 1993), and more.

The two strands of research – the adaptive and the social – both thrived as the archaeology of food expanded gradually during the 1990s and then exponentially after 2000. Today each approach has its own sizable literature, and while researchers embracing one perspective certainly read and appreciate studies following the other, meaningful differences continue to exist between the two.

Many archaeologists employ models derived from human behavioral ecology (HBE). These approaches are generally characterized by cost (generally measured as units of time) vs. benefit (typically calorie and/or protein gain) analyses. Archaeologists employing these approaches posit that past people aimed to maximize their nutritional benefit at the least possible cost. They use this proposition to model ancient foragers' or farmers' most adaptive sets of food behaviors, or as a premise for evaluating ancient settlement systems, technologies, and other developments (e.g., Allen et al., 2016; Elston et al., 2014; O'Connell and Allen, 2012; Stevens and McElreath, 2015; Tremayne and Winterhalder, 2017; Winterhalder et al., 2015). These archaeologists assume that if one knows the search and processing times of various food resources, as well as their nutritional benefits, encounter rates, and reliable availability, one can model microeconomically rational diets for populations of interest.

Modeling microeconomically rational diets generates expectations about what people would eat if they were guided by certain clearly stated principles. Archaeologists can then compare the modeled diets to the floral and faunal remains found in the archaeological record. Doing so allows us to evaluate the extent to which economic rationales drove ancient humans' behavior, as opposed to culturally specific norms (Bettinger, 1991:106; Gremillion, 2015). Optimization models, in other words, identify the dietary choices that ancient people would have made if they were expending as little effort as possible in order to consume as much food (calories and/or protein) as possible. Testing may then reveal that ancient people actually made choices quite different from those identified by the models; when archaeologists find such differences, we can infer that factors other than nutritional net profits shaped how people ate.

Socially oriented food archaeologists focus on exploring those factors: the power relationships, gender norms, and religious beliefs shaping decisions about food; the values different people assign to different foods; and the impacts that foodways have on specific groups' beliefs, politics, and identities. They investigate the ways in which minimizing cost is not everyone's goal, excited by the fact that sometimes people actually seek out foods *because* they are expensive (Gumerman, 1997; Hastorf, 2016). They investigate social motives for economic decisions, discussing how people use food to pay rent, to tithe, to offer tribute, and to dower children, adjusting their food production and consumption in accordance with non-negotiable social requirements (Morehart and de Lucia, 2015). Socially oriented food archaeology focuses on how, within the bounds of feasibility, culture (mediated by individual taste) is the arbiter of what and how people eat.

The two schools of thought are characterized by differences in (a) scale of analytical interest; (b) time periods of interest; and (c) personal taste. Starting at the end of this list: quite simply, different approaches engage different archaeologists. Some people like to study Australia and others Central Africa; some espouse behavioral ecology and others prefer more interpretive approaches (e.g., Bruno and Sayre, 2017:4).

As for (b), picture a timeline reaching from the advent of *Homo sapiens sapiens* on the left to the modern era on the right (Figure 1.1). If we

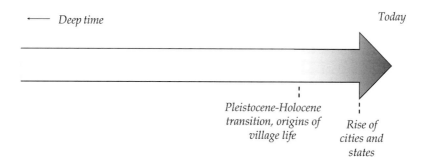

FIGURE 1.1. Timeline showing how archaeologists working in different time periods tend to have different theoretical perspectives on food. White = perspectives derived from human behavioral ecology; black = social perspectives.

picture HBE studies as white, and socially oriented studies as black, the archaeological food literature will map onto this timeline as a long pale smear that shades abruptly into gray around the time that the Pleistocene yields to the Holocene (ten thousand years ago; the earliest settled villages). For the next five thousand years or so, this gray gradually deepens, until another gush of dark color turns the line a rich charcoal hue. (If you split the timeline geographically at this point, areas with cities and states such as Egypt and Mesopotamia would be almost pure black, and areas with foraging populations such as eastern Africa, the Americas, and Australia would remain almost pure white.) From then the line becomes darker and darker in tandem with the spread of sedentism and literacy. It ends with an abrupt return to medium gray in the ethnoarchaeological literature.

The key to this series of color changes, in my opinion, is data availability. How does one link a Paleolithic campsite's sparse stones and bones to status distinctions within the band – or bands, since Pleistocene assemblages are hard to date precisely and often reflect generations of site use and reuse? It's not possible if one wishes to rely more on data than on speculation. At the other extreme, a Babylonian, Roman, or American colonial city affords you not only ample food remains but architectural, artifactual, and often textual data with which to contextualize them. It's easy in such contexts to study social variability and strategies.

As for (a) scale, HBE approaches focus on long-term processes that encompass entire populations. Socially oriented approaches tend to emphasize differences within populations. A few studies even narrow their focus so tightly that they discuss individual people rather than groups of any size (e.g, Lamb et al., 2014). Socially oriented food papers often view society as made up of individuals who strategize and act according to their personal experiences and goals. (In archaeological theory terms, these papers embrace agency and practice.) They emphasize that societies (a) encompass differences of opinion and action, and (b) change when people alter what they're doing. The fit with an interest in intra-cultural variability is obvious. Perhaps less immediately obvious is a focus on everyday food habits: how people farmed, cooked, and ate as they went about their normal lives. Agency- and practice-driven papers commonly explore the politics, symbolism, and gender and identity implications of daily labor and mundane family meals more than special events and feasts (e.g., Atalay and Hastorf, 2006; Hastorf, 2012; Pezzarossi et al., 2012; Pollock, 2015; Rodrí-guez-Alegría, 2005; Russell and Bogaard, 2010; van der Veen, 2014; although see Graff 2018; Hastorf, 2015; Potter, 2010).

Some socially oriented papers address the physical experience of food as well: "food and the senses," as described earlier in this chapter. Archaeologists interested in how people physically experience food do not claim that we can recreate ancient perceptions. Modern plants and animals don't necessarily taste or smell the same as ancient ones – they have different genetics, different diets, and different habitats – plus our own bodies and frames of reference are not those of our ancestors (Hamilakis, 2008; Parker Pearson, 2003). The focus is rather on the range and diversity of ancient sensory experiences, and on their social implications: the ways in which tastes, sounds, smells, sights, and touches enhanced, muted, or changed the messages and feelings that people brought away from their meals and other food-related activities (Beaudry, 2013; Hamilakis, 2008; Hamilakis and Sherratt, 2012; Hastorf, 2016; Robb, 2007:155).

No one denies that humans live in their environments: indeed, many socially oriented researchers explicitly focus on the interactions of ecology and society (e.g., Bruno and Sayre, 2017; Morehart and Morell-Hart, 2015). No one denies that humans have economic and political agendas that they use food to pursue: it's not hard to find HBE-oriented scholars discussing these topics (e.g., Gremillion, 2011; Lupo and Schmitt, 2016). At the same time, the two schools of thought have significantly divergent interests and goals: human adaptation (in the sense of natural selection) versus human history and experiences.

I affiliate myself with the social archaeology of food. This book concentrates on topics such as politics, gender, ethnicity, and faith. I am fully aware that ecologies and technologies constrain options, and I acknowledge that when people acquire, prepare, eat, and excrete food they are expressing and shaping themselves as biological organisms. In this book, however, I focus on how they are likewise doing so as social actors.

Things to Keep in Mind When Studying Food in the Past

What do we need to know in order to understand or to practice food archaeology? Ideally, of course, we must grasp at least the basics of numerous methodologies (see Chapter 2). There are, however, broader concerns that archaeologists must always keep in mind as we explore ancient foodways (see also Twiss, 2012, 2015).

First, an interpretation is only as good as its underlying data. *Pay attention to context and to the character of the sample.* With regards to context, the key issue is whether or not we can reasonably link remains to the activities we wish to investigate. Imagine, for example, an article based on food remains found "in an oven." Were those remains on the floor of the oven, and so plausibly left there at the time the oven went out of service? Or were they floating high up in the soil that filled the oven, and probably just part of the room fill that happened to end up there? The two possibilities have profoundly different interpretive implications. Food remains are archaeologically ubiquitous. They filter from the locations in which people originally deposited them throughout entire settlements. We recover seeds, bone fragments, pollen and phytoliths from middens and from mudbricks, from graves and from gardens. It is vitally important that we be alert to the extent to which food remains' *discovery* locations represent their *use* locations: where they were prepared, eaten, or discarded.

Sample sizes are also crucial, as is the amount of time that each sample represents (i.e., the duration of its deposition). Imagine you're interested in dietary variety in the past, or in food taboos. There were no pig remains in that assemblage! These people ate only three kinds of animals! Both statements are far more meaningful if you're looking at five thousand bones than if you're looking at fifty. And how long did it take for your assemblage to be deposited? A species may be consumed enthusiastically for one season every year and remain otherwise absent from community tables. It may be eaten regularly by one generation and scorned by the next. Consider that in the 1950s Americans periodically ate horsemeat but largely ignored "Chilean sea bass" (i.e., Patagonian toothfish). By the 2000s, norms had shifted and the converse was true. A faunal assemblage that spans that sixty-year period may well contain both species; a similarly sized assemblage that spans only one decade probably does not.

Finally, recovery methods matter. We cannot determine which meats people ate if all we have are animal bones that excavators picked out of the soil by hand. Study after study shows that hand-picking biases assemblages toward large animals (Reitz and Wing, 2008:147–150): we end up seeing plenty of beef and little if any rabbit or duck. Even medium-sized animals like sheep and goats – dietary mainstays across continents and cultures – end up significantly underrepresented (e.g., Russell et al., 2005). Soils must be screened and samples floated (Pearsall, 2015:81–95; Reitz and Wing, 2008:147–151) if we wish to see a site's plant and animal assemblages in anything approaching their true proportions. Organic residues, phytoliths, pollen, and other microremains require other forms of sampling for adequate recovery (Pearsall, 2015). It takes good data to produce good interpretations.

Food is socially ubiquitous. It threads throughout society, knotting together economic strategies, political negotiations, ethnic and gender identities, religious beliefs, and more. Food is also physically ubiquitous. Virtually all aspects of material culture bear direct and indirect traces of foodways. Because no one data set testifies to the entirety of how people ate, archaeologists must employ varied evidence in order to understand past foodways. Let us proceed now to Chapter 2 for a survey of data sets and methods that feature prominently in the archaeology of food.

How Do Archaeologists Study Food?

Data Sets and Methods

Archaeologists use a wide variety of data sets and methods to investigate past food practices. This chapter explains how archaeologists use plant, animal, and human remains as well as architecture, artifacts, and landscapes to reconstruct how people in the past foraged, farmed, cooked, and ate. It discusses what each archaeological method can and cannot reveal about ancient foodways and highlights the complementarity of different data sets.

It is important to note that certain kinds of data cross-cut the subheading categories below. For example, the fats that have soaked into the walls of ceramic pots derive from the plant and animal foods that those pots once held, so they could be considered plant or animal remains. Instead, this chapter discusses them under the general heading of organic residues, because such residues are extracted and studied using broadly similar techniques no matter their foods of origin. None of the subheadings below is comprehensive; as is always the case in archaeology, data sets intermingle and overlap.

Data sets also always require interpretation. A pile of animal bones on a table is just a pile of bones on a table. We can assign those bones to particular kinds of animals, and describe the marks on the bones, but then what we have are lists and descriptions, not understandings of how ancient people cooked and ate. Cut mark descriptions, chemical signature reports, and species lists don't leap up and tell us "this is what I mean with regards to how people ate!" We have to consciously link such data to actual human behavior; we have to build a bridge from our tables and graphs to ancient people's habits and preferences.

We do this in a variety of ways, all of which at their bases involve matching the archaeological data with similar-looking data derived from a known activity or activities. That pile of bones, with cut marks across the ends of their shafts but none in the middle of the shafts? That pattern of cut marks matches the pattern modern peoples have left when they were dismembering an animal. It doesn't match the pattern that they create when they're cutting raw meat off the bones for drying or smoking, and it doesn't match the pattern that they create when they're scraping soft tissues off the bones so that they can break the bones cleanly and suck out their fatty marrow. We therefore infer that the bones on our table are the remains of animals that ancient people dismembered.

We also may note that modern people sometimes dismember animals to make carrying them easier. It's hard to carry a whole deer home; a deer leg is comparatively manageable. Could this be why ancient people cut apart the animals whose remains lie on the table? We can examine this by comparing the specific bones present with the kinds of bone assemblages that modern people produce when hauling around cut-up animals. Modern hunters often find meaty torsos and legs worth carrying home, but not bony feet and heavy heads; we can see if this pattern matches what we see on the table or not.

Archaeologists commonly look for matches with ethnographic, ethnohistoric, ethnoarchaeological, and/or experimental data. Matches are not guarantees: two different activities can produce very similar patterns. Moreover, some ancient peoples surely lived in ways that have no modern equivalents for us to examine. Human history is broad and deep, and very few modern people live in ways even vaguely close to those that dominate our past. Foraging cultures are very few, and everyone everywhere has been touched by Western civilization. (The very existence of an ethnography proves that the documented culture has been in close contact with at least one Western-educated person!) Finally, we archaeologists have no way of conclusively proving that we've made an accurate match. This is why we talk in terms of stronger and weaker analogies: robust correspondences based on multiple lines of evidence, versus flimsier ones that rest on modest resemblances between single data sets.

Botanical Remains

The analysis of plant remains from archaeological sites is called paleoethnobotany in North America and archaeobotany in Britain. Macrobotanical remains – seeds, pods, cobs, and other fragments visible to the naked eye – are typically recovered via flotation and identified by visual comparison with modern specimens. Microbotanical remains – pollens, phytoliths, starches – normally require laboratory processing to be extracted from the soil.

Most parts of most plants don't survive well in the archaeological record. Picture the plant foods that you've eaten recently tossed instead into an outdoor dump, and imagine what would remain of them after a week, a month, a year, a century, or a millennium. In almost all environments soft and seedless produce such as potatoes, bananas, carrots, mushrooms, and salad greens would vanish, or leave only microscopic traces. Hard plant parts such as seeds, chaff, and wood might persist, but in most environments they survive only if charred.

They also, of course, need to have escaped being eaten, which is the normal destiny for edible plant parts. Edible plant remains enter the archaeological record in bulk only on special occasions such as when there has been an accident (e.g., a fire) or a ceremony (e.g., an offering). In contrast, people regularly discard large quantities of inedible plant parts such as chaff, twigs, and weeds. This means that most of the plant remains in the archaeological record represent inedible plants and plant parts rather than what people were actually eating. Fortunately, many inedible remains provide indirect evidence of plant foods. The weeds that people accidentally bring home grow in the same environments as the plant foods they were trying to retrieve; the bits of chaff and twig are the same species as the grains from which people were trying to clean them.

Even more fortunately, people simply eat so many plant foods that despite the many, many factors working against them, the archaeological record is full of edible as well as inedible plant remains. Paleoethnobotanists recover thousands upon thousands of seeds at sites across much of the world, as well as nuts, acorns, legumes, cobs, and other traces of humanity's staple foods. The shapes and sizes of these remains commonly reveal whether they were gathered or harvested (Pearsall, 2015: 136), and sometimes they are damaged in ways that researchers can attribute to specific processing or cooking methods (e.g., Heiss et al., 2017; Valamoti et al., 2011). By examining the anatomical parts in a deposit paleoethnobotanists can tell where barley was winnowed and whether maize was stored as whole cobs or shucked. They can tell whether bread was white or whole wheat, and if they measure the size of its grain, bran, and chaff fragments, whether its flour was thoroughly or haphazardly sifted (González Carretero et al., 2017; Heiss et al., 2017). (Wonderfully, some ancient cooking traditions actually improved plant remains' ability to survive in identifiable forms: archaeobotanists owe a debt of gratitude to the Maya and Aztecs who boiled their maize kernels in wood ash or lime [VanDerwarker et al., 2016].)

Botanical remains thus testify not only to what plants people were eating, but also to how they prepared those plants. One must remain aware, however, that: (a) some plant species are more visible in the archaeological record than others; (b) even the visible species are wildly underrepresented compared to their original presence at a site; (c) ancient cooking choices shape recovered assemblages; and, as previously stated, (d) inedible plant parts dominate the paleoethnobotanical record. The proportions of plant remains found at a site do not approximate their original proportions in ancient human diets. (If you want to reconstruct those, stable isotope analysis is commonly your best bet.) Many plant remains may also relate to activities other than human consumption, such as ceramics tempering, mat weaving, and animal foddering. (It's hard to imagine a more effective way to deposit large quantities of charred plant remains than burning dung – which was, of course, the default fuel source for many past peoples.) Virtually all of a site's botanical remains tell us what plants were *available* there: only plants found in human gut contents and paleofeces are guaranteed to reflect what people actually ate (Riehl, 2015). (Dental calculus reveals what people were putting in their mouths, but we don't necessarily swallow what we chew. Around the world people spit out tobacco, areca (betel) nuts, qat, and more. See also *Dental Calculus, Microbiomes, and Proteins*.)

Paleoethnobotanists identify macrobotanical remains such as chickpeas, rice grains, maize kernels, and berry seeds by comparing the shapes of the archaeological finds with the shapes of modern peas, grains, seeds, etc. They usually do this with a microscope set on relatively low-level magnification. Higher-magnification settings are required to match pollen grains, starches, and phytoliths ("plant stones": tiny silica deposits that develop inside and between cells in some plants) with their modern relatives. Pollen grains, starch granules, and phytoliths commonly preserve far better than macrobotanical remains do, not requiring charring or waterlogging to survive. (This is how researchers explore topics such as Neanderthal plant exploitation [e.g., Henry et al., 2014; Madella et al., 2002], and recover plant parts and foods that don't normally survive charring [Barton and Torrence, 2015; Ryan, 2014]). Moreover, they are small enough that researchers recover them not only from standard soil deposits and ancient feces but also from tool and vessel surfaces – where they reflect what people were *doing* with food, not just what food items they had available – as well as from the calculus that builds up on people's teeth (Barton and Torrence, 2015; Piperno, 2006:98–100). Phytoliths also provide information about ancient growing conditions (i.e., how well-watered the plants were), and can be subjected to stable isotopic analyses (see below).

Microbotanical remains do pose challenges for archaeologists determined to reconstruct ancient diets. Pollen travels – potentially for miles –
and its presence at a site may or may not reflect human actions. Starches
can likewise be airborne, and protocols for avoiding starch contamination
are still being established (Crowther et al., 2014; Mercader et al., 2017).
Heat, moisture, and processing damage starch granules in recognizable
ways. This may be wonderfully informative if the damage derives from
ancient cookery, or alarmingly mis-informative if it derives from accidental
heating or soaking; experiments to help researchers differentiate between
these possibilities are ongoing (Barton and Torrence, 2015; Collins and
Copeland, 2011; Crowther et al., 2014). Phytoliths are not produced by all
food plants (pity researchers wanting to study cassava!), or in all plant parts
(e.g., underground storage organs such as carrots and potatoes – fortunately, they're rich in starch), and species identification can be tricky
(Piperno, 2006:15–20; Ryan, 2014; Shillito, 2013).

Faunal Remains

Animal remains provide tremendous amounts of information about ancient
food habits because they often preserve and because they can be examined
in many different ways (Reitz and Wing, 2008). Zooarchaeologists (or
archaeozoologists, or faunal analysts) only begin by identifying which body
parts of which species are present. That information is excellently useful,
but it doesn't reveal how people hunted or herded their food animals; bone
maturation and tooth eruption patterns reflect that. It doesn't reveal how
people butchered the animals; bone fragments' shapes, sizes, and surface
markings can do this. It doesn't reveal how people cooked their meat
(specimens' shapes, surface conditions, and color patterns), or how they
discarded the unwanted bits and leftovers (fragment shapes, sizes, surface
conditions, and relationships to each other). At most sites only hard tissues
such as bones, teeth, and shells preserve, but given the wealth of information a single bone fragment can provide, from these alone zooarchaeologists construct stunningly detailed images of millennia-old economies,
political maneuverings, ethnic juxtapositions, and religious observations.

How? Consider what knowing only the species and body parts present in
an assemblage can tell us. Zooarchaeologists compare each excavated
fragment against reference specimens or images to determine what skeletal
element (i.e., bone or tooth) they have on the table in front of them, and
what kind of animal, bird, or fish it came from. (This is also how archae-
omalacologists – shell analysts – work.) Taken together, the element and

species information allows analysts to evaluate which meats a group ate, whether different subgroups ate different cuts of meat (for example, if one house dined on leg meat and another ate ribs), and whether people may have been traveling to get their meat. (Large animals are heavy, and if you have to haul one home from a distant kill site you might want to leave its head and feet behind.)

Adding in animal age-at-death and sex data allows zooarchaeologists to investigate whether hunters were targeting prime animals or simply taking anything they could lay their hands on, and whether their strategies were relatively sustainable or were changing the demographics of wild populations. Herders may have slaughtered almost all young males as soon as they reached full meat weight, or they may have kept many alive into adulthood to pull plows or grow wool. To assess these and other animal production possibilities, zooarchaeologists examine many species' bone sizes and shapes. The most reliable indicators of sex are usually pelvic bones and horns/antlers, but in some species males and females also have different average body sizes (although the sexes commonly overlap). Zooarchaeologists determine an animal's age at death by recording which deciduous (baby) and permanent (adult) teeth have erupted and started to wear down, as well as which bones have matured to the point of having their once-separate pieces fused together.

The extent to which animal bones have been damaged or otherwise modified is tremendously valuable information. Zooarchaeologists recognize the traces of long exposure to the elements (e.g., flaky, cracked surfaces), rodent/carnivore gnawing (randomly placed grooves/pits and grooves near limb bones' often-chewed-off ends), and trampling (shallow, often multidirectional striations). These features all testify to specimens' disposal histories: the rapidity with which bones were buried, the extent to which they were disturbed both before and after burial, and the extent to which animals could get at them once they were discarded.

If you cook a chicken leg until its bone is completely black, will its meat still be edible? The same truth – that the meat has long since passed through mere inedibility into carbonized invisibility – applied in the past. Therefore, wholly burned bones are not evidence of ancient cooking practices. They may testify to past trash disposal methods, or kitchen accidents, or myriad other food-related realities, but their carbonized black or calcined white surfaces don't tell us anything about meat cookery. Only patterned burning does that: the discoloration that you see *on the end* of a chicken drumstick or a roasted rib, where the meat has been pulled back prior to cooking and the underlying bone exposed. Zooarchaeologists only use partial and patterned burning such as this to identify past roasting practices.

Even patterned burning won't tell us about meat boiling, drying, or salting, or about the extraction of rich, fatty marrow and grease from inside bones' shafts. To consider those possibilities, we look at the cut marks and bone breakage patterns that people leave as they transform carcasses into food. Butchers often try not to hit bone, especially when using tools that can't be easily resharpened, and cooked meat often slides easily off the bone, so low numbers of cut marks don't mean that ancient people were leaving animals whole. When cut marks do appear, their depths, placements, and cross-sectional shapes vary according to how people were butchering their meat – which of course varies across groups of people and by intended recipe (e.g., Isaakidou, 2007; Kennedy, 2015). Cutting boneless stew meat may leave thin, shallow filleting marks across bones' shafts; cutting a T-bone steak requires sawing a whole vertebra in half.

Dietary Stable Isotopes

Another approach to reconstructing ancient foodways involves identifying the ratios of different stable isotopes in tiny samples of bone or tooth enamel. We are what we eat, quite literally – our bodies are built from the foods we consume – so the elements in our bones, teeth, and hair come directly from the foods we eat. Different foods contain different proportions of certain elements' stable isotopes. (Stable isotopes are atoms of an element that don't decay over time. They maintain set numbers of protons but have different numbers of neutrons in their nuclei.) The proportions of stable isotopes in a person's body are thus products of the foods that he or she consumed. Archaeologists using mass spectrometers to identify stable isotope proportions in human remains can study not only which kinds of foods people were eating centuries and millennia ago, but also the ages at which babies were weaned, the places where people hunted or herded their food animals, the methods farmers used to grow their crops, and more (Larsen, 2015:301–356).

Stable isotope analysis differs from paleoethnobotanical and zooarchaeological analyses in that it allows archaeologists to investigate (a) the diets of individual people, and (b) what those individuals actually ate, rather than what foods were theoretically available to them in and around their settlements. This allows researchers to evaluate the diets of historically interesting characters (see Chapter 4 re King Richard III) and, more commonly, of different social groups that live in close proximity to each other (e.g., men vs. women, children vs. adults, immigrants vs. indigenes).

Human stable isotope values aggregate the values of foods eaten over the course of many months or years; they do not testify to individual meals or unusual short-term habits. It matters whether archaeologists sample bones or teeth for their isotope analyses, as well as which component(s) of bones and teeth they choose to study. Human bone is a living tissue: as long as person is breathing she is resorbing old bone tissue and laying down new. This continually changing bone has both structural protein (collagen) and mineral (apatite) components. Isotope values in bone collagen reflect the protein in a person's diet; apatite isotope values in both bones and teeth reflect the total diet. Meanwhile, teeth form once (growing from the tip toward the root) and their enamel does not remodel. A tooth may wear down, break, or be filed into points, but it will never heal or otherwise change its composition. Thus, while the isotope values in a fifty-year-old's leg bones reflect what he ate when he was roughly forty to fifty years old, the isotope values in his upper front teeth reflect what he consumed when he was about four months to five years old.

The key challenge of stable isotopic analyses is that a wide variety of diets can produce the same isotopic value, and determining which of many possible foods were eaten, and in which proportions, can be extremely challenging. Properly interpreting human isotopic values requires knowing the isotope values of the foods those humans may have been eating. Was the cow grass-fed or corn-fed? It matters if you want to understand the stable isotope values in a hamburger-eater's skeleton! (See *Carbon (C) Stable Isotopes: $^{13}C/^{12}C$, aka $\delta^{13}C$* .) Interpretations also normally rely on isotopes from multiple elements, because different elements' isotopes provide information about different aspects of the human diet. A question unanswered by carbon isotopes alone is often resolvable with nitrogen or oxygen isotope data. Table 2.1 summarizes the stable isotopes commonly used to reconstruct human diets.

Carbon (C) Stable Isotopes: $^{13}C/^{12}C$, aka $\delta^{13}C$

Plants use one of three different pathways – the C_3, C_4, and CAM (Crassulacean acid metabolism) pathways – to extract carbon from the air during photosynthesis. Each pathway takes up a different ratio of stable ^{12}C and stable ^{13}C isotopes. C_4 plants end up with a higher proportion of ^{13}C in their tissues than C_3 plants, while CAM plants are in the middle. When animals (including humans) eat C_3, C_4, or CAM plants, we use the plant nutrients to build our tissues, and so

TABLE 2.1. *Stable isotopes that archaeologists use to reconstruct ancient foodways*

Element	Stable isotopes	What the human stable isotope ratio reflects
Carbon (C)	$\delta^{13}C = {}^{13}C/{}^{12}C$	The proportions of C_3, C_4, and CAM plants in a person's diet (as well as in the diets of the animals that person ate) *C_3 plants include wheat, rice, fruit, nuts, potatoes, rye, and barley. They are generally trees, shrubs, and grasses that grow in temperate climates* *C_4 plants include maize, sorghum, sugarcane, and some millets. They are generally grasses that grow in hot (subtropical) climates* *CAM plants do not normally constitute a significant portion of human diets. They are generally succulents, and include cacti and pineapples*
Nitrogen (N)	$\delta^{15}N = {}^{15}N/{}^{14}N$	The dietary proportions of foods at different trophic levels (plants vs. herbivores vs. omnivores/dairy-consumers vs. carnivores). $\delta^{15}N$ increases as one moves up a food chain The intensity of food production (manuring, irrigation) In some regions, the dietary proportion of marine foods, freshwater foods, or both
Hydrogen (H)	$\delta^{2}H$ or $\delta D^{*} = {}^{2}H/{}^{1}H$ **Different authors use different symbols*	The dietary proportions of foods at different trophic levels. $\delta^{2}H/\delta D$ increases as one moves up a food chain In some regions, the proportion of marine foods in the diet
Oxygen (O)	$\delta^{18}O = {}^{18}O/{}^{16}O$	Mammalian $\delta^{18}O$ values reflect the temperature and amount of precipitation in the source area for the water the mammal drank

Significance re foodways	Important considerations
A person's $\delta^{13}C$ values reflect the proportions of different kinds of plants in that person's food web	Human $\delta^{13}C$ values derive from both (a) the plants that humans eat directly and (b) the plants eaten by the animals that the humans then ate
	Bone collagen $\delta^{13}C$ reflects largely the protein part of the diet
	Tooth enamel and bone apatite $\delta^{13}C$ reflect the entire diet
	Bone continually remodels, so bone isotope values reflect food eaten over the several years prior to a person's death
	Tooth enamel does not remodel. Its stable isotope signatures reflect only the time in a person's life when the tooth was forming. Teeth grow from their tips toward their roots, so different heights on a single tooth have different stable isotopic signatures
A person's $\delta^{15}N$ values reflect:	Equifinality can be a big issue in interpreting $\delta^{15}N$ values. Ecological data may help narrow things down. (If a person lived far from water, fish were probably not a big part of his or her diet)
(a) the proportions of animal foods in his or her diet (and for non-vegetarians, the proportions of herbivore meat vs. omnivore meat)	$\delta^{15}N$ reflects only the protein part of the diet
(b) the conditions in which those food plants and animals lived	$\delta^{15}N$ cannot distinguish meat-eating from milk (or cheese, or yogurt) consumption
(c) the proportion of mother's milk in the diet	
(d) (in some areas) the proportion of aquatic foods in his/her diet	
A person's $\delta^2H/\delta D$ values reflect:	Only ~60% of non-exchangeable skeletal hydrogen derives from food (Reynard and Hedges, 2008)
(a) the proportions of animal foods in the diet	Skeletons incorporate modern hydrogen atoms from water vapor in the air; $\delta^2H/\delta D$ analyses must compensate for this contamination
(b) the proportion of marine foods in the diet (unless the person was drinking isotopically different water)	
(c) local climate conditions (temperature, humidity)	
Human $\delta^{18}O$ values reflect where people were getting drinking water	The water that people consume is not necessarily drunk as pure water: it may be incorporated in breastmilk, beer, etc.

TABLE 2.1. (*continued*)

Element	Stable isotopes	What the human stable isotope ratio reflects
Calcium (Ca)	$\delta^{44}Ca = {}^{44}Ca/{}^{42}Ca$ or ${}^{44}Ca/{}^{40}Ca$	Mammalian $\delta^{44}Ca$ values reflect nursing and weaning
Strontium (Sr)	$\delta^{87}Sr = {}^{87}Sr/{}^{86}Sr$	Plant $\delta^{87}Sr$ values reflect where the plant grew Mammalian $\delta^{87}Sr$ values reflect where the mammal's drinking water originated
Sulfur (S)	$\delta^{34}S = {}^{34}S/{}^{32}S$	The proportion of marine foods in the diet Local geology; rainfall; groundwater; pollution levels; individual and societal dietary preferences

Significance re foodways	Important considerations
Food animals' $\delta^{18}O$ values reflect where people were hunting/ herding	Water moves, both naturally (flowing rivers) and artificially (irrigation canals, aqueducts). Analysts must include such movements in their reconstructions of where on the landscape water with a particular $\delta^{18}O$ value was available
Human $\delta^{44}Ca$ values may reflect consumption of human and/or animal milk Early weaning in herd animals such as sheep and cattle may reflect human dairying	Regional geology affects $\delta^{44}Ca$ values, so one can't directly compare different sites' $\delta^{44}Ca$ values. One can compare $\delta^{44}Ca$ value *patterns* across sites
Plant and animal $\delta^{87}Sr$ values reflect where food species grew/ lived, and thus where people were gathering/farming/hunting/ herding	Foods' $\delta^{87}Sr$ values are determined by the $\delta^{87}Sr$ of the water they take in; the water's $\delta^{87}Sr$ is determined by $\delta^{87}Sr$ values in its geological place of origin. If plants/animals consume water that did not originate locally – water brought in by irrigation canals, or by rivers flowing down from distant, geologically distinct mountains – their $\delta^{87}Sr$ values will not reflect their true home areas Human $\delta^{87}Sr$ values reflect primarily the plant foods a person ate
A person's $\delta^{34}S$ values reflect how much marine food he or she ate In some areas, $\delta^{34}S$ values also distinguish between freshwater and terrestrial foods	$\delta^{34}S$ reflects dietary protein only Modern animals' $\delta^{34}S$ values are often not comparable to archaeological animals' $\delta^{34}S$ values Human and animal $\delta^{34}S$ values can vary significantly within a particular geographic location but be similar at very different locations

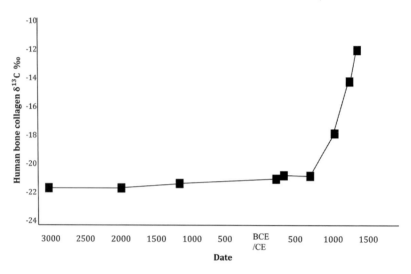

FIGURE 2.1. Aggregated δ¹³C values in bone collagen samples from eastern North America. Modified from Schoeninger, 2009: fig 1.

assimilate the plants' $^{13}C/^{12}C$ ratios (expressed in isotope studies as $\delta^{13}C$) into our bones and teeth. A person who eats large amounts of C_4 plants thus normally has a higher $\delta^{13}C$ in his skeleton than a person who eats primarily C_3 plants. (Figure 2.1 demonstrates the efficacy of this method, presenting what may be the world's least subtle evidence for dietary change. When do you think people in eastern North America started incorporating large amounts of the C_4 plant maize into their previously C_3-based diets?)

Why "normally?" Because humans also acquire carbon from the animal foods we eat – and those animal foods have carbon isotope ratios reflecting the plants or animals that *they* ate. A person who eats exclusively C_3 plants (wheat, rice, apples, nuts, etc.) could develop a higher-than-expected $\delta^{13}C$ signature by eating meat from animals that feed on C_4 plants (maize, sorghum, etc.). Eating fish and shellfish might or might not also raise this person's $\delta^{13}C$ values, because some aquatic species have C_4-plant-like carbon isotope signatures. (Marine species commonly have high $\delta^{13}C$ values, although there are exceptions [Vika and Theodoropoulou, 2012]. Freshwater fish vary depending on where they live.) It is *all* of the plants at the base of a person's food chain – those eaten directly and those consumed by animals that in turn get eaten (or milked, or bled) – that determine that person's eventual $\delta^{13}C$ signature.

Nitrogen (N) Stable Isotopes: $^{15}N/^{14}N$, aka $\delta^{15}N$

Nitrogen's relevant stable isotopes are ^{15}N and ^{14}N; the ratio of the two is written as $\delta^{15}N$. $\delta^{15}N$ values increase along with trophic levels, so that a herbivore has a lower $\delta^{15}N$ signature than does the carnivore that eats it. Of course, meat is not the only food that people get from animals: nursing babies also have high $\delta^{15}N$ signatures, up to a trophic level above those of their breastfeeding mothers (although see Beaumont et al., 2015). Archaeologists can therefore use a skeleton's $\delta^{15}N$ signature to assess the quantity of animal foods in a person's diet – as long as they don't have to worry about any of the other possible causes for a high $\delta^{15}N$.

What other factors may elevate $\delta^{15}N$ values? In some areas – but not all – marine organisms have considerably higher $\delta^{15}N$ values than terrestrial foods (Vika and Theodoropoulou, 2012). Plant foods' $\delta^{15}N$ signatures vary according to the conditions in which the plants grew: manuring and water availability may particularly affect grain $\delta^{15}N$ (Styring et al., 2016). Fortunately, archaeologists can measure $\delta^{15}N$ in plant and fish remains and then use these values to interpret human $\delta^{15}N$ values – as long as the humans, plants, and fish come from the same site, or at least the same vicinity. Because plant and animal isotopic values vary across space, it is important that only local specimens be used as baselines for evaluating human isotope values. Cattle that grazed on coastal plants can have $\delta^{15}N$ values nearly a trophic level higher than cattle that grazed inland, for example (Britton et al., 2008). If you want to study meat consumption in the Scottish North Atlantic a millennium ago, avoid using shorefront-grazed cows from Jarlshof to interpret beef-eating at inland Borlais, lest you seriously overestimate people's carnivory (Jones and Mulville, 2018). Plant and animal isotope values may vary across time as well, and stable isotope analysts must keep in mind the possible impacts of changing climates, ecologies, and farming and herding methods on the isotope values of the foods people ate in the past.

$\delta^{15}N$ values are most frequently presented together with $\delta^{13}C$ values. An example of this is Figure 2.2, which shows that the prehistoric people whose disarticulated skulls and limb bones were buried in the public "Skull Building" at Neolithic Çayönü (Turkey) ate differently from people whose whole bodies ended up buried under house floors (Pearson et al., 2013).

Hydrogen (H) Stable Isotopes: D/H or $^2H/^1H$, aka δD or $\delta^2 H$ (varies by author)

Like $\delta^{15}N$, stable hydrogen isotope ratios (D/H or $^2H/^1H$ = δD or $\delta^2 H$) reflect trophic levels and marine protein consumption (Reynard and

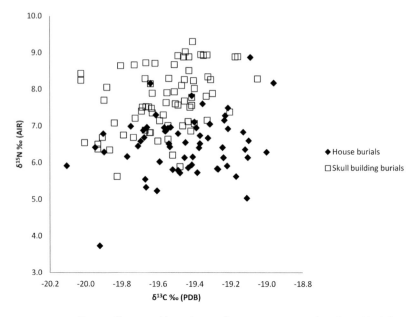

FIGURE 2.2. Bone collagen, stable carbon and nitrogen isotope values from Neolithic Çayönü (ca. 8,200–6,000 BCE) in Turkey. Note the variation in δ15N values in particular: the range represents more than one trophic level. Values reported in parts per thousand (‰) and anchored to the Pee Dee Belemnite (PDB) (carbon) and AIR (nitrogen) international standards. After Pearson et al (2013:fig. 3): figure courtesy of Jessica Pearson.

Hedges, 2008; van der Sluis et al., 2016). When δ15N and δD are both analyzed, δD clarifies the extent to which δ15N ratios were influenced by factors other than diet. δD analysis is comparatively complicated and as yet not a standard part of dietary reconstruction in archaeology (Reynard and Hedges, 2008; van der Sluis et al., 2016).

Oxygen (O) Stable Isotopes: $^{18}O/^{16}O$, aka $\delta^{18}O$

People derive their oxygen isotopes primarily from their drinking water. The stable isotopic signature of that water relates to its evaporation history – which is, of course, shaped by the climate (temperature, elevation, aridity, latitude) where that water flows (Gat, 1996). Archaeologists therefore use stable oxygen isotopes to study where people were drinking (cool mountain springs? sunny flatland pools?), and thus, more broadly, where they were on the landscape. This, of course, is determined to a great extent by how they acquired their food: where they herded their flocks, how far they moved in pursuit of ripe fruit or game, and whether they used canals or aqueducts to irrigate their crops. In helping us place ancient humans (and animals; some species get their water from the plants they eat rather than from drinking per se, but the same idea applies) on the landscape, stable oxygen isotopes help us reconstruct millennia-old subsistence strategies (e.g., Henton et al., 2017). $\delta^{18}O$ values also relate to cooking methods, with boiling and prolonged cooking having particularly well-documented effects, but as yet this discussion centers around cooking's poten-tially confounding effects on geographic signatures rather than on inferring culinary practices per se (e.g., Brettell et al., 2012; Tuross et al., 2017).

Strontium (Sr) Stable Isotopes: $^{87}Sr/^{86}Sr$, aka $\delta^{87}Sr$

Stable strontium isotopes likewise testify to where ancient people and animals spent time rather than to diets per se. As rocks erode, their strontium isotopes enter the water and then the food supply. Varied geologies and hydrologies give different areas divergent $^{87}Sr/^{86}Sr$ ratios. Humans and animals ingest these varied $^{87}Sr/^{86}Sr$ signatures, incorporating location markers in their skeletons (Bentley, 2006). (Plant foods have a far greater impact than animal foods on human $\delta^{87}Sr$ [Burton and Price, 2000; Montgomery et al., 2005].) Archaeologists can thus use stable strontium isotopes to reconstruct where (broadly speaking) people and animals were living, eating, and drinking. How did the Roman Empire feed the legions it sent to keep control over the troublesome Welsh in the early centuries of the current era? Widely varying $^{87}Sr/^{86}Sr$ values in animal bones found at the Isca fortress indicate a military storehouse filled with meat from animals raised in diverse places, not a single supply chain (Madgwick et al., 2019). Stable strontium and oxygen isotopes provide complementary information, and archaeologists are now using them in tandem to narrow down the geographic origins of both people and their food (Bentley et al., 2008; e.g., Bogaard et al., 2014a; Chase et al., 2014; Julien et al., 2012).

Calcium (Ca) Stable Isotopes: $^{44}Ca/^{42}Ca$ or $^{44}Ca/^{40}Ca$, aka $\delta^{44}Ca$

Dairy and plant foods are mammals' main sources of dietary calcium, and they have different isotopic signatures. Milk, whether human or animal in origin, has lower $\delta^{44}Ca$ values than plants (Reynard et al., 2013). (Bones are another source of calcium, but only some populations consume sources such as whole sardines and bone-in salmon.)

Calcium isotope values may thus reflect trophic levels. A nursing child gets his calcium from his mother, but his calcium values differ because he's drinking from her body; from an isotopic perspective, he's a tiny, toothless, predator and his mother his prey. The same can, of course, be said regarding stable nitrogen isotope data, but while $\delta^{15}N$ testifies to consumption of animal *proteins* (from both milk and meat), $\delta^{44}Ca$ values are indicative of dairy's *mineral* component alone (i.e., meat consumption does not affect them). Recent research therefore has archaeologists using bone and tooth stable calcium isotope values to explore weaning and dairy consumption in both humans and animals (Reynard et al., 2013; Tacail et al., 2017; Wright, 2014).

Sulfur (S) Stable Isotopes: $^{34}S/^{32}S$, aka $\delta^{34}S$

People acquire sulfur from the amino acids they ingest, so $\delta^{34}S$ values derive entirely from dietary protein (Nehlich, 2015). The oceans have a known and relatively consistent $\delta^{34}S$ signature, which allows archaeologists to detect diets acquired from or in proximity to the oceans. It is important to note that "in proximity" caveat: sea spray can give coastal and island resources marine-like $\delta^{34}S$ signatures. (Sulfur isotope analyses report the entire island of New Zealand as a marine environment [Richards et al., 2003].) Archaeologists must therefore evaluate $\delta^{34}S$ values in tandem with $\delta^{13}C$ and $\delta^{15}N$ values in order to clarify whether people were eating marine foods or terrestrial ones (Richards et al., 2003; e.g., Nehlich et al., 2011). On land, local geologies influence sulfur isotope values, and several studies use $\delta^{34}S$ to reconstruct people's dietary geographies. Caution is necessary, however, as geology, rainwater, groundwater, pollution levels, cultural norms, and individual tastes all influence human $\delta^{34}S$ values (Nehlich, 2015). Plant $\delta^{34}S$ values are subject to numerous influences as well, so researchers are alert to complications as they begin to use paleoethnobotanical $\delta^{34}S$ values to investigate ancient crop growing conditions (Nitsch et al., 2019).

Other Isotopes

Archaeologists are beginning to use other stable isotopes to investigate ancient diets as well. Copper, zinc, iron, lead, and magnesium isotopes as yet have little presence in the archaeological food literature, but as magnesium, zinc, and iron values relate to trophic levels; magnesium and zinc values relate to leaf versus grass-eating; zinc values may relate to whether a carnivore ate bones or just muscle tissues; and more; we may be seeing these isotopes more in future (Jaouen and Pons, 2016). Jaouen and Pons hold out particular hope for some of these isotopes proving valuable in paleoanthropology, combined with each other and with classic carbon isotopes in studies of millennia-old hominin dental enamel.

Trace Element Ratios

Far more prominent in paleoanthropology than in Holocene archaeology is the use of barium and strontium ratios to reconstruct ancient diets. The ratios of barium to calcium (Ba/Ca) and of strontium to calcium (Sr/Ca) in skeletal remains reflect people's trophic levels. A high Ba/Ca ratio suggests that a person consumed significant amounts of animal protein, whether as milk or as meat; a high Sr/Ca ratio suggests the opposite. Caution is warranted, however, as many, many different factors play into a person's Sr/Ca signature (Larsen, 2015:348–351).

Paleofeces and Gut Contents

Human feces and gut contents appear periodically in the archaeological record, exciting archaeologists who grab at the rare opportunity to examine what individuals ate over a short time period rather than over several months or years. Every stool or set of stomach contents includes a diversity of materials, so researchers examine feces for not only plant and animal macro- and microremains, but also parasite loads and biomolecular and DNA signatures (Maixner and Zink, 2015; Reinhard et al., 2013; Sobolik, 2000). The latter are important, as not all foods are excreted in visually recognizable form. Meat from large animals, for example, is normally taken off the bone and thus rendered zooarchaeologically invisible. Testing feces' biomolecular contents allows researchers to identify such substances as human myoglobin, whose presence in a prehistoric Puebloan stool from Colorado proved cannibalism beyond a shadow of a doubt (Marlar et al., 2000).

Dental Calculus, Microbiomes, and Proteins

A variety of information can be extracted from dental calculus, which is the hardened plaque on your teeth that dentists scrape off with little metal picks. In the absence of modern dentistry, calculus layers gradually build up, sometimes accumulating until a person has visible chunks of stratified calculus adhering to the teeth. Because calculus is not actually part of the human body, it may be analyzable when bones and teeth are off-limits to archaeologists.

Calculus contains proteins, starches, pollen, phytoliths, and DNA from foods and oral pathogens. Archaeologists can submit these data to the same kinds of analyses done on remains found outside of people's mouths – with the added confidence that whatever edibles they identify actually entered people's mouths, and if consumed were eaten by humans rather than by animals. Human fecal remains provide even surer information, but they usually don't preserve, and intact coprolites are rare at best. Dental calculus is nearly ubiquitous among adults over the age of thirty across the globe and through time, and it preserves excellently (Warinner et al., 2015).

Two kinds of analyses that are regularly done on calculus as well as on fecal remains are proteomics (protein analysis) and microbiome analyses (genetic analyses of the microbes that occupy people's bodies). People's dietary choices influence their gut and their oral microbiomes. Eating sugars, for example, promotes the growth of cavity-causing species of oral bacteria (Warinner et al., 2015). Archaeologists analyze the DNA and/or RNA found in dental calculus to identify the bacterial species that lived inside people's mouths. This gives insights into the foods that people were eating. Microbiome analysts can see, for example, that cavity-causing mouth bacteria became more common when farming arrived in Europe, presumably because people started eating more soft, sticky carbohydrate foods (Adler et al., 2013). After that big change, though, Europeans' oral microbiomes stayed more or less the same for *seven thousand years*; only 400 years ago did they change again. Unfortunately, the shift was toward even more cavity-producing bacteria and fewer species associated with good health, as refined grains and concentrated sugars became increasingly available (Adler et al., 2013). The next time your dentist tells you to brush your teeth, you can reply that you're also keeping cavities down by eating like a prehistoric Polish hunter-gatherer rather than a Victorian aristocrat. (Don't actually do this. Your dentist will think you insane.)

Proteomics, meanwhile, entails extracting proteins from their surroundings (dental calculus, but also potsherd residues, bones, etc.), running them through mass spectrometers to identify their peptide "signatures," and matching those "signatures" with others of known origins. Researchers identify milk-drinking among people dead for millennia, discern among pork, venison, and mutton consumption, and find evidence for oats, peas, and cheese eaten centuries ago (Hendy et al., 2018a; Warinner et al., 2014). You might pause at this last statement: how can proteomicists tell cheese apart from fresh milk, since one is made from the other? Hendy and colleagues (2018a) report whey protein in the dental calculus of medieval English people, and casein protein in post-medieval calculus. Whey is the watery component of milk that separates out during curdling: we recognize it as the liquid that floats on top of yogurts. Casein stays in the curd and is the main protein constituent of cheese.

Organic Residues

Lipids (fats, waxes, and resins) are often absorbed into the walls of unglazed pottery. They are found in other locations as well – e.g., on the surfaces of ceramic, metal, and stone vessels as well as on other types of stone artifacts – but absorbed lipids are less subject to loss, and they generally derive from food(s) stored or processed in a vessel rather than from modern contaminants (Roffet-Salque et al., 2017). Organic residue analysts grind up small samples of pots' walls to extract these invisible lipid deposits. They then use ever-developing techniques (gas chromatography, mass spectrometry, selected ion monitoring) to separate out and identify the lipid components in each deposit (Roffet-Salque et al., 2017). Identification relies on matching the archaeological residues' chemical "fingerprints" (Evershed, 2008) with the "fingerprints" of various plant and animal products, from milk to meat to alcohol to beeswax. Organic residue analysis has been used to detect possible taboos on marine foods, ceremonial preferences for certain kinds of meat, the types of foods habitually cooked in specific kinds of vessels, when people started making cheese (at least seven thousand years ago!), and more (Craig et al., 2015; Roffet-Salque et al., 2017; Salque et al., 2013). It is important to note that residues on or in an artifact testify to some of that item's use, but not necessarily to *all* of its uses. In other words, researchers can't assume that a stone knife or ceramic pot was made specifically for cutting or cooking the food(s) revealed by its surface residues: people may also have used it with other foods or tasks that didn't leave residues behind for us to identify.

Human Remains: Paleopathology, Parasites, and Dental Wear

Diets lacking in or oversupplied with essential nutrients leave a variety of traces on human skeletons. Mean adult height and child growth rates within a population reflect the general adequacy of nutrition. Teeth grooves and pits (dental hypoplasias) and thin encircling lines near the ends of arm and leg bone shafts (Harris lines) testify to the temporary cessation of children's growth, often because they were starving (Larsen, 2015; Waldron, 2006). Overeating can contribute to excessive bone formation (diffuse idiopathic skeletal hyperostosis, or DISH): that this condition has been repeatedly identified in monks gives Robin Hood's chubby Friar Tuck an enjoyable ring of historical plausibility (Rogers and Waldron, 2001; Verlaan et al., 2007).

Some pathologies may give more precise information about ancient malnutrition. Researchers have to remember, however, that skeletal pathologies are symptoms, and that many such symptoms have more than one potential cause. Parasite infections, diarrhea, genetic diseases, and traumatic injuries can lead to the same kinds of bone damage as malnutrition (Faccia et al., 2016; Klaus, 2015; Walker et al., 2009). Archaeologists, aware of these caveats, can nonetheless use paleopathologies to identify potential or likely (not certain) nutritional problems in the past. Many researchers, for example, discuss the dietary implications of porotic hyperostosis and cribra orbitalia: spongy-looking lesions on the top of the cranium and in the eye sockets, respectively. Long attributed to iron-deficiency anemias, porotic hyperostosis has more recently been linked to insufficient consumption of vitamins B9 and B12 and, because B12 comes from animal products, to a prolonged lack of animal foods in the diet (Walker et al., 2009). Cribra orbitalia, meanwhile, is linked especially to scurvy (vitamin C deficiency), which can cause porous lesions on arm and leg bones as well as on the skull (Armelagos et al., 2014; Stark, 2014; Walker et al., 2009). Too much vitamin A can induce excess bone production; too little vitamin D can lead to soft bones that bend under a person's own weight (Waldron, 2006; Walker et al., 1982).

Dentists tell you that eating sweets is bad for your teeth: archaeologists tell you the same. Eating a lot of carbohydrate-rich foods increases your risk of dental caries (i.e., cavities). Archaeologically, the transition to crop farming is often marked with a rise in tooth decay and the more an ancient people ate carbohydrates, the worse their dental health commonly got (Larsen, 2015:70–72). Sweet, sticky foods could leave teeth in truly rough shape. In Iron Age Oman, for example, where date palms provided local children with sweet treats, carious decay began very young and affected virtually everyone. Children's teeth show "extensive" damage, adults' teeth can be worse, and tooth loss struck early (Nelson et al., 1999).

As everyone who's ever taken care to wash their vegetables or cook their pork thoroughly knows, food often carries parasites as well as nutrients. Because particular types of parasites travel via specific types of foods, archaeologists can use parasite remains found in human paleofeces, dental calculus, mummies, latrines, and even calcified cysts in skeletonized burials to reconstruct ancient food practices (Reinhard and Araujo, 2016; Reinhard et al., 2013). For example, four species of parasitical flukes found in Joseon Dynasty (1392–1897 CE) mummies transfer to humans only when people eat uncooked fish, crab, or oysters. The fact that eleven out of the eighteen mummies studied were infected proves that raw seafood was an important component of elite cuisine in long-ago Korea (Reinhard and Araujo, 2016; Seo et al., 2014).

Teeth wear down as they are used, in patterns and to extents determined in large part by the foods that they're being used to process (Hillson, 2005:214–223; Larsen, 2015:276–288, 292–297). Gritty foods wear teeth down faster than soft ones, so people dining on bread that's filled with tiny bits of sand from the stones on which the wheat was ground end up with heavily worn-down teeth at relatively young ages. At the microscopic level, hard, brittle foods such as nuts leave tiny pits in tooth surfaces, whereas tougher foods leave thin scratches. Dental microwear is a key line of evidence regarding fossil hominin diets (Grine et al., 2012). In post-Pleistocene contexts, the fact that microwear reflects only foods eaten a few days or perhaps weeks before death gives archaeologists an opportunity to examine short-term dietary differences between individuals and populations (e.g., Gamza and Irish, 2012; Mahoney et al., 2016).

(Humans are, of course, not the only animals whose skeletons bear traces of the foods they ate in life. Paleopathological and dental wear studies on faunal remains provide considerable information about how people produced their meat and dairy: the seasons in which they hunted and feasted, the conditions in which they kept their herds, the fodder they provided, and the ecological impacts of their production strategies [e.g., Henton et al. 2014, 2017; Mainland, 2006; Vanpoucke et al., 2009].)

Lithics

Stone preserves like nothing else. When all other sources of information about how people ate have long since disappeared, stone tools, utensils, and debris remain for us to study. Stone artifacts – lithics – testify to foodways extinct before *Homo sapiens* even existed: meat-cutting and plant-pounding practices from over a million years ago (e.g., Diez-Martín et al., 2009, 2010).

Lithic artifacts provide a variety of kinds of information about past foodways. To begin with, the raw materials that ancient people chose reflect not only practical decisions (e.g., obsidian makes terrifically sharp blades, basalt poor ones) but also economic relationships (e.g., trade routes), the values accorded to particular tools and dishes (raw materials imported from distant lands are generally costlier, in one way or another, than easily available local stones), and potentially their symbolic importance. Archaeologists identify raw materials' source areas by matching an artifact's elemental "signature" – the relative percentages of various elements in its stone – with the signature of a known source area (Andrefsky, 2005, 2009).

As ancient (and modern) peoples designed their tools to work effectively, finds' shapes (forms) generally relate to their intended purposes. Sickle blades have sharp edges for harvesting grasses and arrowheads have pointed tips for penetrating hides. Archaeologists should not, however, rely solely on form to determine what people used a particular item for. People don't use tools for only one thing: they co-opt even tools designed for single purposes for other tasks as needs warrant (Shea, 2013). This was probably especially common in mobile societies, as toting around numerous single-function pieces of stone would have been counterproductive at best (Shea, 2013).

Moreover, ancient people reused and recycled stone tools just as modern people do cans and bottles (Frison, 1968). Knives dulled and were reshaped into darts; simple flakes were retouched to make scrapers (Andrefsky, 2009). Stone tools were rarely "finished" in either shape or use (Dibble et al., 2016). Rather, the shape an artifact has when it is excavated reflects only one moment in its history, like a photograph of you today captures only one era in your life.

Form does not, therefore, necessarily reveal function. How then do lithic analysts link stone artifacts to ancient foodways? Residues (previously discussed) left on stones' surfaces and absorbed into their pores and cracks provide one line of evidence. Another is use-wear. Use-wear analysts inspect artifacts' surfaces for minute or large changes caused by the tools' use. Even stone is altered when it's rubbed, hit, or scraped, so tuber pounding, bone scraping, and other food-related activities often leave traces that archaeologists can identify. Polishes, striations, and fractures are visible under microscopy or even to the naked eye. Archaeologists link specific patterns of damage to particular activities by matching the ancient patterns with modern ones created by experiments using stone tools to undertake everything from tree-chopping to deer-shooting to plant tenderizing.

Admittedly, stone tools can be resharpened, reused, and/or tumbled around during storage or carrying, obliterating some of the original traces on their surfaces (Van Gijn, 2014). Even if this doesn't happen, the phenomenal complexity and diversity of surface traces can make it hard to assign tools to use categories. van Gijn (2014:168) argues that such challenges make microwear analysis "basically interpretive archaeology," but not all analysts agree with her (e.g., Ibáñez et al., 2014). At a minimum, microwear patterns can enhance discovery and interpretation of other lithic data. For example, Nowell et al. (2016) used microwear evidence to select

Paleolithic stone artifacts for residue analysis; seventeen of the forty-four tools chosen on the basis of their microfractures and rounding bore protein traces revealing that roughly 250,000 years ago, hominins in eastern Jordan ate meats ranging from duck to horse, camel, and rhinoceros.

Many people picture slim flakes and blades when they think of lithics, but ground stone tools have also played a vitally important role in food preparation across time and through space. "Ground stone" is a confusing term it refers to either tools' function (grinding things up) or their mode of manufacture (grinding stone down into shape) (Ebeling, 2015: 507) – but archaeologists use it regularly to categorize artifacts widely used in food production, preparation, and consumption. Since the Pleistocene, people throughout the globe have been using mortars and pestles, manos and metates, querns and handstones to process and serve their food.

How do we know that these tools were used to ready food? True, modern people use such tools to grind cereals, meats, and spices, but artists also crush pigments, pharmacists triturate medications, and addicts crush pills. More than that, modern people use individual tools for multiple purposes. Archaeologists do not assume that ground stone artifacts were used exclusively to process food. Rather, researchers expect varied uses, pay close attention to contexts, and examine tools carefully for identifiable residues (e.g., starches or lipids [Copeland and Hardy 2018; Ebeling 2015]) and for use-wear patterns that correspond to food processing (e.g., Fullagar et al., 2017). Experimental archaeologists have published descriptions of the wear patterns produced by grinding maize kernels, seeds, salt, and other foods and non-foods (Adams, 2014; Dubreuil and Savage, 2014).

Many ground stone tools are large and easy to find archaeologically. (Small tools and chips and flakes from tool-making are less so.) However, because grinding stones don't wear out easily – a single item may remain useful for centuries – ancient and modern peoples often reuse them and move them away from their original locations of use. Dating ground stone artifacts is often a challenge as well. Not only can individual tools remain in use for centuries, tool styles and technologies may stay the same for even longer periods of time.

Ceramics

Because much of the pottery in the archaeological record held food at one point or another, virtually everything about pottery can be seen as relevant to ancient foodways. Where the clay came from, and whether potters dug it themselves or traded for it, are parts of the food economy; the same goes for the temper mixed into the clay to keep it strong and stable during firing. Whether pots were mass-produced or individually crafted is not only a technological question, but also about the organization of labor that provided people with storage, cooking, and eating equipment. Vessel forms relate to their intended culinary use(s); vessel decorations to the symbolism attached to particular foods and dining situations; vessel sizes to the numbers of people expected to share their contents. This section offers a brief overview of the pottery analysis methods that are currently most prominent in the archaeological literature on foodways. (For more comprehensive surveys see Hunt, 2016; Orton and Hughes, 2013; Rice, 2015; and Spataro and Villing, 2015.)

Archaeologists interested in ancient foodways tend to focus on three aspects of pottery assemblages. The first of these is the raw materials used to make the pots. The second is the vessels' forms – their shapes and/or their sizes. The third is the style of the vessels: the decorative elements that people added because they wanted to rather than because the elaborations improved vessel function in any perceptible way. Researchers rely on one or more of these pottery characteristics to examine where past people acquired their vessels, what they used them for, and in which contexts they were deployed.

Sourcing Raw Materials and Finished Vessels

People move pottery around constantly (Orton and Hughes, 2013:27). Potters make vessels in one place before trading them away to locals and/or to foreigners. Families bring filled dishes to communal potlucks, feasts, and religious services. Merchants pack preserved foods into sturdy jars that can withstand the stresses of long-distance transport. Travelers carry pretty plates home as souvenirs. Ceramics even relocate before they're made, as raw clays and tempers get hauled sometimes surprising distances to homes, workshops, and kilns.

Archaeologists trace clays and finished pots back to their sources in multiple ways. Clays, like other geological deposits, have distinguishable mineral and compositional "fingerprints" that enable lucky archaeologists to match sherds to sources. A ceramic fragment's color, hardness, and inclusions all provide information, but these days researchers commonly rely on newer techniques adopted from the earth and materials sciences (see chapters in Hunt, 2016: part IV, pp. 238–465). Nonetheless, as Orton and Hughes (2013:169) point out, linking archaeological vessels to specific clay sources remains a difficult task. It is easier to match old pots to old production sites – to find where pots were manufactured, rather than where their raw materials came from. To accomplish this archaeologists don't need to know the "fingerprints" of a potentially enormous number of clay deposits, only those of pottery produced at candidate workshops, or even just in candidate regions.

Vessel Functions

Ceramics are useful in a wide variety of ways. Setting aside items with obviously non-culinary functions such as figurines, bricks, pipes, and sarcophagi, archaeologists are left with pots and plates, ovens and spoons, jugs and goblets, and more. Rice (2015:412) divides culinary pottery containers into three broad use categories: processing/preparation vessels (used for mixing, grinding, pounding, soaking, and cooking), storage vessels, and transfer (serving and eating) vessels. Written records and art can help clarify which categories particular vessels belong in;[1] the contexts in which they were found can be equally informative. Ethnographic and ethnohistoric analogs as well as experiments provide excellent insights (Orton and Hughes, 2013; Skibo, 2013; Villing and Spataro, 2015).

When neither texts nor contexts provide enough information about how ceramics were used, archaeologists sort artifacts into categories based on their forms and compositions, as different pottery attributes suit different uses (Orton and Hughes, 2013:247–260; Rice, 2015:412–425). Vessels meant for shipping sauces or oils work best if watertight (minimally porous), sturdy, and sealable; fanciful decorations are irrelevant and delicate glazes impractical. Vessels meant for stewing work best if sturdy and watertight, as well as resistant to thermal shock (i.e., rounded, with even walls and only certain types of mineral inclusions) and open enough at the neck that cooks can stir, taste, and serve their contents. Mixing bowls benefit from open mouths and strong walls; cheese strainers need numerous small holes for whey drainage; serving platters please or impress diners with eye-catching decorations. Of course many vessels fulfill multiple roles, moving from storage room to wagon cart or from kitchen to table. If such flexibility

---

[1] Sadly, few vessels are thoughtful enough to announce *"DA MIHI VINUM"* ("GIVE ME WINE"); as Orton and Hughes (2013:248) note, such an inscription – found on an early first-millennium CE vessel from Germany – tends to make the affiliation of a vessel with wine-drinking "reasonably clear!"

is expected, potters design vessels to compromise between the demands of their different intended uses (Orton and Hughes, 2013:247; Rice, 2015:414).

Wear and use traces shed light on the functions of pots as well as of stone tools (Skibo, 1992). Soot stains testify to pots' proximities to open fires: a pot propped or hung over a flame often has its entire lower surface blackened, whereas one placed on the hearth among the coals or ashes may have a dark ring around its lower body but not on its actual base (Orton and Hughes, 2013:253, although see Villing and Spataro, 2015). Away from the heat, cooks' grinding, pounding, mixing, and scraping may also leave identifiable marks on pottery, and damage was actually an integral part of some vessels' use: ancient Roman raisin-bread pots, for example, held dough during baking and then were broken open to access the (apparently delicious) cooked loaves (Orton and Hughes, 2013). Accumulated culinary stresses may weaken vessels, sometimes leading to easily identifiable repairs, and sometimes to modifications of vessel design (Orton and Hughes, 2013).

On occasion, archaeologists find ceramics that still contain sizable pieces of foods they once held – olive stones or fish bones in Roman amphorae (van Neer and Ervynck, 2004), sheep and goat bones in Bronze Age tomb offerings (Horwitz, 2001) – but microscopic residues (see Organic Residue Analyses) are a more common source of information about vessel contents and thus uses. As always, archaeologists must be alert to the possibility that a vessel was put to multiple uses, sequentially (reuse, recycling) if not simultaneously. Van der Werff (2003), for example, reports that some olive oil amphorae in the Netherlands were repurposed as dry food storage vessels, while others moved to the end of food's sequence of interactions with humans, leaving their walls impregnated with urine's characteristic phosphate and calcium residues. Even broken sherds may find new life as cheese or honey strainers, fishing net weights, or vessel lids (e.g., Figure 2.3).

Vessel Decoration

A key complexity when it comes to interpreting ceramic assemblages is the fact that people copy items that they like. In other words, if potters in one area make vessels that potters in another area find attractive or appealing, the second group is likely to start making similar vessels. This is why archaeologists can't use basic vessel form to establish where a particular kind of dish was made (Orton and Hughes, 2013:28). There may be small distinctions between regions (Orton and Hughes, 2013:30) that allow researchers to pinpoint production locations, though.

a)

b)

FIGURE 2.3. Recycled food artifacts. (a) Metal food can lid recycled into daikon grater. 1940s CE, Amache Internment Camp, Colorado. Photo courtesy of B. Clark and the Denver University Amache Project. (b) Ceramic vessel fragment recycled into loom weight, Mesopotamia. Photo courtesy E. Stone.

Metals

Archaeologists analyze metal artifacts pots, spoons, knives, plows, and so forth – along more or less the same lines as ceramic items, and with some of the same caveats. Reuse and recycling are particular issues. Metal items don't break easily and if damaged, they can be repaired, so they can have very long use-lives indeed (Mainman, 2015: fig. 63). They can also, of course, be melted down or pounded into entirely new forms. Artifacts' forms, fabrics, and surface decorations all contribute to discussions of food production technologies (e.g., Thomas et al., 2016); cooking methods (e.g., Chevillot, 2007); and the values of various dining accoutrements (e.g., Nelson, 2003).

There are meaningful distinctions between metal artifacts and those of other materials, of course, not only with regards to analytical methodologies (Roberts and Thornton, 2014) but also in terms of the kinds of analyses to which the data sets are well or poorly suited. For example, while metal artifacts can be subjected to use-wear analysis, few are. Metal is subject to corrosion, which obscures or corrupts microscopic damage, and metal is easy to resharpen, which removes use-wear traces (Birch, 2015). A bigger issue for the archaeology of food, however, is that in most areas and time periods we simply don't have very many food-related metal artifacts. Among the cultures that developed metallurgy over the last few thousand years, only some employed it to produce significant quantities of tableware or cooking paraphernalia. Of the items that were produced, many were surely recycled into entirely new goods. Items that were discarded often corroded in the earth, leaving few traces for archaeologists to recover. Only in historical contexts (notably Rome and the medieval and post-medieval West) do metal artifacts feature prominently in the archaeology of food.

Landscapes and the Built Environment

People shape their environments in accordance with their food needs and wants. Farmers channel rivers to irrigate crops; homeowners dig fire pits in their back yards to keep their meals away from the eyes of prying neighbors; architects design banquet halls to seat as many guests as they expect or desire. Archaeologists can therefore gain insight into past foodways by analyzing the spaces in which people produced, prepared, ate, and discarded food. Field boundaries, irrigation canals, herders' pathways, and other large-scale landscape features testify to production areas and methods (e.g., Ur and Colantoni, 2010). The locations and dimensions of hearths and storage facilities reflect cooking and storage strategies and goals (e.g., Bogaard et al., 2009; Howey and Frederick, 2016). The sizes and layouts of homes and public buildings speak to the scale of expected commensalism as well as to how people arranged themselves as they ate – or, in some cases, didn't eat but watched others do so (e.g., Chicoine, 2011:440; Jones, 2007:188). We use the extent to which food facilities were generally visible and/or accessible to infer the public or private nature of related activities; we use facilities' clustering or dispersal to infer the extent of collaboration and the amounts of food involved; and we use the scale and form of environmental modifications to infer labor methods and organization as well as commensal group sizes.

Soil chemistry testifies to the spatial distribution of food activities when no artifacts or features can. Archaeologists take small samples of soil at multiple locations across an ancient surface, and then test those samples for selected elements and chemical compounds. They do this because as any cook can tell you, kitchens as well as dining rooms get spattered with grease freckles, milk droplets, dough crumbs, and other tiny bits of debris. Each of those bits alters the chemical properties of any soil into which it gets incorporated. For example, organic substances raise soil phosphate levels. Places where people cook, compost, and go to the bathroom have higher phosphate levels than abutting places where they don't. Other elements (e.g., potassium, barium, magnesium, calcium) and organic compounds (residues like those found on vessels, tools, and teeth) also testify to food-related activities, from heating/burning to cheese aging (King, 2008; Luke et al., 2016; Pecci et al., 2017).

Texts and Iconography

Texts can provide information about past foodways that no other data set ever quite can. Written documents can provide not only illuminating details but also sometimes emic perspectives on food in the past. Without Roman texts, how would we know that sows' udders were "a delicacy at the tables of the Roman rich" (D'Arms, 2004:432)? Without dynastic writings, how would we perceive the hierarchical rigor of Zhou Dynasty (1046–256 BCE) feasts, or the divine implications of culinary knife work in Muromachi Japan (O'Connor, 2015:154, 181)? Texts are no panacea, however, for reasons enumerated by historical archaeologists the world across. Most people and most meals remain unrepresented; authors have personal biases and agendas; accounts often focus on one aspect of foodways and leave others undescribed (e.g., D'Arms, 2004; Stallibrass and Thomas, 2008b; Moreno, 2007:211).

The same concerns apply to iconographic representations of ancient foodways, from Egyptian models of laboring bakers to Mycenean hunting and feasting frescoes to Maya paintings of bowls heaped with tamales. Tremendously informative about past ways of farming, cooking, and eating, artistic representations reflect only some segments of ancient societies, and they do so in accordance with artists' and sponsors' aims. In ancient Mesopotamia, for example, repetitive crop and livestock motifs advertised the agricultural abundance that underpinned the state. The artists depicted not reality, but an ideal world enabled by rulers acting on behalf of the gods (Winter, 2007).

Artistic conventions also distinguish iconography from cool reportage. D'Arms (2004:437) points out that food abounds in Roman homes' wall paintings and mosaics – cheese and cherries, apples and chestnuts, eggs and radishes – but sows' udders are "conspicuous for their complete visual absence." Homeowners welcomed their guests with images of raw agricultural abundance, not of cooked dishes. Prior to the third century, food is even sparse in Roman images of elite banquets: diners drink but don't eat, and the few foods that are depicted are stylized to the point of unidentifiability (D'Arms, 2004). The texts are full of fabulous delicacies; the art remains silent. As a final note, while the impact of artistic convention is clear here, in many societies archaeologists lack such understanding. Does that painted plant represent simply a plant, or does it signify something else? Is that feast attendee a deity or a human (e.g., Wright, 2004:45)? Images testify to ancient foodways, but they don't necessarily do so in a language that we understand.

Combining Data Sets

It is a truism that combinations of data sets provide the best understandings of past foodways – indeed, of past lifeways on all fronts. A mere skim of this chapter demonstrates the extent to which the data sets that archaeologists use to reconstruct ancient foodways complement each other. Some data testify to plant foods and others to animal foods, some to foods available and others to foods eaten, some to food production and others to food storage, preparation, consumption, and discard. Each data set has different strengths and weaknesses. Animal bones commonly survive better than plant remains, but plants usually constitute the majority of people's diets. Unlike faunal and botanical remains, stable isotopes provide direct evidence of what people ate, but isotopic values cannot reveal the range of foods in a person's diet or how those foods were prepared. Paleofeces can do both, but they rarely preserve for us to find. Ceramics preserve beautifully, but establishing the use(s) to which they were put can be very difficult.

Different food data sets, moreover, often reflect different elements of life in the past (Twiss, 2015). Some provide information about specific segments of society, while others testify more broadly. Only elites might have owned painted walls and metal tableware, for example, whereas everyone ate out of ceramic bowls. Some reflect everyday eating, while others shed light on special occasions. Villagers perhaps ate grain and vegetables every day, but reserved meat for rites and celebrations. To reconstruct more than a sliver of any society's foodways, we have no choice: we must look to as many lines of evidence as we can.

CHAPTER 3

Food and Economics

Where there is money, there are counterfeiters, so pre-contact Aztecs had to keep an eye out for fake cacao beans as they accepted their wages and made their market purchases. A porter whose daily wage of one hundred beans turned out to include fakes made from wax, dough, or avocado pits might have trouble buying those two small rabbits (thirty beans each), and the hundred-bean jackrabbit or turkey hen would be out of reach entirely (Coe and Coe, 2007).

Among the Aztecs and other Mesoamerican peoples, food was quite literally currency (Figure 3.1). The same is true for historic Koreans, who were legally required to pay all state taxes in rice (Kim, 2015). Medieval Europeans paid their taxes in pepper – and the modern University of Bath annually presents a single peppercorn to the regional council as rent for its campus (www.bath.ac.uk/news/2007/11/14/peppercorn.html). But food is entangled with both macro- and microeconomics in many different ways, all of which archaeologists investigate. Do you want to know if prehistoric people had a concept of private property? Take a look at where they stashed their food supplies (e.g., Bogaard et al., 2009). Are you curious about the origins of urban commercialism? Seek out when people began to trade extensively in staple foods – the most basic of market commodities – as opposed to in prestige delicacies (e.g., Barrett et al., 2004). Reconstructing past foodways allows us to explore topics including labor costs and supplies, the extent of professional specialization, resource distribution patterns, economic risk buffering strategies (prehistoric "insurance policies"), and far, far more (e.g., Bolender, 2015; Halstead, 1989, 2014; LeCount, 2010; Mylona, 2008; Orton et al., 2014; Zeder, 1991).

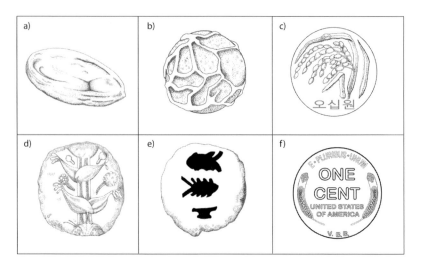

FIGURE 3.1. Food as currency and food on currency. (a) Cacao bean: used as currency in pre-contact Mesoamerica. (b) Peppercorn: used as currency in medieval Europe. (c) Republic of Korea 50-won coin with image of rice (minted 1983–present). (d) Cyrene tetradrachm with image of silphium (a plant exploited to extinction in antiquity), fourth century BCE, North Africa. (e) Pandyan Dynasty (seventh to tenth centuries CE) coin with image of fish, South Asia. (f) United States wheat cent, minted 1909–1956. Images emphatically not to scale. Drawing by K. Thompson.

Production/Procurement

As Hastorf (2016: 84) notes, food production and procurement are huge topics in the archaeological literature. (While "production" can refer to all of the many kinds of work that people do in order to acquire food – cultivating and gathering, shepherding and hunting, weeding and netting, and milking and feeding – I am using it in this section to refer only to the raising of domesticated plants and animals. By "procurement" people generally mean either the collection of wild resources or the acquisition of foods from other groups of people, via trade or exchange; I am discussing the former.) Much of this literature focuses on behavioral ecological issues of nutrition, survival, and adaptation. However, a large subset explores the economic organization of food production in specific cultures. Prominent topics include *how* food was produced or procured (re labor organization, technological developments, investment strategies [e.g., in land]); *which* foods people produced/procured (re valuation of resources, risk/reward balancing); and *how much* of those foods they generated (re risk buffering, surplus mobilization, staple vs. wealth financing). Political pressures and opportunities play into all of these topics, as will be discussed further in the next chapter.

Different food production regimes require different amounts and types of labor, have different ecological impacts, and tend to lead to – and be caused by – different social outcomes. Consider, for example, the contrasting implications and opportunities afforded by small-scale household agropastoralism (individual families tending their own fields and livestock) as opposed to large-scale, specialized crop farming and pastoralism (planters and herders are spatially and socially distinct). People may produce the exact same foods using either strategy: wheat, barley, millet, sheep, goats, and so forth. They may not, however, lead broadly similar lives.

In small-scale household farming, for example, livestock often graze on cropland that's not currently in use, and the animals stay relatively close to home, walking 'banks' of meat, milk, blood, fat, manure, and other products (Halstead, 1996; Russell, 1988). They convert unneeded or spoiled crops into edible food, and their dung fertilizes the fields (Halstead, 1987). Households are largely self-sufficient, although they rely closely on each other for social reasons, for periodic help with large projects, and as backups in case of emergency. Villages thus consist of multiple groups of people with roughly similar economic interests and identities.

In contrast, specialized pastoralists move large herds long distances to pasture, potentially spending weeks or even months away from farmsteads and fields before coming in to exchange their animal products for farmers' grain. Cultivation and herding are thus separate pursuits, potentially conducted by different households or kin groups. Specialized herder/cultivator economies are associated ethnographically with distinct social identities and potential social conflict, despite mutual dependence on exchange (e.g., Bar-Yosef and Khazanov, 1992; Forbes, 1995). Such herder–farmer conflicts may have large-scale political and social implications. Turchin (2009), for example, posits that they underpin the origins of empire in Asia. He argues that conflicts between nomadic pastoralists and settled farmers pushed both groups to increase their group sizes, as nomads tried to keep raiding farmers' crops and farmers sought to protect themselves and their food supplies. The two groups alternated expanding their polities, until steppe confederations were facing agrarian empires.

How intensively people cultivate their land also has profound social implications. When people put significant amounts of labor into improving their farmland (fertilizing, watering, draining it), they are essentially investing in it – adding value to it, and also tightening their ties to it in ways that may enhance claims of ownership or usufruct (e.g., Bogaard, 2004; Currie et al., 2015; Jones, 2005; Netting, 1971). This may not seem like a revelation when one is studying historic cultures, but in prehistory there are serious questions about when people first began to believe that land was something that people could own, or to which they could limit others' access.

Why does it matter if people own the land where they produce or acquire their food? Because different patches of land are commonly more or less fertile, more or less favored by animals, more or less subject to flooding and other natural damage. As a result, when different groups of people (e.g., families) exploit different plots of land, they acquire different amounts of food. If families each use the same plot every year – if they own their land, or maintain durable rights of access – then some families may become considerably richer than others. Moreover, food surpluses produced by relatively successful households can be shared out to less productive ones, incurring debts or obligations that the less productive carry into the future (Halstead, 1989). A system of food production can in this way set the stage for lasting social inequalities (e.g., Halstead, 1989, 2014; Netting, 1971; Sahlins, 1972; see Gurven et al., 2010:53 for qualifying information).

Food production systems also shape whether societies remain stable over the long term, or whether they must reshape themselves dramatically in order to cope with severe environmental degradation. Examples of both abound in archaeology: stories of overhunting, species translocation, and habitat destruction are probably most famous (e.g., examples in Grayson, 2001; Hofman and Rick, 2018), but many scholars illuminate ecologically knowledgeable production methods that remained in use for centuries (e.g., Braje and Rick, 2013; Scarborough and Valdez, 2014). There is also a growing literature that takes neither side, focusing rather on archaeology's potential to inform conservation work (Frazier, 2007; Lyman, 1996; Lyman and Cannon, 2004; Rick and Lockwood, 2013; Wolverton and Lyman, 2012; see also Chapter 8).

An example of how a food production system shapes a culture's ecological impact comes from the 'Opunohu Valley of the Society Islands. For centuries preceding European contact, Ma'ohi chieftains and second-tier elites held sway over landless commoners who produced virtually all of the food that everyone ate (Lepofsky and Kahn, 2011). Elites rarely worked in the gardens or fields – some were, in fact, ritually barred from doing so – but they had a significant impact on agricultural ecologies because they were entitled to limit harvests (Lepofsky and Kahn, 2011). High chiefs imposed *rahui* – restrictions on production – for various reasons, but key among those was a desire to ensure the continued availability of valued foods (Lepofsky and Kahn, 2011).

Commoners subject to these restrictions had to farm strategically, lest they be caught understocked when *rahui* came down and limited the food that they could acquire. Ma'ohi commoners therefore planned carefully how to manage a diversity of resources, from breadfruit to yams, Malay apple to taro (Lepofsky and Kahn, 2011). They tilled and mulched, terraced and irrigated, planted across seasons and in multiple ecological zones. They had learned these methods the hard way, as a century or so after the islands were initially colonized (that is, ca. 1,000 CE) the ancestral Ma'ohi had deforested large areas in pursuit of cultivable land, causing significant erosion and actually rendering sizable swaths of land useless for farming (Lepofsky and Kahn, 2011). These mistakes encouraged subsequent Ma'ohi generations to develop (by ca. 1300 CE) a range of ecologically appropriate agricultural techniques that could produce food enough for both commoners and elites. The combination of elite *rahui* and commoner farming knowledge ensured that even ecologically marginal zones remained productive for centuries (Lepofsky and Kahn, 2011).

This Ma'ohi study highlights the additional fact that food production systems exist within broader systems of production and social segmentation. Archaeologists can use agricultural data to investigate not only status differences, as in the 'Opunohu Valley, but also any number of other social distinctions. Bogaard et al. (2011), for example, report that more than seven thousand years ago, five 'clans' farmed the land around the Neolithic settlement of Vaihingen an der Enz, Germany. Each of these groups cultivated different areas of the landscape. Macrobotanical samples from across the site contain weed assemblages that thrive in varied growing conditions. Some samples grew close to the village in relatively intensively managed plots; others grew further out. The persistence of this variation indicates that Vaihingen's 'clans' maintained their rights to particular fields over the course of generations, giving those who farmed richer zones a distinct advantage over their neighbors. Perhaps this is why all of the non-local 'clans' (one whose fields lay at some distance from the village) left the settlement midway through its occupation (Bogaard et al., 2011)!

Distribution

People need food, so a core preoccupation of any society must be ensuring that it gets produced and that it reaches those who need it. In societies where everyone participates in food production, distribution may not be a major concern. But in societies where many people lack primary access to the food supply – societies with soldiers and sailors, priests and administrators, merchants and artisans – and in those that rely on staples unable to grow locally, food distribution enables both individuals and society as a whole to survive. Longer-distance food distribution also expands the menu of foods available to a group, and allows people to live in nutritionally marginal environments (Lewis, 2015). Food distribution makes complex civilization possible.

Food distribution is not necessarily easy, however, because foodstuffs have shelf lives. Inorganic goods such as ceramics and glassware can sit for centuries without damage, but food is fragile: it spoils, spills, and gets infested with insects and rodents. Food distributors have to consider how well particular foods store in various forms (grapes vs. raisins, hamburger vs. jerky), and how fast they can be sent to various destinations, at what cost. Suppose (counter to most of human history) that a group can rely on sufficient amounts of food being produced and available; they still need a strategy for getting that food to everyone in the group.

Consider the citizens of Tal e-Malyan (ancient Anshan) in the Zagros. During the third millennium BCE, this great city spanned more than 130 ha, with administrators, artisans, and many others uninvolved with food production residing within its walls. A classic study by Zeder (1991) reveals that Malyan's meat came from herds raised in the surrounding countryside. The distribution of this meat constituted one of the specialized segments of the urban economy, with herders, entrepreneurial middlemen, government administrators, and consumers pursuing multiple strategies to get different cuts and kinds of meat to different portions of the population (Zeder, 1991). In the site's Kaftari phase (2400–1800 BCE), for example, high-status citizens dined on young sheep and goats; lower-status citizens ate caprines of all ages. Leg bones predominate in multiple faunal assemblages, indicating that both high- and low-status city-dwellers normally brought home animal segments rather than entire carcasses or live animals. Standardized cut marks on the bones suggest that specialists butchered many – perhaps most – of the animals. In sum, ancient country-folk raised the animals that would feed the urbanites of Anshan; professional butchers commonly cut them apart; people received or purchased different cuts, as their wealth, status, or tastes allowed (Zeder, 1991:197–201).

The system operating at Anshan is, of course, only one possible food distribution strategy. Others have been identified in other areas and time periods, and each such strategy has different social and political implications. For example, market systems push people away from domestic self-sufficiency toward communal interaction, mutual interreliance, and shared infrastructure; growers and herders establish production regimes targeted toward satisfying the markets rather than just their own households and associates (Dahlin et al., 2010). Small-scale domestic and large-scale redistributive economies confer very different pressures and opportunities. Archaeologists are therefore very interested in the specifics of how food reached consumers. Dahlin et al. (2010), for example, challenge the long-standing idea that food moved through lowland Classic Maya society exclusively along redistributive lines: Maya elites collected taxes and tribute that they then redistributed down the social hierarchy. Dahlin and colleagues point out that food could have moved via market exchange as well. Testing this proposition at two Classic Maya trade centers, they find large plazas with rows of market-stall-like foundations as well as soil signatures (phosphorus concentrations) that echo those seen in a modern Maya marketplace. Maya cities may have been economically livelier and more diverse than commonly understood (Dahlin et al., 2010).

Food remains are a terrific data set for studying longer-distance trade networks because unlike artifacts such as amphorae and coins, they don't get reused and relocated (Orengo and Livarda, 2016). Plant foods are a particularly useful data set because local environments place strict limits on the foods that people can grow. (Important food animals such as cattle, sheep, and deer tolerate relatively broad environmental ranges). Moreover, many plants do not preserve well for shipping: thousands of years ago, leafy vegetables and seed-in melons would not have traveled for weeks before they were eaten.[1] Climatically inappropriate and preservation-unfriendly species are thus easily recognizable as imports.

Say, for example, that one is interested in the economy of ancient Britain. We know that the British economy changed dramatically in ~43 CE, when Britain was incorporated into the Roman Empire. In both city and country, people began to import or grow a long list of new foods, including cherries, almonds, olives, apples, figs, grapes, turnips, cucumbers, and cabbages. Shipments of black pepper started to come from India and dates from North Africa; local farmers planted orchards of pear trees, fields of millet, and gardens of lettuce and leeks. Some farmers began to cultivate the new vegetables and fruits in large quantities, which would

---

[1] Of course, one shouldn't underestimate the abilities of people to move perishable foods around, even sans refrigeration, wheeled vehicles, or riding animals. Archaeologists have found marine fish tapeworms in millennia-old Chilean coprolites – 40 km away from the coast (Reinhard and Araujo, 2016)!

only have been worthwhile for people living near markets where they could sell such perishables. Apple pips and plum pits thus testify to the origins of British towns: population centers full of non-farmers eager to buy produce from suburban growers (Van der Veen and Livarda, 2008).

How, though, did these and other goods arrive on British tables? How did Romano-British trade actually work? We know that in Britain, the Romans established a web of roads and rivers along which traveled the goods of the Empire. But which routes carried which goods? And why? Because British archaeologists have excavated hundreds of Roman-era (ca. 43–410 CE) sites, it is possible to create detailed maps of the distribution of the food plants that the Romans introduced to the British Isles (Van der Veen, 2008). These maps reveal, among other things, the existence of at least four separate groups of Romano-British consumers. City-dwellers, military personnel, southeastern English countryfolk, and countryfolk throughout the rest of Britain varied in their consumption of the new plants (Van der Veen and Livarda, 2008).

A focus on merely one of these new consumer groups – the people of London – reveals how Romano-British commerce developed over time. In the early Roman era (first and early second centuries CE), people throughout the city of London consumed the new plant foods. Londoners' economic involvement with the foods largely ended there, though: the distribution of exotic plant remains inside and outside the city indicates that early Roman Londoners were consumers rather than distributors, living at the end of the economic pipeline (Livarda and Orengo, 2015). This pattern shifted during the later second and third centuries, when plant food distributions suggest London's development into southeastern Britain's principal redistribution center (Orengo and Livarda, 2016). Imported foods continued to sail into the London port, but they then entered a commercial sphere that functioned both within and beyond the city itself. Many foods were re-exported to other parts of Britain; those that stayed within London were distributed less evenly throughout the city (Livarda and Orengo, 2015).

In the fourth century CE, Londoners continued to both eat and trade in exotic foods, but the trading system no longer held to its old patterns and locations. In this Late Roman era, the remains of exotic plant foods come increasingly from London's entrance/exit zones and from areas once outside the city's economic core, suggesting that while the trade in imported foods remained important, who controlled that trade may have shifted (Livarda and Orengo, 2015). These developments were part of larger economic changes throughout Britain. During the fourth century, imported foods increasingly landed in Britain's southern ports rather than in London.

From there they traveled northwards on roads, rather than along rivers as they once had. (Orengo and Livarda [2016] suspect that upriver transport made money in the early Roman era because the Romans were paying to ship bulk supplies to their armies and administrative centers. When the Empire ceased shipments, it wasn't generally profitable for individual traders to organize and pay for river shipping.) London probably retained its commercial power because road travelers heading north or west had to pass through it: the Roman road network "seems to force transit through London" (Orengo and Livarda, 2016:31). So London kept its trading power – but different Londoners now held it.

Privatization

To what extent were resources privately owned? Did prehistoric individuals or groups possess and control assets, or were resources communally owned and regulated? Food (along with water) is arguably the most basic human resource there is; everyone everywhere needs food on a daily basis. Every society, therefore, has norms about the extent to which individuals or groups may control their own food supply. Archaeologists investigate communal vs. private control over food in both prehistoric and historic contexts across the globe, reconstructing past economic patterns and considering how they changed as technologies developed, political situations shifted, and ideologies altered.

Consider, for example, the case of Çatalhöyük East, in central Turkey. Çatalhöyük (occupied ca. 7100–6000 BCE) was an early farming town of perhaps a few thousand people, Çatalhöyük (occupied ca. 7100–6000 BCE) was an early farming town of perhaps a few thousand people. Residents lived in abutting mudbrick houses that they entered via ladders down through openings in the roofs. These ladders led down into the main rooms of the houses, in which visitors could easily see hearths, sleeping benches, wall paintings, and assorted tools and decorative displays – but not households' food supplies. Those were generally kept, bagged and binned and basketed, inside smaller side rooms and well outside of easy sight (Bogaard et al., 2009) (Figure 3.2). Food processing tools (e.g., grinding stones) were often highly visible in homes' main rooms, but they seem to have been placed in side rooms when there was enough space to do so, consistent again with the idea that Çatalhöyük's residents liked to keep their food resources as private as possible (Bogaard et al., 2014b; Demirergi et al., 2014). The prehistoric farmers of Çatalhöyük did not, it appears, want their neighbors to know how much food they had.

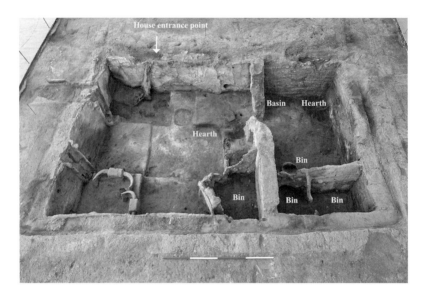

FIGURE 3.2. Neolithic house, Çatalhöyük, Turkey. Building 77. Photo by Jason Quinlan, courtesy of J. Quinlan and the Çatalhöyük Research Project.

Nor did they plan to share their daily dinners. Çatalhöyük's cooking and
serving pots are big enough to feed nuclear families (or their equivalents), not
extended family groups or neighborhoods (Demirergi et al., 2014). The sizes
and locations of grain dehusking deposits, fire spots, and many grinding
stones similarly suggest meals prepared at and for private homes (Demirergi
et al., 2014). This does not mean that households never shared food, of course:
indeed, there is ample evidence for neighborhood or even community events
(Bogaard et al., 2009; Demirergi et al., 2014; Twiss, 2012). However, multiple
lines of evidence suggest that Çatalhöyük households kept and controlled
their own food supplies, which they stored in private spaces and habitually
shared only among themselves. A similar pattern has been identified in the
southern Levant, where over the course of the Neolithic, people gradually
moved their food stores into their homes and ultimately into dedicated
storage rooms (Kuijt, 2015). These two data sets suggest that in southwest
Asia, staple foods have been recognized as private property rather than as
communally owned resources for more than eight thousand years.

Surplus

Archaeologists have been discussing surplus food production for decades,
because such production enables societies to (1) support craftspeople, clergy,

standing militaries, bureaucrats, and other non-food-producers, and (2) treat food as an alienable asset – property that people don't need to keep to themselves, but can trade, share, donate, sell, or otherwise use to advance their social goals. Surplus food is generally seen as a prerequisite for institutionalized social inequality (see Chapter 4), for economic specialization, and for many technological advancements (e.g., Bakels, 1996; Brumfiel and Earle, 1987; Groot and Lentjes, 2013, Johnson and Earle, 2000; Kim and Kusimba, 2008). Its production has often been considered a "trigger" for socioeconomic transformations ranging from the origins of agriculture to the rise of state-level society to the formation of new ethnic identities (Morehart and de Lucia, 2015; although see Forbes 2016; Petek and Lane, 2017). But what *is* surplus food? And how and why do people begin producing it?

Archaeologists debate the most useful way to define surplus. Many – historically, most – archaeologists take an adaptive approach, defining surplus as "production in excess of biological necessity ... [the] amount left over after subsistence needs have been accommodated" (Morehart and de Lucia, 2015:18). Others criticize this approach on the basis that there is no such thing as an *absolute surplus* – no universally applicable subsistence level above which we can automatically identify surpluses (Hastorf and Foxhall, 2017; Morehart and de Lucia, 2015:19). They argue that archaeologists must pay attention to *relative surplus*: the food that ancient peoples themselves saw as additional to their basic requirements. The uniformitarian notion of absolute surplus sheds little light on human economic decision-making, because social norms and goals shape what people consider "surplus" to requirements.

Supporters of absolute surplus retort that restricting ourselves to studying relative surplus precludes our studying some of the most important questions in anthropology (e.g., Halstead, 1989:70). They say that if archaeologists avoid using our own estimates of minimum human biological needs, we have no way of assessing whether ancient groups were producing more food than they needed to survive – and so why and how they were (or weren't) doing so. We need some concept of absolute surplus in order to estimate how much land it took to keep a population alive; we need it to approximate the scale of people's political investments (Morehart and de Lucia, 2015:25).

What, then, can archaeologists do? Should we choose to study absolute surplus or relative surplus? Morehart and de Lucia (2015) argue that this is a false choice. It is important that we recognize absolute surplus; it is also important that we not assume that subsistence goals were more important than social ones. Farmers may grow crops to pay rent or tribute, to tithe or to amass a dowry. Are any of these crops unnecessary, or "extra" in any meaningful way? Surely not. Society places claims on us that we, as social creatures, can't always set aside, even when those claims conflict with our biological urges. Some skip meals to keep the bank from foreclosing on their homes (Morehart and de Lucia, 2015). Others do so to maintain socially approved body types (Counihan, 1999; Parasecoli, 2005). Both absolute and relative surplus are analytically useful concepts. They are also quite different, and it is important that authors and readers be clear as to the difference.

One further point that must be made is that communities may generate surpluses simply as a matter of survival. No political or technological advancement need be intended. Subsistence farmers, for example, need to plant more food than they necessarily will require because rainfall varies, crop diseases strike, insects and fungi attack stores, and field workers face illness and injury (Halstead [1989], Winterhalder et al. [2015], and Panagiotakopulu and Buckland [2018] discuss archaeological evidence for grain weevils and other storage pests). Herders face similar risks, as animals are susceptible to disease, predation, and weather extremes. Producing a "normal surplus" of food enables people to eat even when things go wrong, securing their survival in moderately difficult times (Forbes, 2016; Halstead, 1989; Winterhalder et al., 2015).

Archaeologists have inferred normal surpluses in a wide variety of areas and time periods. A recent example focuses on Bronze Age Greece, where stable carbon and nitrogen isotopes suggest that farmers used varying strategies to produce sufficient food for their families. Human $\delta^{13}C$ and $\delta^{15}N$ values from the site of Thessaloniki Toumba suggest that plants provided the bulk of people's protein intake; animal foods probably contributed to the diet but crops were what kept people alive (Nitsch et al., 2017). Ensuring the food supply meant producing a normal surplus of grains in particular. Households rose to meet this challenge in varying ways. Some farmers laboriously enriched their crops' growing environments, intensively manuring their barley and wheat (and thereby elevating the cereals' $\delta^{15}N$ values). Others managed their crops less intensively, producing cereals with lower $\delta^{15}N$ values. Perhaps these people lacked the labor pool – manure is heavy and hard to move around – to farm more intensively (Nitsch et al., 2017). Some of them might also have been slightly short on fertilizer, as bovine $\delta^{13}C$ values suggest that a non-manuring village's cattle were grazing a few miles away from home in the local salt marshes (Nitsch et al., 2017). These people opted for cattle that grew fat without fodder, which presumably saved more of their crops for their own intake.

Normal surpluses don't suffice when people face severe or long-term shortages, whether caused by natural disasters, raiding enemies, or the loss of working family members to plague or accident. In such cases households may rely on each other, moving food from those with unneeded "normal surpluses" to those who are hungry (Halstead, 1989). It is in everyone's best interests to maintain social bonds across households and between villages, not simply for enjoyment but because such relationships constitute insurance against starvation (Halstead, 1989).

Normal surpluses thus provide a safety net in both good years and bad. In a year when the crops and herds thrive, a household may share its surplus food with neighbors who are less fortunate, knowing that they can expect the same when it's their turn to be in need. In a year when the crops grow poorly and the animals are thin and sickly, the household may eat all of what it produces, either surviving on that amount or supplementing with contributions from better-off allies. Should the year be particularly fruitful for everyone, and storage bins filled to capacity, surpluses still aren't wasted. Animals can always eat extra grain: in twentieth-century Greece, rural farmers planted barley, maize, and rye intending to use it as fodder in good years but as human food in poor years (Halstead, 2015).[2] Surpluses can also be turned to political use (as discussed in Chapter 5).

Surplus is not always easy to handle in either practical or social terms. An abundance of food is surely a net positive, but it comes with costs (Sheets, 2017; Twiss and Bogaard, 2017). If a group harvests or slaughters more food than they need or want to eat at that particular moment, and if they don't wish to simply abandon the extra (as most groups won't), then they have to figure out how to extend the food's availability through time if it is to support its producers. This can be difficult in the absence of modern preservation technologies. Even highly storable foods such as grain and pulses pose challenges: they must be protected from moisture, vermin, and other people, and even then they don't store indefinitely. (Winterhalder et al. [2015:341] select two years as a reasonable estimate of crop shelf-life; Kuijt [2015:325] points out that the proportion of your store that spoils rises with time, and that a mere six months may lose you 10 percent of your grain or more.) Warm, wet weather and perishable foods (leafy greens, milk, poultry) make surpluses even more difficult to manage. Sharing food out

---

[2] Grain isn't the only food that can nourish animals or humans as people see fit. Modern Greek herders gave their goats dried figs in winter; Neolithic Greeks may have done so as well, but it's difficult to tell if the millennia-old fig seeds found at multiple sites derive from people fattening up their animals, or themselves (Valamoti and Charles, 2005).

with friends and neighbors helps with this storage challenge even as it buffers risk, as described above. Archaeologists often call such disbursement "social storage" (Halstead and O'Shea, 1982; O'Shea, 1981).

A sizable archaeological literature reckons with the economics of surplus food production, physical storage, and social storage. A preponderance of this research uses artifactual and architectural storage facilities – bins, jars, baskets – to evaluate how much food was being stored, although we can rarely tell how full such facilities tended to be kept or how much food went into perishable containers or simple heaps that left no archaeological traces (Groot and Lentjes, 2013; Hastorf and Foxhall, 2017). Social storage is often inferred from evidence for food-sharing across households (which we normally call feasting; see Chapter 5): collections of animal bones, for example, representing enough meat to feed tens of people or more, in and amongst houses rather than in palaces or temples (e.g., Demirergi et al., 2014; Twiss and Bogaard, 2017). Larger-scale social storage, involving food exchanges between settlements, is traceable if one can source either food remains themselves or durable goods known to have traveled along the same paths as foods (e.g., Bayliss-Smith and Hviding, 2015).

Archaeologists can think about ample resources in other terms than "surplus". Smith (2017) advocates talking about abundance. She argues that large quantities of food and other goods were regularly present in ancient people's lives, not as the exclusive property of elites but as a widely shared goal and project. Mobile populations traveled to and ate from the richest berry patches, fishing streams, and hunting grounds; settled villagers worked to fill storerooms with grain, nuts, and other preservables. Evidence of food abundance marked the landscape: large, deliberately shaped shell and bone middens rising up under the coastal sun (McNiven, 2013; Thompson et al., 2016); heaps of bones, sometimes meters deep, at recurrently used animal kill sites (Olsen, 1995; Zedeño, 2017; Zeder et al., 2013); communal storehouses posed on hillsides and in villages (Hastorf and Foxhall, 2017; Wesson, 1999). Many (not all) of these abundances were laboriously amassed over time – cumulative rather than momentary bounties – and they had widely varying social meanings and uses.

Food As a Commodity

In market economies food often becomes a commodity, produced for sale or trade rather than for personal consumption or local sharing (Shanahan, 2015). Such commoditization alters food values, labor strategies, exchange patterns,

FIGURE 3.3. Children pretend to be a Roman shopkeeper and customer in Taberna IV.15-16, Herculaneum, Italy. Passersby could buy food from the counter's large jars and perhaps from additional containers ranged on the shelves at right. Multicolored pieces of marble decorate the counter; shop owners invested in such decorations in order to attract well-off customers (MacMahon, 2005). The street is visible in the bottom right corner of the photograph.

and even nutritional statuses (for example, producers sometimes restrict their own diets in order to maximize their sales opportunities [Gijanto and Walshaw, 2014]). The historical archaeological record is full of brand-name as well as generic packaging, food shipping containers, and food sales establishments. Much of the evidence derives from relatively recent time periods (e.g., Jones, 1993), but commercial food sales are visible far back into the past as well (Hartman et al., 2013; van Neer and Ervynck, 2004).

If you wander through the remains of the two-thousand-year-old cities of Pompeii and Herculaneum, for example, you may notice retail service counters installed inside some of the buildings (Figure 3.3). Archaeologists have identified masonry retail counters inside 158 of the properties at Pompeii; 128 (81 percent) of these had associated cooking facilities (Ellis, 2004).[3] These 128 food and drink outlets are located throughout Pompeii,

---

[3] Pompeii's buildings with retail counters have long been called 'bars,' and stereotyped as seedy places full of gamblers, prostitutes, and trouble. However, modern researchers argue

with the notable exception of along one stretch of road. Sixty-three shops sit along the western Via dell'Abbondanza – but only one food establishment. The eastern portion of this road, in contrast, features twenty-two food sellers within the space of 600 meters. The difference probably exists because the western part of the road was used for ceremonial processions; Ellis (2004) surmises that Roman authorities determined which retailers were allowed to open shop along the processional route, and bars didn't meet their moral standards.

If bars were banned from the western Via dell'Abbondanza, they flourished along Pompeii's other main streets. More than half of Pompeii's known food and drink shops sit along the streets that pass through a city gate and run toward the central Forum; 70 percent are located along busy thoroughfares (Ellis, 2004). Furthermore, they concentrate near intersections. Fifty percent of Pompeii's food and drink outlets are positioned at street corners, and as many of these as could constructed their sales counters in places that maximized their visibility to passersby (Ellis, 2004). On the Via Stabiana, for example, where incoming foot traffic flowed north, sales counters sit just inside bars' doors, facing south (Ellis, 2004:fig. 6). Two-thirds of Pompeii's known intersections feature a food and drink shop. Pompeii's food sellers clearly realized the importance of "location, location, location" as they strategized to maximize their profits just as restaurateurs and bar owners do today.

Globalization

Many people point to the era of Christopher Columbus and Vasco da Gama as the era in which humanity began to form a globalized economy, but some archaeologists are using food remains to argue that globalization has far earlier, non-Western origins (Boivin et al., 2012). Thousands of years ago, wheat and barley spread eastwards across Asia; millets spread

---

that some were grocery shops or similar establishments (Beard, 2008; MacMahon, 2005). Ellis (2004) partly disagrees, contending that Roman artwork indicates that shops selling non-food items used wooden sales counters, presumably because they didn't have to worry about fire damage and sloshed liquids in the same way that food-sellers did. Ultimately, everyone agrees that many of the establishments *were* bars. Beard, for example, describes a tavern, its outer walls painted with "election slogans" seemingly for its barmaids/waitresses, and its red-painted counter inset with four large jars and an oven at its end. Hanging over this counter swung a bronze lamp depicting a tiny man with a penis as large as the rest of his body, a second penis springing from the first's tip and bells dangling from the whole: "a combination of lamp, wind-chimes, and service bell. Welcome to the world of the bar?" (Beard, 2008:228).

westwards. By 2000 BCE, all three grains were being consumed in Europe, the Middle East, China, and India. Over the course of the following few centuries, multiple African crops grew in India, south Asian zebu cattle reached the Persian Gulf, and Arabian date palms flourished in Nubia (Boivin et al., 2015). These food sources traveled along myriad routes, including overseas: the African crops that appear in India have not been discovered in contemporary Arabian sites between the two areas (Boivin et al., 2015).

Continental-scale interactions intensified during the first millennium BCE, with Greeks eating chickens (southeast Asia), Indians savoring watermelons (north Africa), and Chinese relishing pomegranates (Mediterranean to the Himalayas; Boivin et al., 2015). Food technologies likewise traveled: Chinese cooks developed new flour mills that probably derived from Mediterranean querns, which turned wheat "from an uninspiring boiled grain into a valued staple for noodle production" (Boivin et al., 2015:353).

Some argue that the prehistoric Eurasian food movements are "comparable in scale of . . . impact on global diets to the Colombian Exchange of historic times" (Jones et al., 2011:665). One might counter that they still don't represent true globalization, as that requires transoceanic travel. Caravans can wander across continents, but as long as they remain landbound they cannot link more than three of the world's continents. This is true, and certainly the Old and New Worlds weren't in significant[4] economic contact until roughly half a millennium ago. One might, however, concede that the prehistoric maritime colonization of the Pacific represents an impressively global-scale accomplishment, and one visible in the progressive spread of pig, chicken, taro, breadfruit, and yam remains across Micronesia and Polynesia (Storey, 2015).

Labor

That food sheds light on past labor conditions is clear at a wide range of sites. One example is the historic Hacienda San Miguel Acocotla in rural Mexico, where during the nineteenth century both landowners and laborers lived on a large agrarian estate. There, Newman (2014:151–152) reveals, hacienda owners brought in village women to spend their days making "mountains

---

[4] Apologies to the Vikings and Polynesians, whose ambitious explorations to North and South America respectively I am deeming too small-scale/short-term (Viking) and archaeologically unresolved (Polynesian) to count as economically significant. Please see Storey et al. (2007), Thomson et al. (2014), and Wallace (2009) for more information.

of tortillas" to feed families who spent their days sweating in huge fields to grow wheat for market. These village women and working families left few and minimally informative documentary traces but plenty of archaeological evidence of lives spent working on and for food. Women in particular are virtually invisible in Acocotla's records – but thousands upon thousands of artifacts testify silently to culinary work so hard and so time-consuming that elsewhere in Mexico and throughout the world it damaged women's skeletons (e.g., Merbs, 1980; Molleson, 1994; see also Chapter 6).

The hard work wasn't the first step of tortilla-making. That was simply boiling dried maize and slaked lime and letting the mixture soak overnight. Someone had to collect the fuel and water, and acquire the ingredients, but that wasn't particularly difficult or time-consuming. (At least it wasn't at historic Acocotla; for Lacandon Maya maize-cookers, acquiring slaked lime involved collecting shells, cooking them for hours over a fire, and then sprinkling them with water [Cheetham, 2010]. The Prehispanic Maya collected chunks of limestone that they baked in hot fires for days [Cheetham, 2010].) Over a hundred of the potsherds found at Acocotla were probably used for boiling and soaking maize.

Tortilla-making's second step, rinsing and hulling the softened maize, wasn't terrible either. (That only two of Acocotla's sherds are from colanders suggests that hacienda women didn't rely on a tool employed by maize-processing Native Americans [Newman, 2014:153].) Nor were the fourth and fifth steps, mixing and cooking the dough. (The griddles used to cook tortillas were the most common ceramic item found at Acocotla: 16,999 fragments!)

The hard work, the labor that filled women's days and limited their participation in other economic activities, was the third step of tortilla-making. Grinding the softened, hulled maize entailed kneeling while pushing and pulling one stone (the mano) over maize scattered over another, larger stone (the metate) until the kernels disintegrated into flour. Women spent hours doing this every day, even as their toe bones grew deformed from anchoring them in place, and their hips, spines, shoulders, and elbows grew arthritic from the repeated motions.[5] Given this it may seem surprising that excavators recovered only seventy-five manos

---

[5] Try kneeling and then rolling something on the floor first forward away from you then back towards you again. Notice how you bend your toes to keep yourself in position. Now imagine that instead of rolling something relatively easily, you are pushing and pulling one rock over another rock. It is supremely easy to understand how one develops "metate elbow" (Merbs, 1980) and other damage, isn't it?

and metates at Acocotla (Newman, 2014:153), but of course these are ground stone tools; they don't wear out at all easily, and they're often removed from sites by people who want to keep on using them elsewhere (see Chapter 2).

Evidence of food preparation labor is common in the archaeological record (e.g., Graff and Rodríguez-Alegría, 2012; Hastorf, 2016 ch.4; Turkon, 2007; see Chapter 6 for a discussion of the gendered nature of this labor). In some cases, such labor constituted occupational specialization. The arch- aeological record testifies to the existence of Roman barkeeps, Greek fishmongers, Classic Maya elite cooks, and Egyptian butchers of various ranks and specialties, from temple workers to estate servants to men with titles such as "Master Butcher," "Director of Butchers," and "Director of Those with Whetstones" (Ellis, 2004; Ikram, 1995:109; LeCount, 2010; Mylona, 2008:81–83). Mesopotamians, who might work not just as bakers or butchers or dairy farmers but also as professional food "embellishers" and "pastry chefs," even referred to one of their gods as the "Cook of Marduk" (Bottéro, 2004:81).

In other situations, cooking labor tangled with other economic under- takings, and archaeologists parse out the food evidence in order to under- stand the labor system more broadly. At the Andean site of Huaca Sialupe (1025–1050 CE), for example, a community of craftspeople built multiple communal cooking fires in areas where they also built shared kilns (Gold- stein and Shimada, 2010). The meals they cooked fueled the artisans as they worked, and some of the cooking debris that they generated fueled the kilns as they burned (Goldstein and Shimada, 2010). Food and craft labor functioned in tandem, and archaeologists cannot understand either with- out reference to the other. Moreover, in this context as well as others the relationship between the two is not simply mutual complementarity. As Graff (2018:15) explains, cooking and craft production often share "tasks, tools, laborers, spaces, fuel, knowledge, social structures, and cultural values" (see also Gokee and Logan, 2014; Stahl, 2014).

Labor Mobilization

Giving out food has always been an excellent strategy for bringing in people to work for you. Such donations don't necessarily constitute direct payment for work: few people would consider pizza slices and soda to be a fair swap for spending a day helping someone move. In such cases the labor is voluntary; the food is courtesy rather than recompense. In other cases, both the labor and the provisioning are mandatory. The Inka, for example, required their subjects to work for them, but those subjects expected to be fed as they did so (Gumerman, 2010).

The classic anthropological example of food being used to mobilize labor is the "work feast," at which the host's hospitality generates debts that the guests repay with their labor. Attendees gather to work; the host feeds them and keeps the proceeds of their work (Dietler, 2001:79-80). Prior to the advent of monetary economies, such feasts were virtually universal in agrarian societies and "the nearly exclusive means" of mobilizing volunteer labor for large-scale projects (Dietler, 2001; Dietler and Herbich, 2001: 240). Work feasts can mobilize hundreds of people from numerous social groups, as participants come for the food and drink more than for the chance to socialize with those close to them (Dietler and Herbich, 2001). The workers that one attracts are relatively unskilled, but if a host wants something large built or some heavy objects moved, they can make it happen (Dietler and Herbich, 2001). Food and drink[6] thus get the stones hauled, the canals dug, the ore mined, and the fields tilled.

Archaeologists have inferred work feasts in a wide variety of cultures and time periods and in service of an astonishing range of goals. Mycenean palaces may have hosted feasts in order to recruit men for military service, Mississippian chiefs in order to build and maintain Cahokia's huge mounds and sacred spaces (Fox and Harrell, 2008; Kelly, 2001). Of course, most work feasts would have been relatively small events, and many would be archaeologically invisible. Feasts held where the work is actually done often leave their remains in areas that archaeologists rarely excavate (e.g., offsite, in agricultural fields). Even if they occur inside settlements, their traces get scattered or destroyed by the work itself (e.g., at construction sites) (Nash, 2010).

Archaeologists nonetheless do manage to identify some smaller-scale work feasts. Researchers working at the Moche farming village of Ciudad de Dios, for example, found not only a wealth of agricultural tools but also ample evidence for feasting. Llama bones, big grinding stones, brewing urns, and oversized hearths combined with noisemakers such as whistles and rattles suggest that the villagers regularly held parties. These were probably small events hosted by elites, as the evidence for them is

---

[6] Let's not forget the work required to provide these (Brown and Kelly, 2015; Jackson, 2015). It takes labor in order to produce a feast that will mobilize further labor.

concentrated in modestly-sized patios in a privileged area of the site. Gumerman (2010) thus posits that at Ciudad de Dios, elites used work party feasts to reward agricultural workers for their labor.

Food's Power to Cause Economic Change

Among the most prominent and widely cited archaeologists of foodways is Dr. Brian Hayden. Hayden is particularly well-known for his theories about how foodways – specifically feasting – have driven many of the most profound economic (and social and technological) changes in human history.

Hayden's argument is that people hold feasts because feasts are excellent tools for ambitious individuals who want to advance themselves politically. Hayden posits that there are self-centered "aggrandizers" in every society, even the most egalitarian hunter-gatherer bands, who constantly maneuver to gain power and advance themselves over other people (Hayden, 2014:14–17). These aggrandizers may constitute only a small percentage of a population, but they can amass considerable power with their determined, aggressive, and manipulative self-promotions. In gaining power and wealth, aggrandizers improve their positions not just socially but in evolutionary terms as well, "typically hav[ing] multiple wives and large numbers of children" (Hayden, 2014:19).

In societies that do not strictly enforce egalitarian principles, aggrandizers can pursue power in a variety of ways. Feasting, Hayden argues, is an especially common and powerful strategy for self-advancement, "probably … the single most important way of utilizing surpluses to acquire other desirable forms of wealth and power" (Hayden, 2014:18). To explain: feasts enable hosts to convert their surplus food into assets other than food, such as material wealth or positive relationships with other people. Some feasts attract guests who will serve their hosts as laborers, soldiers, or political allies; some feasts pull in people who owe their hosts tribute or taxes; some feasts display and reinforce existing ties of kinship or cooperation (Hayden, 2014).

Hayden (2014:12) says that hosts draw people to feasts primarily by distributing food. (This is why, in Hayden's model, feasts occur when surplus food is available, not when people are hungry or uncertain of their food supply.) There is, moreover, no limit to the amount of food that aggrandizers can convert through feasting. There is never a reason to slow or stop surplus food production; there is always a reason to increase it (Hayden, 2014:19).

Success in feasting breeds further success, as the power and wealth gained by successful feast-hosting is reinvested in marriages, land rights, labor control, and, of course, more feasts. Feasting "spirals inexorably upward," with wealth and power becoming ever more concentrated and food and economic production intensifying further and further as aggrandizers keep competing and competing (Hayden, 2014:19). It doesn't matter what technologies are available, it doesn't matter what inventions do or don't occur: competitive feasting propels production to keep increasing and increasing.

What if production cannot increase? What if aggrandizers call for ever more food, ever fancier dishes, ever more impressive decor, and none exists? Then, Hayden argues, people develop ways to get them. In particular, Hayden has long contended that the origins of food production are rooted in ancient peoples' desires to expand their supply of feasting foods (e.g., Hayden, 1992, 2003, 2014). Animals were domesticated in order to ensure the availability of delectably fresh and ideally fatty meat (Hayden, 2014:123). Plants were domesticated either to serve as feast foods, or to feed the animals that would eventually become the feast foods (Hayden, 2014:125, 130–140).

Furthermore, in order to attract as many people as possible to their feasts, self-interested hosts make their events as pleasurable as they can. This involves using or inventing technologies "probably including the first use of metals, beads, tailored clothes, musical instruments, pottery, and elaborate architecture" (Hayden, 2014:13).

If Hayden is correct, then foodways have been the proximate cause for many, even most, of humanity's major economic developments. Ethnographic and sociological data demonstrate that feasts can and do spur social and economic change. In the early twentieth century, for example, competitive feasting among the Papua New Guinean Enga led to bloody conflicts over pigs and pig-raising land, as well as to (in some areas) a rise in the value of pearl shells (Wiessner, 2001). In the late twentieth century, birthday party "feasts" played a key role in McDonald's successful entry into China. Adults often found the food "strange and unappealing," but the chain marketed itself directly to their children as a great place for birthday celebrations complete with food, cake, and toys (Watson, 2000:122).

Many archaeological data sets are also consistent with Hayden's arguments. Consider his best-known theory, that feasting led to domestication, and exclude those of his criteria that are essentially unfalsifiable, such as his contention that the first domesticates were feasting foods. (Feasting foods vary tremendously across cultures. One can therefore plausibly interpret *any* food as having been intended for festal consumption; this criterion is impossible to disprove.) Hayden expects domestication to have arisen in feasting societies that were sedentary, occupying rich environments, and long familiar with the species they would domesticate. These expectations are often borne out, although African herders remained mobile.

Is Hayden right, then, that feasting has motivated humanity to change everything from how we get our food to what technologies we live with? Few (any?) archaeologists accept the scope of this model that links such a tremendous variety of political and economic developments to a single root cause. Many archaeologists challenge Hayden's belief that competition is the fundamental goal of feasting (e.g., Craig et al., 2015; Dietler, 2011; Halstead, 2015; Hamilakis and Harris, 2011; Kim et al., 2016; Reinhart, 2015; Rowley-Conwy, 2018). Some also note that ethnographies exist only post-Western contact and lack time depth, making them inappropriate bases for explaining origins (e.g., Wright, 2014:9). Finally, many of the falsifiable criteria that are consistent with Hayden's model, such as (for the origins of domestication) sedentism, a favorable environment, and long-term familiarity with each domesticate's ancestors, are equally consistent with other, very different perspectives (e.g., Zeder, 2016:334, table 2).

Yet many archaeologists agree that feasting could have propelled important economic (and political) developments. Several researchers have raised the possibility (but not claimed certainty) that feasting motivated cattle domestication in Asia and in Africa (Marshall and Hildebrand, 2002; Simoons and Simoons, 1968:233; Twiss, 2008). More broadly, Spielmann (2002) argues that communal feasting has propelled economic intensification in many small-scale societies: that diverse foragers, farmers, and horticulturalists have ratcheted up and/or specialized production in order to supply food and paraphernalia for ritual feasts. Others have linked feasting to changing trade patterns and economic production strategies. As feast-hosting spread through fifteenth and sixteenth century Philippine society, for example, demand for feast-appropriate plates and bowls expanded, leading to a trade boom in imported porcelains (Junker, 2001:289–293). Not all households could afford high-quality Chinese porcelains, though, having to settle for "aesthetically inferior" Annamese and Siamese copies instead. This loss of market share perhaps explains why Chinese manufacturers began mass-producing lower-quality porcelains for export to the Philippines, establishing big, export-focused kiln sites and ceasing production of many delicate forms in favor of more compact items (Junker, 2001:293). Whether or not one accepts the particulars and the scale of

Hayden's arguments, he is indubitably correct that feasting has changed economies, across space and through time.

Whereas once archaeologists discussed food and economics largely in terms of subsistence strategies, today we see research on topics from household investments to urban market systems to intercontinental trade networks. Pick an introductory economics textbook, flip to the table of contents, and drop your finger at random: chances are good that you have landed on a topic that some archaeologist, somewhere, is investigating through the lens of food. Many of these investigations explore not just how ancient economies functioned (or malfunctioned) but also how those economies shaped and were shaped by politics, religion, and other aspects of life in the past. As you proceed through the coming chapters, you will see that the converse is true as well. The topic at hand may be ritual, gender, race, class, diplomacy, ethnicity, or inequality, but economics will also appear. On that note, let us move along to the next chapter, on food and inequality – and as we talk about fancy mouse- and swan-eaters touch also on wealth, trade, and labor.

CHAPTER 4

Food and Inequality

Richard Plantagenet was born at Fotheringhay Castle, the twelfth child of the Duke and Duchess of York. The year was 1452, and power struggles roiled England: a mentally incapacitated king reigned while noble families feuded, corruption flourished, and civil discontent soared. Richard was two and a half years old when open fighting broke out and Richard's father, whose royal descent made him a plausible heir to the throne, captured the king. Richard's father escorted the king to London to rule as a figurehead and took control of the nation as Lord Protector. This situation lasted less than a year, however, and England slid into a series of civil wars (the Wars of the Roses). When Richard was eight, enemy fighters killed his father and seventeen-year-old brother Edmund and left their heads to rot on display at the main gate of the city of York. When Richard was eight and a half, his nineteen-year-old brother Edward fought back and won, becoming king himself.

Not yet nine, Richard became Duke of Gloucester. As he grew, he became one of his royal brother's most powerful defenders, taking on more and more responsibility as he matured. By seventeen he led his own army. At eighteen Richard joined Edward in fleeing England, their enemies having resurged. Six months later, the brothers battled back and restored Edward's throne. Richard's scoliosis did not prevent him from being a skilled soldier, and he spent his twenties alternating between military command in support of his brother and administration of the north of England.

Then, when Richard was twenty-nine, Edward died, leaving a twelve-year-old child as heir to his dangerous and politically riven kingdom. Richard was named Lord Protector of the Realm. Richard escorted the pubescent king to London, housing him and his younger brother in the Tower of London's Royal Apartments. (This was where kings traditionally awaited their coronations.) In June of 1483 the children were pronounced illegitimate, which meant that Richard was his brother's legal heir.

The citizens of London petitioned Richard to take the throne. And on June 26, 1483, he accepted.

Richard thus became Richard III, King of England. At the age of only thirty he had attained the highest status, an achievement he celebrated at a coronation banquet attended by perhaps 3,000 people. Diners savored peacocks in their plumage, roast swans and cranes, and roe deer "reversed in purple (turned inside out and colored purple)" (Sutton and Hammond, 1984:287).

The pomp did not preface a long and fruitful reign. Richard had many enemies, including some who were wealthy and well-armed. A mere 26 months after his coronation, Richard III died in battle, hacked and stabbed at the Battle of Bosworth Field. Historical documents record his corpse being stripped naked, put on display, and eventually interred, but over the course of centuries his resting place was lost (Buckley et al., 2013).

Then, in 2012, archaeologists discovered Richard's skeleton underneath a parking lot in the city of Leicester. He had been stuffed unshrouded into a too-short grave, inside a friary church where the public could not generally go (Buckley et al., 2013). Nine head wounds testify to a death by sword and halberd; cuts to his rib and pelvis probably represent postmortem "humili-ation injuries" (Buckley et al., 2013:536).

Lamb and colleagues (2014) took samples from multiple portions of Richard's skeleton in order to get data related to his diet at different times of his life. Stable carbon, nitrogen, and oxygen isotope values in his teeth reflect his diet during childhood. Values in his femur average his diet from late adolescence until his death; they are dominated by what he ate in his twenties, prior to becoming king. Values in his rib reflect his diet during his kingship (roughly his last two years).

Richard was born to a wealthy and noble family, and all of his carbon and nitrogen isotopic values are consistent with those of Late Medieval English elites. Aristocratic diets of the era were rich in meat and fish, and Richard clearly ate plenty of both. (Richard's meat was probably eaten well-cooked, as there's no evidence for him having been infected with pork, beef, or fish tapeworms. His cooks would have benefited from washing their hands, though, as Richard did have roundworms [Mitchell et al., 2013]. People get roundworms by eating food contaminated with human feces.)

Indeed, Richard's $\delta^{13}C$ and $\delta^{15}N$ values place him at the pinnacle of medieval English society, even prior to his ascension to the kingship (Lamb et al., 2014). Yet becoming king – reaching the apex of the status hierarchy – changed what Richard ate. The difference is not apparent in his $\delta^{13}C$ values, which hover between 18.5 and 19‰ throughout his adult life and during most of his childhood as well (Lamb et al., 2014). It appears in his $\delta^{15}N$, which rises dramatically as he passes from his twenties (femoral $\delta^{15}N$ = 13.5‰) into his thirties (rib $\delta^{15}N$ = 14.9‰) (Lamb et al., 2014). His $\delta^{18}O$ values climb as well, which Lamb and colleagues suggest may reflect increased wine-drinking.

The rise in Richard's $\delta^{15}N$ suggests that kingship brought him a considerable increase in high-trophic-level terrestrial foods. Game birds and freshwater fish (which have terrestrial $\delta^{15}N$ values) are prime candidates for the foods in question, as both were considered delicacies and status symbols (Lamb et al., 2014). Large freshwater fish were valued so highly that they were stocked in royal fishponds; swans, cranes, and herons featured at royal and ecclesiastical banquets (Albarella and Thomas, 2002; Lamb et al., 2014). Uneasy may lie the head that wears a crown, but the stomach rests full of delicacies.

The subject of this chapter is the archaeology of food and social status. By "status" I mean position in a formal or informal hierarchy or rank order; the topic here is inequality. Food is an effective tool for displaying status distinctions – and for challenging them (Goody, 1982; Mennell, 1996; Wiessner and Schiefenhovel, 1996). Elites may display their positions by eating high-value foods, supping from elaborate serving vessels, or dining in prestigious locations. Subordinates may be barred from these actions, while also being required to complete time-consuming or laborious food tasks. Many food-related activities occur daily, making them particularly informative about status distinctions. From time to time one can splurge on a costly meal, or take a day off from doing the cooking, but it's difficult to do so on a regular basis. As Sunseri (2014:168) writes, "it is much easier to express status aspirations through a few, big-ticket items like ceramics or ornamentation than to eat outside of one's means repeatedly." It is also worth noting that in many societies lower-status people are ideologically barred from seeking or consuming high-status foods (Ashby, 2002). Widely shared moral proscriptions can reinforce dietary boundaries; people may even believe that consuming foods unsuited to one's social status leads to dire health consequences (e.g., Grieco, 1999).[1]

Archaeologists can and do, therefore, use food to reconstruct social status in the past. We explore how people produced, prepared, and ate food in order to assess their relative positions within social hierarchies – and we are often thrilled by what we learn. But using archaeological food data to

---

[1] A sad late-sixteenth-century Italian tale depicts the fate of a peasant adopted by a king and fed an aristocratic diet. He begs for turnips and fava beans, and, not receiving them, dies (Grieco, 1999). Eat your vegetables, commoner kids.

establish social organization in the past is a tricky prospect. Researchers interested in doing so must determine how they will link particular foods or foodways to high or low social status; if and how they will separate the dietary effects of status from those of wealth; and the extent to which they equate specific foodways with specific statuses (as opposed to modeling a looser relationship between food and social standing). Let us begin by considering the first of these challenges: how do archaeologists identify high-status foods and foodways in the archaeological record?

High-Status Foods

> And so [Robin Hood] came to dwell in the greenwood that was to be his home for many a year to come, never again to see the happy days with the lads and lasses of sweet Locksley Town; for he was outlawed, not only because he had killed a man, but also because he had poached upon the King's deer, and two hundred pounds were set upon his head, as a reward for whoever would bring him to the court of the King.
>
> H. Pyle (1883), The Merry Adventures of Robin Hood

It is hard to imagine a more effective demonstration of relative status than the performance staged by eleventh- and twelfth-century English deer hunters. In the years after the Norman Conquest in 1066 CE, England's new kings instituted laws limiting who could legally hunt forest animals. Wild game became the legal province of the elite, who reinforced the special nature of their activities by using French terms to describe their complex and ritualized pursuits (Sykes, 2006). Hunting forest animals without permission was punishable by maiming or imprisonment (Sykes, 2006).

Contrary to popular imagination, commoners did participate in deer hunts. Sykes (2006) notes, for example, that seven of the ten hunters depicted in a medieval hunting manual are yeomen or servants rather than aristocrats. All of the men (and at least some of their dogs) received portions of the deer they brought down. Manuals provided varying rules about who got what, but in general the forester received one shoulder and the best hunter the other; the dogs got most of the offal[2] and the pelvis was offered

---

[2] Humans did eat some offal ("numbles") too – a humiliating experience, apparently, and the root of our expression "to eat humble pie" (Goody, 1982:142). I am aware of no equivalent expression for the elevating experiences of eating deer noses or testicles, both prized by medieval lords (Sykes, 2006; Thomas, 2007a).

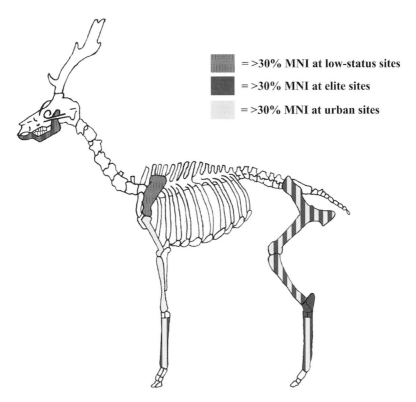

FIGURE 4.1. Deer bone representation at medieval English sites occupied by people of varying social positions. Colored elements appear regularly (>30 percent of the Minimum Number of Individuals [MNI]) among deer remains found in sites. Medium-gray and textured = low-status sites; dark gray = elite sites; pale gray = urban sites. Antler data excluded. Data from Sykes (2007); image redrawn by Kate Thompson and modified by K. C. Twiss.

to the raven (Sykes, 2007; Thomas, 2007a). Sykes calculates that medieval aristocrats ate only around two-thirds of the venison legally consumed in medieval England, or less if one includes illegally hunted (poached) animals as well.

These conclusions aren't mere hypotheses. Elite sites dating to the years following the Norman Conquest contain disproportionately low numbers of deer pelvic and forelimb (shoulder) bones (Sykes, 2006, 2007) (see Figure 4.1). Conversely, forest workers' residences have a plethora of forelimb bones, but few hindlimb elements (Sykes, 2007). The foresters' leftover bones are also primarily from the left sides of the deer, archaeological data confirming the medieval *Tretyse off Huntyng*'s statement that after a successful deer hunt the left shoulder was the forester's fee (Sykes, 2007). It is nearly impossible to track down the right shoulders given to the "best hunters," because these yeomen resided in rural villages together with other commoners. Medieval village faunal assemblages are few, deer bones scarce within them, and none can be associated specifically with a hunter's household (Sykes, 2007). Rural deer remains generally accord with expectations – high proportions of shoulder blades and right-side bones – but these conclusions are based on extremely small samples (Sykes, 2007).

Overall, the patterning is clear. Elites and non-elites may have hunted together, and both may later have dined on the venison they took. But the similarities between commoner and aristocratic experiences were limited, as social status determined both how much and which cuts of meat people legally received, cooked, and ate. As Sykes (2007:156) says, "at every stage … people knew, and were reminded of, their place within society: different ranks had different roles within the hunt itself; the cut of venison they were given … would have been a meaty symbol of social position, and even at the level of consumption different people were offered different venison dishes according to rank."

The word "legally" is important in that last paragraph, for some English people subverted both laws and unwritten rules to hunt, sell, and eat venison. Despite norms dictating that venison could neither be bought nor sold, historical and archaeological evidence shows that discontented foresters periodically hawked their portions on the black market (Sykes, 2007). More ambitiously, poaching gangs – venison traffickers – took down deer and sold their meat in urban alehouses and taverns, producing urban faunal assemblages that include all deer body parts (Sykes, 2007). Peasants trapped and scavenged deer behind authorities' backs as well: one butchered red deer was discarded down a village well, perhaps to conceal its remains from patrolling foresters (Sykes, 2007).

Texts clearly reveal the status value of deer in medieval England. How do archaeologists identify high-status foods in prehistoric contexts? How do we tell if a particular food was symbolically or socially valuable? We cannot safely project our own ideas about values and costs into the past, because (as will become increasingly apparent as you read through this chapter) what we appreciate is not necessarily what members of other cultures want (DeFrance, 2009; Ervynck et al., 2003:437).

Foods' values also change through time within cultures. Consider the case of rice in Korea. Many scholars have argued that, historically, Korean rice was a luxury good, eaten largely by elites. Thousand-year-old texts depict rice as the food of aristocrats, centuries-old laws require that taxes be paid in rice, and in the early modern era rice farmers couldn't afford to eat their own crops (Kim, 2015). Yet paleoethnobotanical data demonstrate that rice wasn't always a high-status food in Korea. Roughly 2,500 to 3,000 years ago, rice was eaten in both rural farming villages and prominent settlements, by people living in small houses as well as in large ones. Beginning around 2,000 years ago, rice's availability decreased and its status rose (Kim, 2015). And today, of course, rice is Korea's staple food. Food values change as cultures do, and we cannot take a food's status at one moment in time as indicative of its status throughout time.

Archaeologists sometimes rely on criteria for identifying elite foodways that derive from ethnography or other external sources (van der Veen, 2003b; e.g., Jamieson and Sayre, 2010; Kirch and O'Day, 2003). Those approaches carry their own challenges. How do we sort out which elements of an ethnohistoric food-ranking system represent genuine indigenous perspectives as opposed to observers' biases (Leach, 2003; Staller, 2010)? How do we account for observers' potential blindness to quality differences within unfamiliar food groups? Polynesian cultures recognize high- and low-value strains of breadfruit, taro, and sweet potato (Leach, 2003); West African Songhai differentiate between prosaic *tuo* (sour dough balls) and delectably well prepared ones (MacLean and Insoll, 2003).

Many researchers rely primarily on evidence available in the archaeological record itself. In order to avoid circular arguments archaeologists commonly identify "elite foodways" by first identifying "elite-associated contexts," then characterizing the food remains and paraphernalia found therein (Peres, 2017). This approach has meaningful limitations. Curet and Pestle (2010:416) point out, for example, that it can only be used in situations where there *are* elite contexts. It strands researchers who work in sites and cultures without institutionalized status differences, or without identifiable higher- and lower-status areas of settlement. It may also overlook high-status foods that elites periodically distributed out for communal feasts or other rituals (Curet and Pestle, 2010). Nonetheless, contextual evidence is our first, and often best, line of evidence for determining foods' status values.

When identifying elite foods on the basis of their find contexts is not possible, archaeologists often broaden the scope of their contextual analyses, examining the uses to which foods are put. Those uses establish foods' values. The meaning and the worth of any food is shaped by how it is acquired, how it is accessed, how it is processed, and how it is consumed (Table 4.1; Curet and Pestle, 2010; Hamilakis, 1999; Hastorf, 2003; Sykes, 2014a).

TABLE 4.1. *Criteria commonly used to identify high-status foods; these are the criteria cited by the authors (authors do not necessarily endorse all criteria)*

Criterion	Specific signatures	Curet and Pestle (2010)
Scarcity	Unavailable to most people, for ecological or social reasons	X
Abundance	Lots of food	X
Periodicity of availability	Available only occasionally	X
Exotic/non-local		X
High labor costs (acquisition or preparation)		X
Prepared by specialists	For complex/skilled work, not mass production of staples	X
Food wastage	Edible food left uneaten	
Scarcity of processing debris		
Tastiness		X
	Younger animals	
	Meaty/fatty (often re specific animal body parts)	
Diversity	Numerous species	X (when ecologically feasible)
Symbolic prominence		X
	Wild taxa	
	Domesticates	
	Birds	

deFrance (2009)	van der Veen (2003b)	Ervynck et al. (2003)
X	X	X
X	X	
X	X	X
X	X (refined foods)	X
X		
X		
X (note tastiness is culturally determined)	X (but culture can override innate preferences)	
X		X
X	X	X
X (note: this varies culturally)		X
X		
X		
X	X	
X		

A widely respected approach entails looking at food iconography, in the expectation that artistically prominent foods were valuable foods. Two-thousand-year-old Moche painted pots depict presentations of maize, beans, potatoes, and peanuts; Hastorf (2003:549) infers that these featured foods were politically as well as symbolically important. Thousands of pomegranate seeds and fruit fragments were found in a fourteenth century BCE shipwreck at Uluburun off the coast of Turkey. Were these pomegranates luxuries intended for aristocrats, or were they just fruit? Ward (2003) argues that they were high-status foods partly because bronze, gold, ivory, and glass pomegranates feature across the Late Bronze Age eastern Mediterranean; two ivory pomegranate finials were even found on the shipwreck itself.

Archaeologists often also consider the intrinsic natures of foods when evaluating their possible social implications. This is generally considered the weakest strategy for inferring foods' social status, but sometimes we work with very limited contextual information and this is the best we can do. In such situations, archaeologists often rely on anthropological data indicating that animal fat and protein are highly valued in many cultures and/or biological data confirming that humans are predisposed to like sweet foods (Curet and Pestle, 2010; Hastorf, 2003; van der Veen, 2003b). Researchers may also cite ethnohistorical and ethological data demonstrating that some foods are inherently challenging to obtain or prepare; finding them in an archaeological site tells us that people invested significant time in these particular foods (van der Veen, 2003b).

This approach is risky, because a single food can be associated with high status in one cultural context and low status in another (DeFrance, 2009; Hastorf, 2016:204; Kim, 2015; Sykes, 2014b). Deer heads, for example, are associated with elite settlements in Early Medieval England, and with low-status settlements in later Medieval times (Sykes 2014b: 370). Additional reasons to be wary include the facts that an ostensibly low-quality food can be delicious when cooked a particular way; that animals' culinary appeal depends not just on their species but on their bodily conditions; and that youth and tenderness appeal only to some (DeFrance, 2009; Hastorf, 2003; Leach, 2003; Reitz et al., 2006).

An effective illustration of the complexities involved comes from American historical archaeology. A strategy that many zooarchaeologists have used to assign food status values involves identifying which bones in an animal's body carry plenty of meat and which do not. We assume that the former (e.g., ribs, upper limb bones) represent valuable meat cuts and the latter (e.g., lower limb and foot bones) represent low-status cuts. We expect that high-status people ate a greater proportion of high-value cuts than low-status people did. Yet many historical documents refer to affluent households cheerfully consuming heads and feet: calf's head soup, pigs' trotters, and more (Reitz et al., 2006). Reitz and colleagues (2006) therefore decided to test the reliability of the valued bones = high-status assumption, examining more than two thousand pig specimens from forty-seven different historically documented contexts in Charleston, South Carolina. They found no consistent differences between the pig bones in upper-class residences and those in lower-status ones. They concluded that at least in cities, where factors from urban trash management strategies (pigs as garbage disposals?) to employment norms (servants living with their employers?) may shape residents' meat acquisition, "high-value" pig bones do not testify to high-status people. The situation is not entirely hopeless – cattle bones might work better than pig bones do – but zooarchaeologists must still recognize that urban faunal assemblages are shaped by factors beyond simply consumer status (Reitz et al., 2006).

Let us focus, however, on Reitz and her colleagues' point that incorporating cattle bones into the study might strengthen it. It is odd, when one thinks about it, to focus on individual foods when studying ancient hierarchies. Can you identify a single species whose modern production, distribution, and consumption you would recommend to ethnoarchaeologists as fully capturing today's social inequalities? Researchers know the limitations of such narrow foci and avoid them when they can. Many even conclude that food remains in general are not enough: we must work with as many different data sets as we can if we hope to untangle the social significance of particular foods in the past (Sunseri, 2014; Sykes, 2014b).

This is surely true, but simply broadening the scope of one's study to include multiple food taxa enriches our understandings of past social organization. Even a few taxa may not tell much of a story. Goldstein and Hageman (2010), for example, point out that Mayanists' traditional focus on maize, beans, and squash handicaps people's ability to investigate social complexity in the Late Classic (600–900 CE). Authors who present this dietary triad as the essence of all Maya subsistence struggle to explain how plant foods reflected and upheld Late Classic inequalities (Goldstein and Hageman, 2010). Therefore, when comparing and contrasting plant remains from lineage-feasting and residential middens at a Late Classic Maya site, Goldstein and Hageman make sure to include fruits, leafy greens, and other non-staple plants. Finding taxonomic similarities as well as differences between the middens, they infer that the rural Maya reserved some tastes for settings wherein the local lineage head affirmed his position. Maize, beans, and nance fruits were widely consumed, but *Psidium* (perhaps guava) and *Guazuma* fruits "coded for" distinctions (Goldstein and Hageman, 2010:437).

Some important articles discuss "luxury foods" rather than high-status foods per se (e.g., Hastorf, 2003; van der Veen, 2003a, 2007). As van der Veen (2003b:406) notes, luxury foods are commonly associated with elites: "they are seen as the preserve of the upper classes, who use expensive and exotic foods to mark social status, to identify distinction." Indeed, Van der Veen (2003b:420 – italics mine) defines luxury foods as "foods that in any particular time and place are regarded as an indulgence *and a status indicator*." Curet and Pestle (2010:416) "hesitate to fully equate" high-status with luxury foods, but embrace a close relationship between the two. All agree that at the least luxury and high-status foods share important characteristics, such as limited availability.

A common element of identifying a food as a luxury is identifying it as enjoyable but not indispensable (Curet and Pestle, 2010; van der Veen, 2003b) – a difficult proposition for archaeologists. Our own assessments of past peoples' biological or economic baselines don't necessarily match their perceptions (see *Surplus* in Chapter 3). How, then, does one determine what ancient people considered a need as opposed to a desire? One strategy advocated by van der Veen is identifying foods that represent *refinements* of standard foods: white bread rather than bran-filled black, perhaps, or unusually large pomegranates and melons (e.g., Bosi et al., 2009; Halstead, 2014:163–165).[3]

Isaakidou (2007) takes this idea and runs with it, seeking 'haute cuisine' at Bronze Age Knossos in Crete. She examines how animals were butchered for cooking, focusing in particular on the size of the 'parcels'

---

[3] Low-status unrefined foods receive little explicit attention, probably because they are difficult to identify archaeologically. One possible exception was a televised taste test of a broth recipe based on the gut contents of northern European bog bodies. As Jones (2007:237, 315) describes the 1954 event, the archaeologist taste testers quickly washed their mouths out with brandy and one later commented that "with meals like that, perhaps they had thrown themselves into the bog"(phrasing from Jones, not an original quotation).

On a more serious note, culinary refinement can take various forms, many of which do not leave perceptible traces (for example, icing on a cake). We archaeologists therefore struggle to differentiate between (a) an absence of evidence for refinement and (b) evidence of its absence. This doesn't lessen the social importance of unrefined foods. Halstead (2015:35) fascinatingly describes hungry Greek villagers eating the low-status grains and cereal byproducts that would normally feed the livestock, and paying the social price for doing so: "elderly villagers in Greece can still name the neighbors who resorted to demeaning ingredients for bread in the winter of 1941-42."

into which carcasses were divided. She finds that cut marks on cattle, caprine, and pig bones rose significantly through time, roughly tripling over the course of the third and second millennia BCE (Isaakidou, 2007). This means that as the Minoan period passed and the age of palaces arose, meat at Knossos gradually got cut into smaller and smaller packages. No longer were whole haunches habitually roasted in pits or over open fires; much of the meat was now filleted into pieces that could be combined with other ingredients in stews, fry-ups or other more complex dishes (Isaakidou, 2007). Equidistant transverse marks along the lengths of several bones suggest that some meat was cut into on-bone sections as well. Perhaps Minoans favored their pork and mutton marinated with herbs prior to roasting, or perhaps they occasionally decorated it for serving (Isaakidou, 2007).

This brings us to an important point: standard foods may be turned into special ones by being cooked or served in particular ways. Species does not determine status when it comes to foods. Some societies use the quantity of food, more than its quality, to mark status (e.g., MacLean and Insoll, 2003). Others focus on how standard foods are presented or on how they're prepared (Gijanto and Walshaw, 2014; Leach, 2003; MacLean and Insoll, 2003; Mennell, 1996: 75; Morán, 2016:47).

Any food might thus become something whose consumption elevates people above the norm: a dish that elites will not only eat but learn to appreciate. Those who fail to appreciate such dishes mark themselves as having lower-class tastes (Bourdieu, 1984). It is common for members of different social classes not only to have access to, but also (since tastes are learned) to prefer, different foods.[4] Low-status people, growing up without much access to high-status foods (or table manners), don't acquire a taste for them (Bourdieu, 1984). Their lack of appreciation can, in turn, be used to discount calls to expand their access to haute cuisine and to level the social, as well as culinary, playing field. Food inequalities can thus beget taste inequalities that, in turn, reinforce the original food inequalities.

Sometimes archaeologists identify high-status eaters not on the basis of specific dishes or food quantities, but on the basis of a diverse diet – one that includes a wide range of different kinds of not necessarily "special" foods. Wari elites in the seventh-century CE Andes; Mississippian elites in

---

[4] In 2019, how do you feel about caviar? Extremely dark chocolate? Sea snail broth, "plankton mousse under a toasted-milk crumble," and "slivers of giant squid just cooked in hot seaweed butter," as served at the internationally famous, months-long-waiting-list-for-a-table restaurant Noma (Redzepi, 2018, Wells, 2018)?

the southeastern USA; Ndele and Grima chiefs in modern Central Africa –
all typically ate more varied diets than their lower-status peers (DeFrance,
2014; Jackson, 2015; Schmitt and Lupo, 2008). However, archaeologists
wanting to use dietary diversity[5] to assess status must consider whether
the additional plants or animals found in "high-status" assemblages were
in fact eaten (e.g., Curet and Pestle, 2010; Jackson, 2015; Jackson and Scott,
2003). Ancient elites often owned valuable pelts, pets, costume elements,
and ritual paraphernalia.

This question, unlike the "was this human food or animal fodder?"
conundrum mentioned in Chapter 2 (section on Botanical Analyses) and
Chapter 3 (section on Surplus), has a correct answer and can be addressed
archaeologically. Ethnographic and ethnohistoric data often help narrow
down whether people in a specific culture are likely to have eaten a
particular species. Sometimes the nature of an animal species provides
insights (e.g., colorful birds in the Americas); sometimes the taphonomy of
remains or the animals' ages or health statuses clarify matters (e.g., Jackson,
2015; Jackson and Scott, 1995; Kirch and O'Day, 2003; Wallis and Blessing,
2015).

An additional concern is that hungry populations often broaden their
diets because their preferred foods no longer suffice to keep them fed
(Halstead, 2014; Stiner and Munro, 2002; Sunseri, 2014). Can we tell if
dietary diversity represents a luxury or a necessity? Contextual evidence is of
course the ideal clarifier, but taphonomic data can also provide valuable
information. They allow researchers to evaluate whether ancient people
were extracting every nutrient they could from their foods (e.g., bashing
bones to smithereens to get at every last drop of marrow or grease), as we
assume hungry people would do (Sunseri, 2014). One final caveat is that
the "luxury of variety's" archaeological signature matches that of opportun-
istic hunting – commonly a low-status activity (DeFrance, 2009; Schmitt
and Lupo, 2008; Sunseri, 2014).

Diversity may stem from how foods are prepared, not simply what they
are. Polynesians living on Tongareva ate a limited range of species, but they
could make a variety of dishes out of a single one. Leach (2003:450) reports
a Tongarevan feast featuring young coconuts and mature ones, assorted
cooked coconut dishes and "frothy coconut cream."

Archaeologists thus face numerous complexities when we want to identify high-status foods, especially in the absence of texts or other strong

---

[5] This is measured in terms of both taxonomic richness (total number of taxa) and evenness
(how evenly those taxa appear throughout the assemblage).

contextual information. In such situations we rely on the fact that "animal carcasses are, by nature, hierarchical" (Sykes, 2014b: 356) – different body parts have different values even if those values vary across time and space – and plant species and parts likewise vary in utility. We do our best with the data available to us, and we make sure to investigate not just the status values of particular foods and recipes, but food in general. I therefore turn now to status and diet: the intake of elites.

High-Status Diets

In some situations archaeologists may struggle to identify what foods high-status people were eating but be absolutely confident that they were eating (or working) differently from mere plebeians and peasants. The example of Richard III demonstrates how stable isotopes allow us to examine status-related dietary distinctions; dental wear and calculus, paleopathologies, and other bioarchaeological data also provide relevant information. Researchers first use non-food data such as mortuary treatments to assign status to human remains. They then compare and contrast high-status and low-status skeletons' (or mummies') dietary signatures in order to examine differential foodways in the past.

One of the best-known examples of such research examines status distinctions at the immense Mississippian site of Cahokia, just outside of St. Louis. Among Cahokia's many, many mounds is one – Mound 72 – that contained more than 270 human burials dating to approximately 1015–1150 CE (Ambrose et al., 2003; Emerson et al., 2017). Their burial treatments imply differing social positions: a person buried atop twenty thousand shell beads probably outranked someone stacked with twenty-three other people in tidy layers. Ambrose and colleagues (2003) analyzed the stable isotopic signatures of bone collagen and tooth apatite from four high-status skeletons (including one of the bead-resting gentleman's retainers) and five low-status ones. Three of the high-status individuals have higher collagen $\delta^{15}N$ (meat) than all of the lower-status people, most of whom have modestly higher $\delta^{13}C$ (maize, the Mississippians' sole important C_4 plant). Interestingly, high- and low-status people's apatite $\delta^{13}C$ values – deriving from the entirety of the diet – diverge more than their collagen values, which, deriving primarily from dietary protein, drastically underreport low-protein foods such as maize. The $\delta^{13}C$ and $\delta^{15}N$ isotopic data thus indicate that in this time and place low-status people ate tremendous quantities of maize, supplemented by C_3 plants (the source of most of their protein) and small amounts of meat (Ambrose et al., 2003). Higher status people generally ate more meat and relied substantially less on maize (Ambrose et al., 2003). These dietary differences meant that elites enjoyed better health than their lower-status neighbors, whose skeletons are more frequently affected by pathologies related to malnutrition.

It's important to note that one cannot use the *extent* of food-related inequality to measure the *extent* of social differentiation in ancient cultures (Cuéllar, 2013). Social distinctions can be expressed in a variety of ways and using a variety of material culture; food may or may not be involved. Beyond that, though, social rankings and unequal foodways may originate at different times, develop at different rates, and peak at different levels. In prehistoric northern Peru, for example, Moche elites might have dressed in elaborate costumes, lived in impressive homes, and been interred in large tombs accompanied by rich offerings and sacrificed retainers (Castillo Butters and Castillo, 2007; White et al., 2009), but they dined no more frequently on valuable llama meat than did anyone else living at the site of Pacatnamú during the first millennium CE. Only in the later Lambayeque period (ca. 1100–1370 CE) did high rank mean better access to llama meat (Cuéllar, 2013; Gumerman, 2002). We cannot, therefore, take a lack of evidence for dietary distinctions as proof of egalitarianism. Nor, given the multiplicity of factors that shape foodways,[6] can we assume that the most pronounced distinctions in what people ate occurred in the civilizations with the strongest hierarchies.

Without inappropriate equivalences of scale, food archaeology can still shed light on complex status distinctions: we're not limited to simplistic Elite vs. Commoner models. Consider the work of Emery (2003), who was interested in elucidating status differences within the Maya elite. Some archaeologists had argued that the ancient Maya were either aristocrats or commoners, but Emery concurred with scholars who believed that Maya society included multiple social tiers: rulers, gentry, middle and lower classes, serfs and slaves. She decided to examine the complexities of Classic Maya social ranking by analyzing faunal assemblages from the Late Classic (600–800 CE) site of Aguateca in Guatemala. These assemblages came from five households known to have belonged to elites of varying status. Aguateca's highest aristocracy inhabited the Palace; noble artisans occupied the Houses of the Axes, Mirrors, and the Scribe; and elite hangers-on resided in the small house known as Str. M8–13. The houses were all abandoned quickly when Aguateca was sacked, so their contents reflect

---

[6] Ethnicity, religion, occupational specialization, gender: please just refer to every other chapter in this book.

relatively normal elite life rather than special abandonment deposits or other atypical behavior (Emery, 2003).

Their contents also prove Emery right that Classic Maya social status was complex and involved in foodways. Aguateca's highest elites ate differently from the mid-range elites, who in turn ate differently from those lower than they. To be more specific, residents of the Palace ate primarily deer meat: no other vertebrate contributed anywhere near as many bones to the Palace assemblage. At the Houses of the Axes, Mirrors, and the Scribe people balanced their deer consumption with turtle and dog meat. (The faunal similarities between these three houses indicate that people's occupational specializations didn't determine their diets [Emery, 2003].) And, interestingly, the people living in Str. M8–13 ate rather like the elites of the palace, with plenty of deer meat and far less of anything else (Emery, 2003). This last result may indicate that M8–13's residents were palace servants, able to bring home the highest status foods, or it may reflect something unknown about abandonment behavior at Aguateca. It also raises the possibility of emulation, which is an important topic in the archaeology of inequality (Emery, 2003).

Emulation

What people do with food isn't simply a reflection of their positions within a social hierarchy. People also use food to try and reposition themselves, eating as the elites do in order to present as elite themselves. (The next chapter discusses this at length.) The social power of such dietary emulation is apparent in people's willingness to compromise not just their finances but sometimes their family wellbeing in its pursuit. For example, contemporary American food stamp users exacerbate their hunger by spending their limited resources on "heavily advertised, status-invested foods" rather than on generic bulk goods because eating brand-name foods asserts their membership in the social classes they see celebrated on television and in other media (Fitchen, 1998:324). Similar calculations were surely made in the ancient world – at Bronze Age Lachish, perhaps, where local Canaanite elites seem to have begun dining on geese in emulation of their imperial Egyptian overlords (Koch, 2014).

Low-status people eating high-status foods are not, however, necessarily social climbing (Emery, 2003; van der Veen, 2003b:409). Sometimes people work or live with elites, gaining access to their food and cooking equipment. This is why deer bones from multiple sites indicate that medieval English forest workers ate considerable amounts of venison: proportionally more, in fact, than nobles did (Sykes, 2007). From Classic Mesoamerica to Imperial

Rome to the historic United States, archaeologists studying foodways express caution about palace servants, domestic slaves, and others (Baumann, 2009; Crader, 1990; Emery, 2003; Killgrove and Tykot, 2013; Turkon, 2007).

Past commoners also celebrated with special foods. Historical documents show that (Robin Hood notwithstanding) medieval peasant poachers took deer not because they were starving but because they wanted their food to be special. Poachers hunted deer specifically for festive occasions, and gifted venison to their friends and neighbors (Sykes, 2007). Additional potential factors include lordly donations to the less fortunate; lordly profiteering off of the less fortunate via forced purchasing; under-classes' resistance against elites' expectations; culinary creolization (when higher- and lower-status people belong to different ethnic groups); and practical considerations such as work hours (if, for example, purchased as opposed to gathered foods signal status) (Jamieson and Sayre, 2010:215; Mennell, 1996:56; Scott, 2001a: 685). Archaeologists must therefore be cautious about assigning a motive when they identify low-status people eating like their elite brethren.

It can be easier to see elite defensiveness against culinary boundary-narrowing than to explain that narrowing. Prestige foods commonly lose status over time, becoming more and more broadly available: once luxuries, white bread, sugar, and chocolate no longer symbolize elite dining (van der Veen, 2003b). Elites do not habitually welcome this. If they cannot effectively defend food boundaries with sumptuary laws or similar prohibitions, they often move them, developing new eating habits to set themselves off from the underclasses (van der Veen, 2003b). Such maneuvering is visible in the archaeological record. A particularly engaging example comes yet again from medieval England.

In the eleventh and twelfth centuries CE, deer was definitely a signature food of the English aristocracy – but all meat was valuable and its ample consumption was one of the means by which lords differentiated them-selves from peasants (Albarella and Thomas, 2002; Thomas, 2007b). Aristo-crats ate beef, pork, mutton, and venison regularly and in large quantities; peasants ate cereals supplemented by only a little animal protein. This distinction remained generally in place over the course of the thirteenth century as well, despite economic, agricultural, and demographic troubles that shook English society.

Then, in the mid-fourteenth century, came the Black Death (bubonic plague). The English population plummeted, to the point that peasant labor became a valued resource (Thomas, 2007b). Recognizing this, peasants started to demand payment for their work, claiming an income that allowed them to afford meat. Historical accounts indicate that in some areas the proportion of animal calories in peasant diets more than quadrupled, from 5 percent to 23 percent (Dyer, 1988). The aristocracy was losing its exclusive access to meat in large amounts. This clearly bothered them: a (never enforced) 1363 law limited the underclasses to one meat or fish meal a day (Thomas, 2007b).

Examining the animal remains from forty-eight castle, manorial, ecclesiastical, urban, and rural sites, Thomas (2007b) finds that castle deposits from both before and after the Black Death are relatively rich in deer (no surprise) and pigs (used only for meat); urban and rural sites generally have higher proportions of (multifunctional) sheep. Elites ate peacocks (they tasted terrible, but they looked spectacular served with their feathers on) and members of the lower classes did not. Even so, the taxonomic distinctions between castles and lower-class sites were limited in the early medieval era (Thomas, 2007b). Meat-eating marked status: aristocrats didn't need to eat a specific type of meat in order to display their social bona fides.

After the Black Death (fifteenth and early sixteenth centuries CE), this changed. Late medieval animal bones found at castles include newly high proportions of high-status birds (Albarella and Thomas, 2002; Thomas, 2007b). No such rise is apparent at lower-status sites. The English aristocracy had not taken the lower classes' dietary insurgency lying down. Once meat was "democratized and devalued," the nobility developed a new dietary signature (Thomas, 2007b:144).

None of this is to say that emulation is rare or socially unimportant, or that archaeologists should avoid considering it as a potential influence on past foodways. For example, recalling that imitation foods are not a modern invention, we might consider the possibility that cheaper versions of high-status foods represent attempts at social climbing instead of fraud. Were all of the twelfth-century inhabitants of Calatrava la Vieja in Spain really fooled when they bought cheap sardinellas instead of costly sardines (Ervynck et al., 2003; Roselló Izquierdo and Morales Muñiz, 1991)? Did Romans living at the northern edges of Europe buy locally made fish sauce instead of imported *garum* because they couldn't taste the difference, because they liked it better, or because it was a way to claim elite tastes at affordable prices (Ervynck et al., 2003)?

Using the Good China: Inequalities of the Table

Foods themselves testify to inequalities, of course, but so do the means and materials of their service. Status is marked in where meals take place, and in the arrangement of people at the table (Gero, 2003; Gumerman,

1997; McCann, 2009:69; Mennell, 1996:57; O'Connor, 2015). The materials out of which dishes are made – silver or wood, porcelain or earthenware – their technical sophistication, and their design elaboration relate to diners' social standing as well, although wealth can be a more important influence (see below). That ceramic dishes (commonly the largest such data set) reflect social status may seem obvious today, but less than twenty years ago archaeologists were thrilling to work that "rescue[d] ceramic assemblages from their century-long appointment as chronometric indicators and put[...] them firmly back into the hands of people, connect[ing] them to their intended contextual functions" (Gero, 2003: 285, although see Gumerman, 1997:120). Prominent in this new work were papers that discussed ceramics as culinary equipment involved in gender expression, political negotiations, and, of course, social status (e.g., Junker, 2001; Mills, 1999).

Since then, three aspects of ceramic assemblages have featured prominently in the discussions of serving dishes and social status: vessel forms, vessel surface decorations, and vessel wares. (Vessel sizes are discussed more frequently in the contexts of economic organization – e.g., household sizes – and political maneuvering.) The diversity of vessel shapes is used to assess status in largely the same way as the diversity of food remains: more variety is interpreted as signaling higher status. Archaeologists see specialized cooking equipment and diverse shapes as reflecting culinary activities whose biologically unnecessary complexity would have advertised people's social standing (e.g., Villing and Spataro, 2015). Specific shapes may also be associated with high-status dining. Dormice were a delicacy in ancient Rome, served at the finest tables, so when archaeologists recover fragments of *vivaria in doliis* – airhole-pocked jars with channels running around their interiors, used to house dormice being fattened up for consumption – they have found evidence of a food produced specifically for the highest strata of Roman society (Meulemans, 2015).

The forms and diversity of tablewares may reflect social status as well. The dishes from which one eats reflect the manner in which one dines, and manners certainly reflect status. Two hundred and fifty years ago at Presidio Los Adaes (Texas), the governor and his lower-status neighbors ate essentially the same diet, but the governor's household alone used a variety of platters, plates, saucers, and bowls to dish the foods out as individualized servings. Lower-class people ate out of bowls or scooped from communal pots, while Los Adaes's elites dined "from the proper kind of plate at a well-appointed table" (Pavao-Zuckerman and Loren, 2012:222).

How do vessel decorations testify to status in the past? They do so in multiple ways. Some archaeologists focus on design symbolism (e.g., Borgna, 2004:180); others on the costliness or elaboration of particular decorative choices. In Classical Greece, for example, fine black-glazed pots shared their shapes with prosaic stew and cooking pots, but their gleaming dark surfaces made them fit for the tables of respectable families (Villing and Spataro, 2015). Reents-Budet (1998) describes multifaceted status signaling on Classic Maya elite pottery. Highly trained, literate artisans painted historically or ideologically significant images and texts on small, cylindrical vessels, adding patrons' names and titles (and occasionally their own as well, signing their work like ancient Michelangelos). An owner who brought such an exceptionally high-quality vessel out at a feast displayed his elite status; patronage of the highly regarded artists who created them lent prestige as well (Reents-Budet, 1998).

Even the scale of a vessel's decorations may matter. In situations where people want attention focused on food-related activities, they often give serving vessels attention-grabbing decorations. If the target audience will be physically close to the vessels, the decorations can be small, but if viewers will be several meters away, any designs must be relatively large or eye-catching if they are to be seen (Mills, 2007). Roughly 900 to 750 years ago in the American Southwest, Puebloan peoples made a variety of beautifully and boldly decorated bowls. The designs on these bowls – high-contrast in highly polished black on white or white on orange – covered most of the bowls' exterior surfaces and made them easily visible through crowds or from tens of meters away (Mills, 2007). Then, beginning around 1275 CE, Puebloans started to decorate their bowls more subtly. They painted smaller designs, many of which were only visible at short distances, and some only from certain angles. Mills (2007) argues that this results from open spaces yielding to smaller, enclosed ones inside Puebloan settlements and communal feasts declining in size. The select attendees could get close to the bowls, whose designs no longer needed to shout across plazas.

Easily recognized distinctions such as shape and decoration aren't the only ones that can matter when it comes to identifying special or valuable pots. Vessel wares are commonly analyzed with an eye to either their places of origin (imported items commonly being viewed as higher status than local goods) or their functional or aesthetic merits. Sometimes, however, wares' values are rooted more in symbolism than in functionality or beauty. At the historic site of Juffure in West Africa, special occasions featured ceramics that were heavily tempered with oyster shell – and only oyster shell, not other kinds of shell – as opposed to the sand used as temper in everyday vessels (Gijanto and Walshaw, 2014). (Layers of oyster shells were found in the feasting deposits too. Apparently people were using the remains of a special food to make their special pots [Gijanto and Walshaw, 2014].) Feasting pots were not just bigger or more dramatically decorated than quotidian ones; they were technologically distinct.

Conducting Oneself in Accordance with One's Station

Table manners constantly reinforce people's social positions. Who gets served first, and who last? Who says the pre-meal prayer? Who takes the first bite, and who determines when a meal is over? Such rules distinguish clearly among those who dine together. Manners also distinguish among people who don't share food: different social tiers employ different etiquette. Manners are, however, excruciatingly difficult to reconstruct using archaeological evidence, and only in historical contexts are they normally discussed (e.g., Gray, 2008; Mylona, 2008; Pavao-Zuckerman and Loren, 2012; Pollock, 2003).

In contrast, many archaeologists can take advantage of the fact that inequality is manifested in how people work with food. Who does the farming? Who does the cooking? Who cleans up? Never are these tasks distributed equally across society. They may be assigned on the basis of age, gender, caste, or other social distinctions – but in many situations the answer to who does the hardest and least publicly rewarding food work is people of relatively low status. Archaeologists therefore use patterns of food labor to investigate ancient status differences.

What, for example, was social life like at Epiclassic (ca. 650–900 CE) La Quemada in Mexico's Malpaso Valley? Its architecture and artifacts indicate that the residents of this imposing site were part of a Mesoamerican cultural sphere in which hierarchies are well documented. Yet La Quemada's burials and craft goods fail to reveal meaningful differences in social status. Throughout the entire Malpaso Valley, archaeologists have found few prestige goods or specialist crafts, and those that they have found are scattered rather than concentrated in particular structures or areas (Turkon, 2004, 2007). Elaborated burials and distinctive homes are virtually absent as well. The classic archaeological signatures of inequality are thus sparse in the Malpaso Valley. How to investigate the topic?

Turkon (2004, 2007) decided to investigate maize grinding, reasoning that anyone who could do so would have avoided this dull, tiring, and extraordinarily time-consuming[7] work. Maize was the staple food in the Malpaso Valley, and it was commonly ground using heavy stone manos and metates. Tallying the numbers of *manos* and *metates* in different areas within La Quemada and two other Malpaso Valley sites could therefore reveal where people were preparing food (Turkon, 2004). So could the ratio of edible kernels to inedible cupules (cob fragments): in areas where kernels dominate, people were doing more eating than cooking, and in areas where cupules dominate, more food preparation was taking place. Turkon found both cupules and kernels everywhere, suggesting that people were cooking in all households – but not necessarily to the same extent. Two of La Quemada's middens were distinctly richer in kernels than in cupules, and middens near those two were among the lowest in *manos* and *metates*. These middens were also located near the ceremonial core of the site, which features monumental staircases, a votive pyramid, a hall of columns, and a ballcourt (Turkon, 2004). Were the people who dumped their trash in these central middens elites who spent less time laboring over their food than others?

Turkon turned to the ceramics. Assuming that people who didn't do much food preparation would have relatively few storage and cooking vessels, she compared proportions of sturdy preparation vessels and decorated serving wares across her three Malpaso Valley sites. Her results surprised her: none of the La Quemada middens was cooking-vessel-poor. Nor was any of them particularly rich in serving vessels, as might be expected of elites involved in culinary display. Fascinated, Turkon decided to combine all of her lines of evidence, adding data about the diversity of food remains in each midden as well. The resulting statistical cluster analyses identified multiple status levels in the prehispanic Malpaso Valley. Elites produced middens relatively poor in grinding tools and rich in edible maize kernels: they indeed lived near La Quemada's ceremonial core. Members of the middle class deposited middens containing more traces of food preparation. People of lower social standing left relatively high numbers of grinding tools and inedible maize cupules (Turkon, 2004). Traditional archaeological evidence for status differences may be sparse in the Malpaso Valley, but by incorporating food labor data we can see complex social distinctions.

---

[7] Brumfiel (1991) suggests that in order to feed their families, Aztec women spent six to eight hours a day grinding maize. See also Chapters 3 and 6.

The Pimp and Nun Complication

Although high status and economic wellbeing are commonly linked, they are emphatically not the same thing. As Lyman (1987:58) points out, "a person may have low status or prestige and a high income, such as some pimps." Highly esteemed people may have limited incomes as well, with priests and nuns being classic examples. Archaeologists must therefore be wary about distinguishing status levels on the basis of wealth: a rich person is not necessarily a respected person, and vice versa.

Indeed, archaeological evidence exists for people using their purchasing power to eat like their "betters." I previously mentioned that zooarchaeological evidence exists for medieval English poaching gangs selling deer meat in urban taverns and alehouses. Faunal assemblages from medieval English cities include deer forelimb bones – officially the province of rural hunters and foresters – and deer remains with widely varying stable carbon and nitrogen isotope values (Sykes, 2007; Sykes et al., 2016). These data reveal that poachers sourced venison from multiple rural locations in order to supply the urban black market. They are also evidence of Lyman's "pimps": people using their purchasing power in order to eat like their social superiors.

It is best, therefore, to consider both status and wealth together. This is because while the two don't travel together, they do interact in archaeologically and socially important ways. On the archaeological front, people's opportunities to express their status are limited by their economic situations. (The same is true, of course, of their attempts to express other aspects of their identities [Peres, 2008].) High-status people are not always capable of acquiring high-status foods (Gumerman IV, 1997; Peres, 2017). Nor are they necessarily interested in doing so: excavations of modern American trash demonstrated that affluent households don't necessarily purchase expensive food or tableware (Rathje and Murphy, 1992; Wilson and Rathje, 2001; see also Chapter 8).

Low-income households, meanwhile, often face constraints that wealthier ones don't. They are limited to particular purchasing channels and can afford to take fewer economic risks. They may find themselves cornered into buying relatively expensive meat simply because it is the only meat that they can acquire. (Wealthy households, meanwhile, may eschew purchasing meat altogether, relying on livestock that they own themselves [Reitz et al., 2006:105].) Households that can't easily afford costly foods buy them sometimes in order to celebrate a special occasion or to claim a position in society not entirely congruent with their economic resources (Fitchen,

1998). As a result, food cost is an unreliable measure of economic status, let alone social standing (Rathje and McCarthy, 1977; Reitz et al., 2006).

Some archaeologists have suggested that given the economic and logistical constraints of poverty, archaeologists interested in economic status would do better to consider the *quantity* of meat consumed, and the relative proportions of fresh vs. preserved meat, than the specific cuts (Landon, 1996:17; Reitz et al., 2006). Yet quantities are a complicated signal as well.

During the spring of 1973, American beef temporarily became expensive and hard to find. Fortunately that spring also marked the start of the University of Arizona's Garbage Project, which had professional and student archaeologists sampling the dumpsters of Tucson in order to explore modern American behavior via its material correlates (Rathje and Murphy, 1992). Over the course of the next fifteen months, Project archaeologists were stunned to see the amount of wasted beef in Tucson's garbage decline. Rechecking the data, they came to the same conclusion: Tucsonites wasted three times as much beef when it was expensive and hard to find as they did when it was cheaper and readily available (Rathje and Murphy, 1992:60). A similar pattern appeared again in 1975 during a sugar shortage: the price of sugar doubled and Tucson sugar wastage tripled (Rathje and Murphy, 1992:61). The Garbage Project attributed this pattern to "crisis-buying," people buying all the limited-availability food they could and then finding themselves unable to cook or store some of their purchase. In such a situation, the only way for an archaeologist to approach a correct interpretation is to consider the quantities *and* the types of foods recovered (i.e., meat cuts and sugar types), and to examine how those change through time.

We thus end in the same position we're always in: the more information the better. Archaeologists interested in reconstructing status through foodways have the best chance of being accurate if they combine multiple lines of evidence: not just bones or seeds, but also culinary settings and paraphernalia as well as texts if they're available (Peres, 2017 and many, many more).

Establishing how members of a particular culture used food to mark and to claim high status is a challenging task, but it is also an exciting one. Success means insights not only into entrenched hierarchies but also into shaky and contested social distinctions. Today archaeologists use the remains of bread and beef, mutton and millet to explore topics ranging from the origins of social complexity to the effects of social status on religious behavior (see Chapter 7). The archaeological literature on food and inequality is extensive and fascinating. It is also an important contributor to an even larger discussion about food and power. We are ready now to discuss the archaeology of food and politics.

CHAPTER 5

Food and Politics

Power is about people's positions *in relation to other people*, not in isolation (Dietler, 2001:77). An absolute monarch alone on a desert island has no power: only when others are around can he or she exert influence. The extent of one's power, authority, or influence is the extent to which one can direct others. Politics, for the purposes of this chapter, consists of activities intended to enhance personal or group power. It includes community-building and cooperation as well as competitive maneuvering and contention. It occurs at all levels of society, from family relationships to international affairs. This chapter is thus about how individuals social climb, how families affirm their prestige, how communities come together, how chiefs attract followers, and how empires subjugate their conquests. It's about how political realities influence foodways, and how foodways influence politics – sometimes to the point of reshaping nations.

Every day, people produce, prepare, serve, and eat food. In doing so, they daily act out power relationships: peasants weed lords' fields, servers dish out equal or unequal portions, and parents shush children at the table. When studying foodways, we study politics. We study the tiny, mundane interactions that, repeated thousands upon thousands of times, saturate people's lives with potent messages about authority and about togetherness. We study the dramatic performances that over the course of hours or days shake old political alignments into new patterns. And we study myriad other scales and forms of food activities that bring people together and push them apart. The globalization of food discussed in Chapter 3 was a political as well as an economic undertaking; the gendered habits discussed in Chapter 6 are as well. Politics is one of the most commonly discussed topics in the archaeology of food. Let us now turn to exploring why.

Feasting

"Feasts are inherently political," writes Michael Dietler (2001:66). Christine Hastorf (2016:179, 195) calls the feast "the archetypical political meal … the material manifestation of political action." Many, many archaeologists clearly agree: not only is the archaeological literature on feasting voluminous, it's also heavily slanted toward politics. You can read about political feasting among Vikings, Shang, and Inca; in Africa and in Amazonia; from the Paleolithic to the present day. Why such scholarly enthusiasm? I argue that there are three key reasons.

First, feasting is indeed inherently political. Feasts aren't only about politics, but because people participate in varying ways, feasts reinforce or adjust social asymmetries (Dietler, 2001; Hastorf, 2016; Hayden, 2014). The social distinctions built into feasting – people sitting in various locations, contributing varying amounts of labor and goods, using varying tableware, and so forth – express interpersonal relationships both as they exist *and as participants wish them to be.* This is important: festal distinctions don't necessarily reflect existing social realities. They present relationships as people believe they are, or as they should be. As a result, the ways in which feasts are supplied, staffed, served, consumed, and cleaned up can naturalize, mask, or challenge power asymmetries (Dietler, 2001:71). Habitually serving the aristocrats before the peasants normalizes the status chasm between them; intermingling the two groups camouflages the chasm and may lessen social tensions; serving the peasants before the aristocrats may challenge the status quo (revolution time!) – or not, if it's the season for temporary and religiously mandated aberrations (Saturnalia time!).

Feasts thus represent opportunities for people to present themselves to others not just as they are, but as they wish or believe themselves to be, as well as to try and change the status quo (Dietler, 2001:72). Many different attendees may be doing this at any one feast, and as they don't all necessarily adhere to the same agenda, considerable jostling may ensue. A single person or group may even pursue multiple goals at a time, contending (for example) for both personal advantage and societal restructuring (Dietler, 2001). Feasts are often, therefore, veritable symphonies of political action: many performers, each with his or her own music to play, combining to produce a single composition. If numerous players hit discordant notes a cacophony may result, but individuals adjusting pitch, volume, and tone as they play along in the score can shape the music without destroying the overall harmony.

This brings up another key point, which is that with all of the political maneuvering that can go on at a feast, the overall event is nonetheless a shared experience. That sharing binds people together even if they are also overtly competing. Conversely, feasts celebrating communal identities and common interests also distinguish among participants in at least some ways. Those distinctions may be all-but-invisible to attendees, but even subtle distinctions make statements about people's relative positions in society. "[N]early all feasts actually serve in some ways to define social boundaries while simultaneously creating a sense of community ...[they define] distinctions between social groups, categories, and statuses while at the same time establishing relationships across the boundaries that they define" (Dietler, 2001: 88).

At this point readers may argue that when they go to a dinner party, they feel neither slighted nor impressed by the seating arrangements or the order of service; they feel mildly uncomfortable if they get invited over repeatedly without hosting a reciprocal meal, but it's not a big deal. Dietler (2001:77) explains that the competition inherent in feasts isn't always aggressive or dominating; it's often just about not falling behind one's peers. Hosts may simply aim to affirm their own standing, companionably sharing food with others in order to maintain their reputation in the eyes of the community (Dietler, 2001:77). This is not a definition of "competition" that attracts much archaeological attention: virtually all of the literature on competitive feasting assumes oppositional if not combative efforts. However, it's good to be clear on what Dietler meant in his often-cited paper, and more importantly on the full range of politicking that can take place through feasts.

What exactly do people gain by hosting feasts, or by making some other kind of valued contribution to them? Specific answers to that question obviously vary across cultures, but archaeologists often subsume the specifics into admittedly imprecise terms such as "prestige" or "symbolic capital." Dietler (2001:78) explains that symbolic capital enables people "to influence group decisions or actions." It is, in other words, power. It derives not from force of arms or legal diktat, but from guests' feelings of obligation to their hosts. These feelings may be temporary and quite subtle ("Thanks for having us over! It's our turn to host next time"), or they may be strong enough that hosts earn real deference and the right to take the lead in group decision-making (Dietler, 2001:78). Guests incur obligations to hosts, and until/unless they reciprocate they remain subordinate or otherwise "less" than those who provided the hospitality (Hastorf, 2016:195, e.g., Mauss, 1990 [1925]). In many societies, therefore, people host feasts in order to earn community respect and endorsements for their leadership (Dietler, 2001:78–79).

Holding on to that leadership requires further effort, because political power shifts and flows. If a former guest throws a feast that outshines his erstwhile host's, who now has the symbolic capital – the standing to exercise leadership? Not the original host. Political standings require continual maintenance and renegotiation, even if the goal is only to avoid falling behind (Dietler, 2001). Dietler (2003) argues that this is true even in societies with institutionalized power roles. Without at least some consent from their subjects, states and empires fall; feasts help build that consent, enhancing social solidarity or class differences, patronage relationships or tributary obligations as powerful hosts prefer (Bray, 2003b; Dietler, 2003).

When Vikings arrived in Iceland, they entered a landscape empty of other humans and scarce in the resources that they used at home to negotiate political leadership (Zori et al., 2013). Back in Scandinavia, the Norsemen competed for political support by impressing potential supporters with their munificence: ambitious Vikings distributed gifts and hosted splendid feasts. Beef and beer weighed down chieftains' tables as they opened their doors to peers and supporters: "þorkell hosted a Yule-drinking feast at Helgafell, and a large number of people attended. He showed great magnificence with everyone that winter. [His wife] Guðrún ... said that this is what wealth was for – to increase prestige..." (*Laxdaela Saga*, ch. 74: Sveinsson, 1934, cited in Zori et al., 2013).

In newly colonized Iceland, though, beef and beer were hard to come by. Both cattle and barley were ill-suited to the long, cold winters, requiring months of indoor shelter and foddering (cattle) or significant soil improvements (barley) in order to survive. Only wealthy, high-status farms could afford to raise either, and even they couldn't necessarily produce enough to satisfy themselves. Facing shortages of their primary feasting foods, could motivated Vikings demonstrate the kind of lavish hospitality necessary to attract supporters and build coalitions? Excavations at the rich farmstead of Hrísbrú in Iceland's Mosfell Valley suggest that the answer was yes – for some, and for a while. At Hrísbrú, cattle remains outnumber caprine remains by almost 2:1, despite the far greater ecological suitability of the latter, and pollen and seeds testify to barley cultivation. But these data come from relatively early in the Viking settlement (approximately the tenth century CE), before human-induced environmental degradation made Icelandic cattle- and barley-raising increasingly costly. Sagas record Mosfell Valley chieftains thriving until the late twelfth century; after that they disappear from the stories (Zori et al., 2013). Barley cultivation ceased at roughly the same time, as Hrísbrú's last barley pollen dates to the early thirteenth century. Zori and colleagues argue that this cessation reflects the fall of the Mosfell Valley chieftainship. As their power faded, leaders had a harder and harder time attracting labor. What labor they could attract, they could no longer afford to spend on raising risky and expensive feasting foods – which meant further decline in supporters and allies. Their power spun downwards, as waning hospitality led to weakening allegiances led to less food production led to still further deteriorations in festal hospitality. Beef, beer and power traveled together: losing the former meant losing the latter.

Losing the ability to host a feast may mean losing the ability to lead, but it's worth noting at this juncture that feast-hosting is no guaranteed route to prestige or power. Feasts can fail (Smith, 2015). They can do so because guests argue or fall ill; because hosts can't muster adequate food or enter-tainment;[1] because a torch falls and sets the mats on fire; or simply because no one comes. (Poorly attended dinner parties are no modern invention.) Myriads of things can go wrong, any one of which may damage or even destroy a host's social standing. Hosts and supportive guests can watch for oncoming problems and attempt to head them off, but feast-hosting is a risk (Smith, 2015).

Dedicated readers of the archaeological literature often see feasts being classified according to their primary intended purposes (Table 5.1). Those who create these categorizations acknowledge that feasts simultaneously define social distinctions and bind participants together. They argue, however, that appreciating different feasting categories helps us (a) further our thinking about how feasting and politics interrelate and (b) recognize past political situations and complexities (Dietler, 2001:75; Hastorf, 2016:202; Hayden, 2014:11). I am, at present, largely unconvinced by this argument. My skepticism does not lie exclusively in the fact that the boundaries between some categories are blurry to the point of obscurity, or in the fact that feast participants may not all recognize the same agenda, or in the reality that different households can celebrate similar occasions with very different kinds of feasts, or in the fact that what starts as one kind of feast may end up quite something else (Dietler, 2001; Hastorf, 2016:202;

---

[1] Or hosts just get the food wrong. Beaudry (2010:65) mentions an eighteenth-century American host who, in order "to regale … French [guests] with a delicacy of their own country" served them bowls of soup with whole, full-grown frogs in them. Stunned Frenchmen lifted the dripping amphibians up by their legs and started to laugh hysterically. Perhaps the host intended a joke, but the dinner went down in history as "an episode recounted to ridicule the ignorance of Americans" (Beaudry, 2010:65).

Morán, 2016:17; Phillips and Sebastian, 2004:247). Nor am I primarily concerned with the challenges of recognizing different feast categories in the archaeological record. Hastorf (2016:202) says three of her four categories are neither materially distinct nor archaeologically identifiable, while Dietler [2001:75] states that his classification is not intended as a typology, nor should his categories be expected to have archaeologically recognizable signatures. Hayden [2001] classifies feasts by purpose and then, separately, by expected material signature: the two lists cross-cut each other.) Perhaps, though, this is why I can cite virtually no archaeological studies that successfully apply feasting categories much beyond "essentially competitive," "essentially integrative," "a mix of both competition and integration," or "for labor mobilization." My discomfort is a product of all of these factors. I completely accept the importance of understanding the ways in which feasting intertwines with politics and endorse wholeheartedly people's attempts to elucidate them. But I remain dubious that feast classifications are particularly useful to archaeologists, despite their widespread application.

How, for example, would one categorize the famous Mound 51 feast from Cahokia? Cahokia (ca. 1000–1350 CE) is the largest known Mississippian settlement. It features a massive, 19-ha Grand Plaza and well over a hundred mounds of varying sizes and shapes. Among these mounds is a small, nondescript-looking construct called Mound 51. Mound 51 sits on a huge filled-in pit that was dug by ancient Mississippians in order to acquire dirt for building other mounds (Kelly, 2001; Pauketat et al., 2002). Only a small percentage of this pit has been dug (five 3×3 m units in a pit known to be at least 53×20 m in area), but its phenomenally well-preserved contents are revelatory when it comes to Cahokian life. A majority of the pit faunal remains derive from only one of its layers, called Zone D2 (Kelly, 2001). Zone D2 also yielded a variety of exotic and valuable items as well as oddities such as a drilled alligator tooth (Kelly, 2001; Pauketat et al., 2002).

In sharp contrast to Mississippian faunal assemblages from other levels, elsewhere at Cahokia, and across the Southeast, Zone D2's mammalian assemblage is 99.7 percent deer: not small fragments, representing a relatively limited number of actual bones, but large pieces and even entire elements. Fragile bones remain unusually intact, and vertebrae articulate to form segments of multiple animals' spines (Kelly, 2001). Ninety-seven percent of the elements are meaty, high-value bones, indicating that the deer were butchered elsewhere and only the best venison brought to this location. At least some of this venison was then cut off the bones for stewing

TABLE 5.1. *Selected feast categorizations.*

Key proponent	Feast type	Goal	Participants
Dietler (2001)	Empowering feasts (*aka entrepreneurial feasts*)	Acquiring/creating social and economic power	Donors and receivers → superiors and subordinates
Dietler (2001)	Patron-role feasts	Maintaining existing power inequalities	Donors and receivers → superiors and subordinates (equal reciprocity not expected)
Dietler (2001)	Diacritical feasts	Maintaining existing power inequalities	Insiders only; outsiders excluded
Hayden (2001, 2014)	Alliance and cooperation feasts	Social bonding	Variable
Hayden (2001, 2014)	Economic feasts	Material gain	Variable

Character	Notes
Effective but not necessarily overt goal: use commensal hospitality to get and maintain symbolic and sometimes economic capital Not inherently aggressive; often about positively reaffirming host's prestige and social standing	Participants may see as harmonious communal celebration, even as feast is also arena for prestige and influence acquisition. Feasts "unite and divide at the same time" (Dietler 2001:77). Can also be used to gain economic power, e.g., work feasts (labor mobilization) If large-scale, requires lots of planning, time, labor, and surplus stocks of food/drink
Formalized use of commensal hospitality to symbolically reiterate and legitimize institutionalized power asymmetries Redistribution: obligations incurred via hospitality, but no expectation of equal reciprocation. A continually unequal hospitality pattern expresses and naturalizes unequal relations	Obligation exists in return for generosity; failure to be generous weakens status Can challenge leaders via such feasting Chiefs raise food resources in various ways: tribute, work feasts
Differentiated cuisine and consumption styles used to reify and naturalize ranked differences in status Doesn't involve unequal commensal partners; rather, it involves separated commensal circles (insiders and outsiders) Style distinctions may be culinary (special foods, dishes), manners-based, or in tableware/settings, etc.	Subject to emulation; sumptuary laws fight back
Solidarity feasts (intra-group) Reciprocal feasts (inter-group) Political support feasts (to attract political supporters) Promotional feasts (to attract labor/ economic support or display success)	Goals include enhancing group solidarity and effectiveness; creating alliances; bonding for military activity; acquiring/validating political support; attracting affiliates to the group
Solicitation and punishment feasts Competitive feasts (profits from loans/ interest) Feasts required for political advancement (when a formal criterion for a position) Maturation feasts (investments in children) Work party feasts Tribute feasts	Goals include mobilizing labor; investing in children; investing in exchanges; compensating for losses or transgressions; extracting resources from others

TABLE 5.1. (*continued*)

Key proponent	Feast type	Goal	Participants
Hayden (2001, 2014)	Diacritical feasts	Creating distinctions between groups	Superiors and subordinates
Hastorf (2016)	Celebratory feasts (*Dietler's 'entrepreneurial feast'*)	Solidarity; empowerment	Group members
Hastorf (2016)	Potluck feasts (*similar to Dietler's and Hayden's "solidarity feasts," but not identical*)	Reaffirming group membership	Self-identified group members; equals
Hastorf (2016)	Alliance-building feasts (*aka patron-client, patron-role, promotional/ alliance feasts*)	Maintaining/ enhancing existing power inequalities	Donors and receivers → superiors and subordinates (equal reciprocity not expected)
Hastorf (2016)	Competitive feasts (*Dietler's and Hayden's "diacritical feasts"*)	Reifying existing power inequalities	Superiors and subordinates

Character	Notes
Status/power display	Hayden (2014:12) unconvinced that status distinctions are *ever* the primary goal in pre-industrial societies. Argues that feasts aim to attract people, not distance them; exclusions are byproducts, not central agendas
No overt political agenda, though some symbolic capital can be maneuvered. Minimally distinctive In some cultures, hosting = the main strategy for getting/holding any authority position	May morph into alliance-building feasts Harvest festivals, "reciprocal aid feasts" (two equal groups exchange help, e.g., at harvest), weddings, work feasts
"Politically covert" feasts among equals; everyone brings food to share in an atmosphere of communality and solidarity	Potential for competition, as cooks try to outshine each other
Overtly political. People of superior status provide formal and gracious hospitality. Equal reciprocity not expected, but reaffirmation and renewal of subordination and political/economic debt	E.g., potlatches: prestige performances, elaborate preparations, extensive funding; they reposition the host socially Incurred debts mean alliance feasts = "common political devices used to firm up insecure positions and weave people together" (Hastorf, 2016: 201)
Differentiated cuisine and consumption styles used to reify and naturalize ranked differences in status Overt displays of differences among the elite, as hosts know everyone is judging their performance and success	ACTIVE stylistic competition; emulation and style-sensitivity are factors The most archaeologically recognizable feast type. Special, high-value foodstuffs/ quantities; exotic goods; unusual or highly standardized utensils These are the feasts that most archaeological feasting studies discuss

or drying, because blowflies and flesh-eating beetles – whose remains were discovered alongside the bones in large numbers – eat almost nothing but raw, decaying flesh (Kelly, 2001).

The non-mammalian fauna in Zone D2 are also noteworthy. An unusually limited bird assemblage is dominated by swans, which are uncommon in Mississippian contexts. This domination is despite the fact that there are no swan wing bones in the pit: the Mississippians removed those for other uses, it seems (Kelly, 2001). The birds were probably valued primarily for their ritually important feathers, and may not have been eaten (Kelly and Kelly, 2007; Pauketat et al., 2002).

The bones in the pit tell us that more than nine hundred years ago Mississippian cooks stood on a floodplain and stripped meat from bones, cut the wings from swans, and filleted fish. They probably also cleaned squash: clumps of seeds and pulpy material resemble the scoops we take out of jack-o-lantern pumpkins at Halloween (Kelly, 2001). They cooked maygrass, maize, and other plant foods, and ritually painted ceramic vessels red, black, and white (Beehr and Ambrose, 2007; Kelly, 2001; Pauketat et al., 2002).

Researchers agree that the pit remains represent the leavings of people cooking primarily for community-wide feasting. (Beehr and Ambrose [2007] suggest that the feasts may even have drawn attendees from farmsteads and villages miles away.) But – and this is important when we're contemplating categorizing this event – such feasts were no neighborhood potlucks. Chiefs may have coordinated the venison supply, arranging for selected deer parts to be the only mammal meat served. They might also have hosted the feasts, perhaps in the nearby Grand Plaza. At the very least, elites contributed luxurious goods such as crystals and engraved pottery, thereby distinguishing themselves from the masses of more plebeian participants (Kelly, 2001). Pauketat and colleagues (2002:275) believe that Zone D2 testifies to the Cahokian population's coming together as they formed "a Cahokian … identity, or way of life." Kelly (2001:357) broadly concurs, but notes that elites may also have used these feasts to advance their social standing. The Mound 51 deposit is skillfully studied and wonderfully informative about Mississippian life at Cahokia, but in my opinion assigning it to a particular category of feast (solidarity? promotional? work party?) is neither justified by the data nor beneficial to our comprehension of what was probably occurring. The Cahokians were simultaneously uniting and dividing themselves. Different people surely had different ideas about which goal was primary. And the event itself might not have proceeded according to plan, producing results that diverged widely from what people went in expecting.

Second, feasting provides insights into politics at multiple scales, from domestic maneuvering within households and among friends up through imperial strategizing across class and cultural boundaries. Of particular note is feasting's ability to provide information about how abstract and sometimes large-scale political systems shaped and were shaped by actual human experiences (Bray, 2003b; Dietler, 2001; Hastorf, 2016; Mills, 2004). How did people actually compete for power? How did they strengthen – or challenge – existing power structures? What did people *do* in order to advance themselves and their interests? And how did their actions shape the grand trajectories of their societies? Studying feasting allows us to address these questions at what Hastorf (2016:195) terms the "human scale." The remains of a feast represent the remains of a specific political event (or series of events). We can evaluate the size of these events; hosts' strategies for impressing their guests; variation in participants' experiences; and more. In studying feasting we study how people negotiate authority and influence, bridging the gap between on-the-ground human experiences and big political themes (Dietler, 2001; Hastorf, 2016:195).

An example of archaeology shedding light on different scales of feasting at a single site comes from China. The northern Chinese city of Yanshi Shangcheng flourished in the years between 1500 and 1400 BCE. This Erligang (early Shang) center, with its central palace compound and thick enclosing wall, was home to warriors and to artisans, to cooks and to administrators (Reinhart, 2015). Royals and other elites dwelt in the walled palace complex; more modest residents lived and worked north and east of them, in the outer city. Yet Yanshi's politics were far more intricate than a simple two-tier hierarchy. Reinhart (2015) examined ceramic and faunal remains from two kinds of site contexts: (1) pits in the palace area, rich in bones, sherds, plant remains, and ritual paraphernalia, and (2) middens and other deposits in a "potters' area," where simple houses lay near kilns. Both areas yielded evidence for feasting. Ceramics from the palatial area were varied and often large; they were also associated with the remains of sacrificed animals, human burials, and as stated before, ritual paraphernalia. Vessels were generally smaller and simpler in the potters' area, but excavators recovered a handful of special "meat" and "wine" vessels as well. Reinhart supports her contention that these ceramics reflect feasting by noting multiple lines of evidence supporting ritual activity as well as ritual food use in the potters' area, albeit mostly later in the site's occupation. She infers that Yanshi elites held large-scale diacritical feasts that Yanshi workers chose not to emulate, opting instead for small-scale feasts perhaps emphasizing family ties and shared ancestry. The accuracy of this specific inference is hard to assess, given the depositional differences between the palace and potters' contexts (pits versus middens; ritual versus residential areas). However, it's clear that there were multiple scales and multiple kinds of feasting going on at Yanshi, involving various ranks of people.

As for linking grand political developments to on-the-ground human activities, i.e., life on the human scale, let us cross continents to the Andes, where archaeologists have uncovered feasting remains at a site whose early centuries are broadly coeval with those found at Yanshi. In the middle of the second millennium BCE, Chiripa was one of four thriving, independent villages on the Taraco Peninsula (Hastorf, 2010). For a thousand years, people periodically walked from other villages to Chiripa to feast and honor the ancestors, reaffirming their shared memories and identities. Together they ate, burned incense, and conducted ceremonies in and around big walled enclosures (Hastorf, 2010, 2015). Every time villagers or visitors walked through the center of Chiripa, they passed these spaces, triggering recollections of communal activities and shared symbolism.

As time passed, however, civic structures grew smaller and less accessible. Highly visible walled enclosures capable of holding a hundred people yielded to sunken enclosures able to contain only fifty; additional participants would have stood around their edges to watch ongoing activities (Hastorf, 2010). Chiripans eventually built and then repeatedly rebuilt a space ringed by small, decorated rooms, in which people stored ancestors, foodstuffs, and ritual valuables. The architecture indicates that the entirety of the village could gather in the open space in front of this complex; roughly 100 people could proceed into its core; only ten or so could enter the storerooms and spend private moments with the ancestors (Hastorf, 2010). These rooms – which had the only doorways in the entire settlement – were normally kept closed, their outer walls reminding passersby of the families whose ancestors lay within. This experimentation with distinction and segregation soon ended, and by roughly 100 BCE the rooms were all buried under a big new surface open to all (Hastorf, 2010).

Chiripan feasting data thus connect human-scale experiences with big political developments. Changes in who was able to feast, where, and with whom may not have driven social segmentation and later re-integration, but they certainly contributed. Picture yourself sharing food, music, and worship with everyone you know; now picture yourself sharing these experiences with only some of your friends and acquaintances, as others process past you into an enclosure where they will eat, dance, and pray by themselves. You probably feel how the latter experience doesn't just *reflect* social distinctions but also *enhances* them.

Elsewhere, archaeologists have argued that feasting can and does propel major political (as well as economic and technological: see Chapters 1 and 3) developments. For an example let us turn again to the Mississippian and to Cahokia.

What caused the "Big Bang" in American prehistory? How did it actually happen? During the eleventh century CE, people across much of the American Midwest and Southeast abruptly and profoundly changed how they lived. Archaeologists working in this area see rapid and dramatic expansions of settlement size (Cahokia's population multiplied five- to tenfold [Pauketat and Lopinot, 1997]), technological innovations, economic reorientations, and ritual reorganizations. Researchers have been debating why it happened for decades, with scholars offering explanations including immigration, contact with distant cultures, the rise of the bow and arrow, and the institution of maize agriculture (Brown and Kelly, 2015). However, none of these potential influences can fully explain the social processes through which the Bang might have occurred (Brown and Kelly, 2015).

Brown and Kelly (2015), focusing on Cahokia, see feasting as an important part of the answer. Over the two centuries leading up to the Bang, multiple groups moved to Cahokia. Once there, they developed communal rituals to cope with the increased frequency and scale of social interactions. One important such ritual was feasting, Brown and Kelly argue, because food-sharing is a particularly effective bonding activity. Participating in communal feasts united the new urbanites – at least at first. Over time, the bonds between Cahokia's various groups weakened, as groups short on healthy adult laborers proved unable to produce enough food and other resources to contribute as much to the feasts as others. Unwilling to risk damaging the ritual feasting that cemented their social solidarity, richer groups came to the rescue and loaned workers to those in need. This placed the understaffed groups in social as well as economic debt and eventually led to social stratification (Brown and Kelly, 2015).

Brown and Kelly believe that communal feasting "gravitate[s] toward inequality" because group sizes and proportions of working adults naturally fluctuate over generations. If equal relationships are to be maintained, strong leveling mechanisms must be put into play: without these, inequalities will naturally arise. Groups' labor potentials determine their social opportunities, and if chance causes a group's demographics to shift in an unfavorable direction for a few generations, they may not be able to recover socially (Brown and Kelly, 2015). (This argument echoes one that others have made about agricultural land as well as labor: see the next section on the politics of food production.) Many scholars disagree that large feasts inherently lead to inequality (e.g., Dietler, 2001; Twiss, 2008). Brown and Kelly may be correct about Cahokian feasting, however, and they certainly demonstrate how the archaeological study of food can link specific, on-the-ground activities such as Mississippian feasting to grand political developments.

Third, feasting is relatively archaeologically identifiable. I use the word "relatively" because identifying feasting in the archaeological record often isn't easy. True, it can be: sometimes one finds the remains of five hundred or more kilos of butchered beef in a single Neolithic interment (e.g., Goring-Morris and Horwitz, 2007), or a Phrygian tomb containing fifteen pieces of wooden furniture, the body of a king laid out on purple and blue textiles, and bronze vessels still containing the dregs of a spicy lamb and lentil stew (not to mention a potent mix of mead, wine, and beer; McGovern, 2017). But then one runs into situations like the prehispanic Southwest, where people cooked and served the same foods in the same pots at feasts and at home (Potter and Ortman, 2004; Van Keuren, 2004), or the contact-period Southeast, where circa 1700 CE Sara people bound themselves together in the face of European diseases and Seneca raiding by feasting on their most common, basic staple foods (VanDerwarker et al., 2007). Multiple papers therefore wrangle with how best to identify feasts in the archaeological record, especially in prehistoric and non-state societies (Hayden, 2001; Reinhart, 2015; Twiss, 2008; Wills and Crown, 2004). Emphases vary, but most generally embrace one or both of the following approaches. The first consists of identifying food remains or culinary deposits that are atypical for the culture and site being studied: unusually large piles of bones, unusually elaborate dishes, unusually located dining facilities. (Atypically small or simple deposits are justifiably excluded from consideration.) The second involves searching for the material traces of feasting behaviors that appear commonly in the ethnographic and ethnohistoric records (Table 5.2). Both approaches are widely accepted, with the usual caveat that multiple lines of evidence are best.

Feasting is thus both deeply and inherently political, and something that we can access archaeologically. Feasts are not the only meals where people affirm or negotiate authority and influence, however. *All* meals have political implications (Hastorf, 2016:180). Some meals overtly acknowledge power and status distinctions – royal feasts, for example – and some do not, but politics pervade them all. We turn now to the many ways in which politics and foodways interact beyond the register of the feast.

TABLE 5.2. *Material correlates of ethnographically or ethnohistorically documented feasting. After Twiss 2008: Table 1. Not all feasts include many of these signatures. Textual records and scenic art, which are not included on this list, may testify to any or all of the listed aspects of feasting.*

Common aspect of feasting	Material correlates
Consumption of large quantities of food and/or drink	○ Unusually large and dense concentrations of food remains ○ Special disposal practices to cope with tremendous quantities of trash ○ Facilities for collecting food (storage bins/pits/containers, granaries, animal pens) ○ Atypically large or abundant food preparation/serving equipment ○ Numerous or large cooking facilities (hearths, ovens)
Consumption of an unusually wide variety of foods	○ An unusual variety of cooking or serving equipment
Consumption of rarely eaten and/or symbolically important foods	○ Remains of rare or labor-intensive species or preparations ○ Remains of iconographically prominent foods or species ○ Remains of foods associated with ritual contexts
Culinary emphasis on large animals	○ Remains of large animals (wild or domestic)
Consumption of domesticated animals	○ Remains of domesticated animals
Consumption of alcohol	○ Brewing equipment ○ Elaborate drinking paraphernalia ○ Residues of alcoholic beverages ○ Depictions of alcoholic beverages
Use of special locations ○ special sites ○ special structures or spaces within sites ○ special locations within structures or spaces	○ Non-habitation sites ○ Unusually large, numerous, or elaborate facilities; atypically located facilities ○ Unusually elaborate spaces inside structures
Public rituals	○ Ritual items large enough to be visible from a distance ○ Food remains associated with graves/human remains ○ Spatial association of food remains/cooking facilities with ritual sites or structures

TABLE 5.2. (*continued*)

Common aspect of feasting	Material correlates
Performances (singing, dancing, music, oratory, etc.)	○ Costume elements ○ Musical instruments
Displays of wealth and/or status	○ Presence, relative abundance of prestige items ○ Special display facilities
○ destruction of wealth or prestige items	○ Destroyed/damaged wealth or prestige items
○ food wastage	○ Discard of edible material, articulated joints, minimally processed bones
Use of special serving paraphernalia	○ Unusual quality, decoration, or materials of serving equipment
Production/display of commemorative items	○ Artistic representations of food taxa ○ Trophy bones ○ Memorial constructs

Quotidian Politics

Feasts and everyday meals are related (see Chapter 1), and daily foodways are as saturated with politics as festal ones. Some people eat more or better than others; some people are served first; some people do the cooking and others merely the eating. Families bond as they eat, but power relationships are also clear: Father sits at the head of the table, Mother says grace, and both chastise children whose manners slip. An entire literature exists on the politics of family meals and school lunches (e.g., Allison, 1991; DeVault, 1991:227–243; Weismantel, 1988).

Archaeologists therefore investigate the politics of daily meals as well as feasts. Hastorf (2012) provides a notable example as she reminds us that food work isn't inherently low-status. A family cook, like a feast cook, may derive power and prestige from her position. Hastorf advocates examining the placement of homes' cooking facilities to establish cooks' prestige and power. Were hearths and ovens prominently located or hidden from view? (Iconographic depictions of cooks or cooking facilities can provide excellent insight into the visibility of cooking and, by proxy, its social value [Graff, 2018], but such imagery is rarer than hearths and ovens are.)

At Neolithic Çatalhöyük in central Anatolia, hearths and ovens featured prominently in homes' main rooms. People placed these cooking facilities where everyone would see them – and cooks crouching over them could see everyone in return (Hastorf, 2012). At times, therefore, cooks were "physically in the center of the house, watching all that goes on, orchestrating all activities that relate to food" (Hastorf, 2012:79). At those times, we infer, cooks held domestic power.

Cooks weren't always seated by the fire, supervising their households, however. Many did considerable work away from the fires, in small, private and probably poorly lit side rooms. These rooms, as discussed in Chapter 3, are where we find most of the site's plant processing debris and grinding facilities (Demirergi et al., 2014). The Çatalhöyük story is more complex and interesting, it turns out, than simply "cooks had power." Yes, at least some food preparation was highly visible and therefore presumably socially valued. But other food preparation was relegated to side rooms, out of sight and away from centers of conversation and debate. Were the fire-tenders and the food-grinders different people? It's extremely unlikely that such tasks were anyone's exclusive responsibility. However, certain people undoubtedly did more grinding than others, probably in relation to their age, gender, and/or health status. As grinding was not a publicly valued activity, these people's work earned them little power or prestige. Fire-tenders, in contrast, were spatially and socially central in domestic life. They also controlled the food during its final stages of preparation, so perhaps they decided when as well as what others would eat. Time spent baking and roasting, but not grinding, contributed to one's social position.

I argued before that the intentions behind ancient feasts are difficult to access archaeologically. We know that feasts were political arenas, but their original aims and effects are usually only broadly reconstructible. (Even then, fair-minded scholars may disagree about interpretations.) The same can be true of quotidian foodways. We sometimes recognize politics in action, but have difficulty eliciting what power relationships were involved: who was doing something in pursuit of what agenda.

Researchers once thought that mass-produced food equipment might testify to rationing, as in the case of the bevel-rim bowls of fourth-millennium-BCE Mesopotamia. These coarse, plain bowls were mass-produced, used and discarded in astonishing numbers (Goulder, 2015). Several archaeologists have cited logical reasons to identify them as containers for distributing grain or bread rations. In addition to the bowls' sheer numbers, cuneiform texts record ration distributions; the cuneiform ideogram for rations resembles a bevel-rim bowl; the bowls themselves are cheap and easy to make; and some scholars identify standardized bowl sizes and shapes (Goulder, 2015; Pollock, 2003). This last point is strongly contended, though, and there are other arguments against interpreting the bowls as rations containers. The bowls are sometimes found in small quantities rather than en masse, and they're normally found in central areas rather than in worker's homes. It's also hard to imagine why rations would be distributed in heavy, open, breakable containers (Goulder, 2015). (Pollock [2003:31] infers that workers had a "fast-food mentality" and ate at work.)

Experiments conducted by Goulder (2015) support the idea that the bowls were used to bake bread. If they were rations containers, then the huge stacks of bowls recovered at some central sites might represent centralized bakeries' stored or surplus equipment. How, though, to explain sparse and scattered bowl finds, as seen in early fourth millennium levels at numerous sites on the Mesopotamian peripheries? Goulder argues that the evidence best fits the idea that the bowls were used to bake leavened bread for administrators or merchants, not for humble workers. Leavened bread, especially if made of wheat, was relatively costly to make, and plausibly a delicacy for bureaucrats rather than field workers. Large collections of bowls are commonly associated with administrative buildings. And prestige cooking equipment could have filtered gradually into peripheral regions as they increasingly echoed the culture of the urban heartland (Goulder, 2015). The bevel-rim bowls may, therefore, track not worker rationing but the rise and spread of bureaucracy, wherein leavened bread constituted part of administrators' "differentiating 'salary'" (Goulder, 2015:359). The case of the bevel-rim bowl thus illustrates both the opportunities afforded by cooking equipment when it comes to the study of ancient politics, and the challenges involved in identifying the actors and agendas at work.

The Politics of Food Production

Who has the right to pick those grapes? Who decides which crops to plant, and in which proportions? Who may hunt that stag, and who gives that permission? Power and access are inextricably intertwined with food production (Hastorf, 2016:10). This is true at all levels of society, from the household ("no picking all the strawberries, kids") to the nation and beyond.

Food production is fundamental to political success: regimes have risen and fallen on the basis of their ability to ensure that their people eat (Friedel and Reilly, 2010; Gill, 2001; Paulette, 2016; Scott, 2017). Food production also plays a central role in scholarly debates about the origins and bases of power. In the Near East, for example, early states' power has often been attributed to centralized control over food resources. The idea is that in Mesopotamia and Egypt, small groups of people controlled agriculture and husbandry from inside their palaces or temples. They coerced the populace to produce surpluses that went into central storehouses. Administrators then redistributed the food as rations (Scott, 2017; Weiss et al., 1993).

Ur and Colantoni (2010) use food data to challenge this model. Arguing that other data sets have been biased in favor of centralized state control, they examine agricultural and food storage evidence from early urban (third millennium BCE) northern Mesopotamia. In this region shallow "hollow ways" radiate out from ancient sites, marking the tracks along which farmers and livestock walked to and from their fields and pastures. Around them the countryside is littered with sherd scatters, the remains of manure or midden mixes dumped onto fields as fertilizer. The density and continuousness of these scatters, as well as the plethora of hollow ways, testify to high-intensity cultivation around northern Mesopotamia's early cities (Ur and Colantoni, 2010). But the resulting food wasn't all stored in institutional warehouses. Inside the city of Hamoukar, private homes held both grain storage jars and grinding stones; evidence of animal dung proves that animals lived inside the city and probably inside house compounds too (Ur and Colantoni, 2010). Nowhere in the region have archaeologists found institutional food storage facilities large enough to provision entire cities. Early cities' temples and other institutions resemble larger versions of normal households: bigger stores, more grinding equipment, but the difference is in scale rather than in kind (Ur and Colantoni, 2010).

Ur and Colantoni thus argue that the early Mesopotamian state was no centralized bureaucracy. The food evidence accords with a different political model, one in which the state was the largest of a nesting-doll hierarchy of "households." A successful man's household might include numerous smaller, dependent families' households, even as he himself was part of the king's household (Ur and Colantoni, 2010). At each level of this hierarchy, households maneuvered to support themselves economically and advance themselves politically. Food was a key part of this maneuvering, and the third millennium's intensive production may reflect numerous households working toward hosting politically useful feasts (Ur and Colantoni, 2010).

Recently published stable isotopic evidence enriches the political picture set forth by Ur and Colantoni. Worried about the difficulties of dating hollow ways and sherd scatters, Styring and colleagues (2017) turn to northern Mesopotamian crop stable isotope values. They remind us that high $\delta15N$ values are associated with fertilization, and thus with intensive crop production. As far back as the Neolithic age, Mesopotamian crop δ15N values vary, indicating that some crops were being grown on fertilized fields and some weren't. In general, however, the amount of manure put on the fields was lower in the third millennium than in earlier periods, suggesting that as cities boomed, their populations were fed by farming more and more land rather than by intensifying production on the same land they'd always farmed (Styring et al., 2017).

This expansion was probably undertaken by households rather than managed by a centralized administration (Styring et al., 2017). But the expansion may also have helped fuel the concentration of political power in fewer and fewer people's hands (Styring et al., 2017). When the amount of food one produces reflects the amount of land one farms (rather than the effort one sinks in), land becomes increasingly important as a source of wealth. Heritable land is wealth that a family can transfer through the generations. Because land varies dramatically in its agricultural potential, heritable land means that family incomes are likely to differ across generations. Agricultural expansion may therefore have enhanced inherited inequalities. It may also have helped centralization efforts, because land is easy to tax (Styring et al., 2017). Food production strategies may have helped turn the Mesopotamian ziggurat of households increasingly hierarchical.

Diplomacy and Political Messaging

The year was 879 BCE. The Neo-Assyrian emperor had established a new royal capital, and the grand palace at its center was finally completed. To consecrate it, Ashurnasirpal II hosted what O'Connor (2015:57) calls "the greatest feast yet known in history," so splendid that a list of its provisions – more than 15,000 sheep and 1,000 deer; 300 oxen and 10,000 fish; 32,000 birds and 10,000 eggs; 1,000 boxes of greens and 10,000 of grain; oil and nuts and bread and grapes; garlic and cumin and pomegranates and onions – was inscribed on a stela depicting the emperor under the aegis of his gods (Figure 5.1). Ensuring that everyone would understand the scale of Ashurnasirpal's power and the extent of his political reach, inscriptions reported that

When I consecrated the palace of Calah [Kalhu, modern Nimrud], 47,074 men and women ... were invited[2] from every part of my land ... 5,000

---

[2] "Invited" does not mean that they were given the option of an RSVP. According to Wiseman (1952:28), these "guests" (quotation marks his) were largely captives who had been put to work renovating Kalhu and then became the nucleus of the city's residents. The foreign delegates may also have been unenthusiastic attendees who, as hostages, didn't

FIGURE 5.1.   Banquet stela of Ashurnasirpal II (879 BCE), Nimrud [Calah/Kalhu], Iraq.
Reproduced from Wiseman (1952:fig. 1). © The British Institute for the Study of Iraq
1952, published by Cambridge University Press.

> *dignitaries [and] envoys ... 16,000 people of Calah [and] 1,500 zariqu of
> my palace, all of them – altogether 69,574 including those summoned from
> all lands and the people of Calah ... thus did I honor them and send them
> back to their lands in peace and joy.*
>
> Grayson, 1991:292

The stela was installed near a doorway leading to the new palace's throne
room, a political message inscribed on stone for eternity (Wiseman, 1952).
Other kings hosted feasts: indeed, feasting was so politically important that
Assyrian victors looted losers' large bronze vessels, not just to acquire
valuable booty but also to deprive enemies of a key political tool (O'Connor, 2015:59). But anyone who saw that stela knew that Ashurnasirpal
reigned supreme. (A bit more than two hundred years later another Neo-
Assyrian ruler, Ashurbanipal, would decorate his palace at Nineveh with
another political message featuring food. On a stone relief commonly
called "the Banquet Scene," Ashurbanipal and his queen sip wine and
nibble delicacies in a lovely garden. Birds sing in the trees; servants play

have the option of returning home afterwards. The food was lavish, the palace spectacular,
but who knows how many of this feast's participants actually had a good time?

music and fan the diners; and the head of the vanquished king of Elam swings from a nearby tree. Please visit the British Museum's website to see a color photo.)

These archaeological finds silently inform all who see them that the kings who sponsored them are magnificent beyond compare; that they possess wealth and respect as well as military might; and that those who oppose them fail – and die. They intimidate opponents, and woo potential allies. And they are far from unique in the archaeological record, where extensive artistic as well as artifactual evidence testifies to communities and governments using food to intimidate, to negotiate, and to attract foreign and domestic groups.

In first millennium-BCE southwestern Arabia, for example, the kingdom of Saba strung along watercourses edging Yemen's great interior desert (Lewis, 2007). Trade caravans linked Saba's towns and cities, but were vulnerable to raids by hostile desert nomads. Pursuing peace and economic security, the Sabaean government would meet occasionally with desert tribespeople at the border-zone sanctuary of Jebel Lawdh. There, agriculturalists and nomads gathered inside a pair of buildings designed for ritual banqueting, seated on rows upon rows of long stone benches. Around them was a sanctuary dedicated to numerous tribal gods, not to a single local deity as per South Arabian norms (Lewis, 2007).

The Inka used food storage facilities as political advertisements, "symbolic stand-ins for Inka power" (Hastorf and Foxhall, 2017:32). Communities erected rows of *qolqa* storage units on hillsides, so that any time passersby looked up, they would see a sturdy stone testament to Inka wealth and power. The "banks of the Inka state", *qolqa* held potatoes, maize, quinoa, and other foods to sustain Inka state employees as well as (on occasion) needy locals: enough food, alongside other goods, that only a great power could possibly assemble so much wealth in a single location (Hastorf and Foxhall, 2017:30). Placing the *qolqa* in highly visible locations meant that the Inka's subjects received constant visual reminders that they labored for a rich and politically effective state, and that said state occasionally sustained them in their times of need.

Archaeology thus demonstrates that food has been a diplomatic tool for millennia. It has been used to establish peace, to foster alliances, to improve governmental security and stability, and to warn off potential challengers. Sometimes, however, diplomacy has failed, and war has ensued. We turn now to how warfare affects foodways, and how food shapes – and sometimes causes – war.

Food and War

> … *Lucullus was not carrying on the war in any theatrical way, nor for mere display, but, as the saying is, was "kicking in the belly," and devising every means for cutting off food.*
>
> Plutarch (1914), *Life of Lucullus*, In *Plutarch's Lives*, ch. 11, transl. B. Perrin

War does not stay on the battlefield. It seeps into every aspect of civilian as well as military life, including of course foodways (Keeley, 2016; Wilson and VanDerwarker, 2016). Wartime shortages may lead to starvation or milder malnutrition, certainly, but violent conflicts have far broader and more complicated effects on foodways. War keeps people where they think themselves safe, limiting where they can go to gather, hunt, or farm their food. When food is chronically scarce, the vulnerable and the socially marginalized – children, women, minorities, the poor – often suffer far more than the powerful, exacerbating social differences. Military purchasing influences farmers' decisions about what to plant, military imports introduce locals to novel flavors and species, and military pillaging ravages civilian food supplies.

We see all of these patterns archaeologically. In North America, for example, food remains testify to war's impacts on civilian populations. Plant and animal remains from the Central Illinois Valley reveal that eight hundred years ago, people collected fewer wild fruits and nuts and fished less during an era of intensifying violence. Too scared to range far from their defended villages, and unable to increase their crop production, they narrowed their diets and accepted that they would be periodically hungry and malnourished (VanDerwarker and Wilson, 2016). In the American Southwest, masses of incinerated maize at the eponymous Burnt Corn Pueblo silently testify to Ancestral Puebloans' embrace of a devastatingly effective military strategy (Snead, 2016). Much of the pueblo's burnt maize was relatively green, probably set aflame while drying on the rooftops so that it could be stored. In setting fire to it, the arsonists obliterated the community's food supply and ended occupation at Burnt Corn Pueblo (Snead, 2016:145).

(As a side note, strategic destruction of enemy food supplies is widely known historically – the armies of Assyria, Rome, England, and the United States have been among its practitioners [Keeley, 2016] – but it is difficult for archaeologists to identify destruction or theft that occurred outside of sites themselves. Livestock theft, tree ringing, and crop burning leave few or no traces in the areas likeliest to be excavated. Most of the archaeological information we have about "kicking in the belly" therefore comes from destroyed food stores inside settlements, which reflect only a tiny portion of the cross-cultural nutritional devastation wrought by ancient warfare.)

Other sites prove that chronic violence affects different parts of a population differentially. In South America, the collapse of the highland Wari Empire in the eleventh century CE introduced an era of social unrest and violence. During this era, some people's skulls – not everyone's – were deliberately modified, bound tightly in infancy so that throughout their lives they would have visibly elongated heads. These people ate far worse than people with unmodified skulls did: over half of the Andahuaylas province modified skulls studied by Kurin (2016) have cranial lesions caused by nutritional problems, whereas only a quarter of the unmodified skulls bear lesions. Whatever the social difference marked by skull modification (possibly ethnicity or kin group), it clearly correlated with elevated food insecurity during a violent era (Kurin, 2016).

Soldiers need food: as either Napoleon or Frederick the Great said, "an army marches on its stomach." Societies provision their warriors in a variety of ways (e.g., Allen, 2016; Fales and Rigo, 2014; Roberts et al., 2012; Stallibrass and Thomas, 2008a). Some amass foods that troops can carry with them as they travel. Archaeologists sometimes recover such food stores, which can be analyzed to learn about military supply chains and logistics. When the English warship *Mary Rose* was recovered from the sea floor where she had lain since July 19, 1545 CE, when she sank during a battle against the French, archaeologists found thousands of cod bones among the provisions sent along with its sailors. The fish were probably decapitated and then salted or dried for storage, since there were no cranial bones and some of the remains were found associated with baskets and casks (Hutchinson et al., 2015). Stable isotope and ancient DNA analyses of the cod remains indicate that the English navy was sourcing military rations from multiple locations as distant as Iceland, Atlantic Europe, and possibly even Newfoundland: none of the *Mary Rose*'s fish was caught anywhere near southern England (Hutchinson et al., 2015). King Henry VIII's sailors set off for battle victualled with British beer, biscuits, beef – and imported salt cod (Coy and Hamilton-Dyer, 2005).

Other cultures expect their warriors to live partially or wholly off the landscape. The famed warriors of Sparta, for example, used to schedule their invasions for harvest time. When in 425 BCE they accidentally invaded Attica before the grain was ripe, they had to abandon their plans and, hungry, retreat home (Oliver, 2007:114).

Archaeologists commonly evaluate whether the food remains found at military encampments were locally produced by examining (a) their stable isotopic signatures and (b) in the case of animal remains, the body segments represented: foods intended for transport are often processed for portability and durability in ways that remove heavy and/or decay-prone parts such as heads. Of course, armies and navies have frequently traveled with livestock, so body part representation can only be one line of evidence, not a complete argument. Wild plant and animal remains can indicate local acquisition if they come from species that are unavailable in troops' homelands or are found in large enough quantities that it's unlikely that warriors were hauling them across significant distances. Even in historical contexts, analyses such as these can reveal surprising information about how warriors were and weren't fed. George Washington's freezing, hungry soldiers mournfully recorded "[a] general cry thro' the camp among the soldiers. 'No meat! No meat! … (Waldo 1897:309)" at Valley Forge, but that didn't prompt them to go hunting: they left virtually no wild animal bones behind at the camp (Campana and Crabtree, 2006).

Food remains themselves are not the only data set that reflects provisioning strategies. According to Allen (2016), Maori war parties carried little in the way of rations, preferring to attack, sack, and then eat a community – its food stores, and also potentially some of its occupants. "Te Ika a Tu" – the fish of the war deity Tu, aka human flesh – was a reward for routing the enemy, and successful warriors might eat it for days, such that "war parties quite literally lived on their enemy"(Allen, 2016:51). Eating Tu's fish not only provided nutrition but also humiliated the enemy, converting them as it did from humans to cooked food in a culture where men not only didn't cook food, they didn't even carry cooked foods on their backs. Victims' heads might also be smoked and carried home to be displayed next to victors' ovens, a placement that shamed the losing warriors still further by installing them officially in the feminine sphere of cookery. Village fortifications are material signatures of such conflicts, built as they were to defend both people and food stores.

Food is also a cause of conflict. Prominent in the archaeological literature is the idea that food shortfalls can lead to violent competition. Archaeologists commonly look to see if high proportions of violent trauma in a population correlate with either skeletal markers of nutritional stress or evidence for environmental degradation. Many such correlations have been found, such that "some archaeologists have … argued that almost all wars are associated with difficulties in obtaining or producing food (e.g., LeBlanc 2003)" (Keeley, 2016:300). This is not a position that all archaeologists embrace, because correlation is not causation, and war leads to hunger as often as the converse. However, it certainly highlights the extent to which nutritional strain is associated with violence across both space and time.

Of course, people don't need to be facing hunger in order to fight on food's account. Competitions can spiral out of control, and competitive feasts have been ethnographically reported as (a) devolving into armed battles, or (b) motivating participants to go raiding for feasting supplies (Junker, 2001:281, 298). Non-competitive feasts can also enable violence, as hosts mobilize non-professional fighters by inviting them to dine. Invitees may or may not have a choice about attending. Such corvée labor is extremely challenging to see archaeologically, but an inscription on a Mycenaean tablet from Pylos records the palace's military leader contributing to a feast held at the palace; his rooms, decorated with the palace's only frescoes showing warfare, are next to rooms interpreted as feasting halls (Fox and Harrell, 2008).

Finally, food needs direct the timing, organization, and success of violent conflict (Keeley, 2016). Among the Maori, finishing the planting of the sweet potato crop freed the men from gardening duties to go to war; harvest time marked the end of the war season (Allen, 2016). Aztec troops waited to march until after harvest, and departing groups included not only fighting men but also huge numbers of porters, whose job it was to haul everyone's maize (Hassig, 2016). Many Inka warriors left the siege of Cuzco to get their crops sowed before the start of the rainy season; the siege eventually failed, in part because Inka troop numbers declined (few of the crop-sowers returned) and in part because they failed to deprive the besieged Spanish of food and water (Flickema, 1981).

Expansionism

Food may cause conflict within societies. It may also motivate groups to expand their territories. Rome, for example, pushed into new territories specifically to acquire farmland, and never extended its empire beyond regions capable of producing agricultural surpluses (Hastorf, 2016; Jones, 2007:228). Both the Maya and the Aztecs fought for lands rich in salt (Williams, 2010).

No matter their motivation, political expansions bring together people of different cultural heritages. The resulting interactions change how people eat for economic reasons as well as cultural ones: new ingredients and equipment become available, new social pressures emerge, and personal and group identities develop in new directions. (See Chapter 6 for discussions of food and identity.) Such developments leave clear traces in the archaeological record. For instance, ceramic griddles reveal that women in the Valley of Mexico embraced tortilla-making only when their towns came under Aztec rule and they needed portable food to sustain family members working away from home (Brumfiel, 1991).

Sometimes foodways even shift as part of the expansionist agenda. The Inka brought distinctive state pottery to conquered regions, deploying it as they offered their subjects food in return for tributary labor. Food storage, cooking, and serving vessels communicated imperial authority as they helped the Inka obligate their subjects to work for them (Bray, 2003b). In some locations the Inka also established new maize farms, evicting locals in favor of more-easily-controlled immigrants and using irrigation to extend the agricultural year and increase yields (Hastorf, 2016:157–163). State farms' produce went into the highly visible *qolqa*, where, as previously described, it sat until it was doled out to soldiers, state administrators, and occasionally the subject peoples who had labored to produce it (Hastorf and Foxhall, 2017).

Colonizers and colonized negotiate the boundaries between them using food. The Roman Empire relied on indigenous middlemen to rule in Britain and Gaul: there simply weren't enough Romans to staff the provinces without local collaborators (Beard, 2015:491–498). Provincial Britons and Gauls aided the imperium not as employees or conscripts but as participants in the Roman project, identifying culturally as well as politically with Rome (Beard, 2015). As part of their Romanization, native-born Romans introduced the conquered to their homeland's foods and foodways, importing new flavors and in some cases dining together with the vanquished. Food-sharing "played a key role in the process of *becoming* Roman" (Jones, 2007:216). (The colonized didn't necessarily welcome Roman outreach, of course, and economic, political, and geographic differences resulted in distinctly variable cuisines across the Empire [e.g., van der Veen, 2008].) Spaniards in the New World, in contrast, sought to keep barriers between themselves and all but the highest-ranking American peoples. Pursuing this agenda, they attempted to keep "Indians eating only New World foods and Spanish eating Old World foods" (Morán, 2016:81–82, although see Chapter 7 on wheat). They even tried to legislate this difference, with laws like a 1553 regulation stating that indigenous Mexicans could not sell, trade, or slaughter pigs; many Spaniards felt that locals shouldn't even eat pork – or beef, or mutton (Coe, 1994:233–234).

It's important at this point to clarify that "the colonized" don't begin to eat new foods: *individuals* do. (The same is true, of course, re "the colonizers.") Those individuals choose their foods for many reasons, only one of which is their ethnic or national affiliation (Dietler, 2007). Moreover, different segments of society have varying access to, and are more or less open to, foreign foods. (The Britons invited to Roman tables were men of status and power, not poor farmers [Hastorf, 2016].) History, archaeology, and social anthropology document foods being taken up first by aristocrats and later by plebeians (as well as the converse); by soldiers and then by civilians; by men before women and/or by children before their parents (e.g., Coe and Coe, 2007; Dietler, 2007; Somerville et al., 2017; Weismantel, 1988).

Culinary adopters consume their new foods in various forms and contexts, but rarely for the same reasons and in the same ways as the foods' original consumers. Coca-Cola entered Kenyan Luo society as a luxury drink; Pepsi has been adopted as a Communion beverage in rural San Juan Chamula, Mexico, where priests say that carbonation fends off evil spirits, villagers hang Pepsi posters together with crucifixes in their homes, and one villager explains "when men burp, their hearts open" (Dietler, 2007; Pilcher, 2002:234). The important point here is that new foods are only adopted when they have meanings relevant to the culture at hand, and when locals can fit them into their social relationships (Dietler, 2007). Only people who see themselves as benefiting from a new food take it up. If no one perceives a benefit, a newly available food will be ignored or even turned into a symbol of ethnic or national difference (Dietler, 2007). The same is true of culinary equipment, recipes, manners, and eating habits.

Consider the southern frontier of ancient Egypt. The pharaohs' empire expanded during the early centuries of the Middle Kingdom (2040–1650 BCE), with armies spreading into and establishing control of lower Nubia. To protect their gains, the Egyptians built a series of fortresses so massive that they loomed as symbols of royal power and domination over the land (Smith, 2003). These immense fortifications were given names such as "Destroyer of Nubians" and supplied with ample weaponry, but mere structures could not prevent the seventeenth-century BCE fall of the Middle Kingdom and the ascent of the Nubian state of Kerma. For a hundred years the Kermans pushed the Egyptians back north, only to fall back south again with the rise of the New Kingdom circa 1550 BCE. Kerma itself fell in 1500 BCE, sacked by Egyptian troops who went on to establish a new frontier deep into Upper Nubia. Throughout these turbulent times, people continued to occupy the ancient fortresses (Smith, 2003).

The Egyptian state legislated a hard border, threatening its citizens with punishment or death if they failed to respect political boundaries (Smith, 2003). The fortresses' occupants lived far away from the capital, however, and government pronouncements do not necessarily reflect on-the-ground realities. Smith (2003) therefore decided to investigate the extent to which people living at the "Destroyer of Nubians" (now a site called Askut) enacted state policies and ideology. Egyptian and Nubian ceramics differ, so archaeologists can determine Askut cooking and serving vessels' cultural antecedents. Smith found that the Middle Kingdom denizens of Askut used few Nubian vessels. When Askut came under Kerman control, Nubian wares rose from 3 percent to 12 percent of all culinary ceramics. They then declined to 9.5 percent during Egypt's New Kingdom reign over northern Nubia (Smith, 2003).

These data raise three interesting points. First: Middle Kingdom Egyptians were indeed "aloof overlords" to Nubia (Smith, 2003:51). Few chose to cook or eat Nubian-style, which suggests little intermingling with people living nearby. Middle Kingdom Egyptians generally obeyed state policy. Second: Askut residents largely continued to "eat Egyptian" under Kerma's sway. Kerman conquest didn't entail a new population living at the fort (that is, Nubians didn't seize it and settle in as the Egyptians fled northward). Nor did it entail strict colonial control over fortress lifestyles. Smith (2003:51) suggests that Askut's residents simply changed allegiance from Egypt to Kerma, and/or the Kermans took a 'minimalist' approach to colonialism.

Third: New Kingdom Egyptians at Askut maintained relationships with Nubians who kept much of their own culinary culture. This is fascinating. The return of Askut to Egypt did not result in a major decline in Nubian cookware; indeed, Smith reports, the proportion of Nubian wares in Askut's cooking vessel assemblage actually *increased*. Nubian ceramics constitute 83.5 percent of all cooking vessels at New Kingdom Askut. Nor are these ceramics confined to a single area of the site, as one would expect if an enclave of Nubian servants or traders were in residence (Smith, 2003). Nubian wares are spread throughout the settlement, indicating that people across Askut were using Nubian cooking pots and serving bowls. The fact that at this time Egypt controlled the entirety of lower Nubia adds another element to the story. During the New Kingdom, a "massive acculturation effort" deliberately drew northern Nubians into Egyptian economic, social, and political systems. This should, one would think, lead to the gradual disappearance of traditionally Nubian crafts and cooking styles (Smith, 2003:44). The presence of classic Nubian ceramics – inside an Egyptian settlement, no less – indicates no such widespread acculturation. Only some New Kingdom Nubians adopted Egyptian styles, as current archaeologists would expect.

Back though to the myriad people at Askut using Nubian ceramics: who were they? Perhaps some were locally born elites, feasting with Egyptians in pursuit of status and trade deals. In that case, one would expect the Nubian wares to be serving vessels, suitable for display and commensality (Smith, 2003). (Kermans made beautiful, delicate, red and black polished bowls and beakers that they used in elite feasting [Smith, 2003].) But most (more than 60 percent) of Askut's New Kingdom Nubian wares were cooking pots; serving vessels total less than 30 percent of finds (Smith, 2003). Smith infers that some Egyptians were not just socializing with Nubians, but also probably marrying them. The Askut culinary assemblage thus testifies to Egyptians' and Nubians' having made variable choices about whether or not to adopt elements of the other culture. In doing so, it illuminates the complexities of politics along the ancient frontier.

The archaeology of food explores how people have used food to advance themselves politically, how political developments have changed cultures and individual lives, and how people have responded to those changes. Researchers explore power and influence inside private households and across the boundaries of empires, taking advantage of food's prominent role in all scales of political activity. People's political actions are, of course, shaped by their genders, their ethnicities, and other aspects of their personal and group identities. Let us turn now to how archaeologists are using food to investigate the complex topic of identity in the past.

CHAPTER 6

Identity: Food, Affiliation, and Distinction

Food is an inordinately powerful tool for expressing and negotiating virtually any aspect or component of identity. Gender, ethnicity, status, religion: all are both created and challenged through food and foodways. In producing, cooking, and eating particular foods in particular combinations, using characteristic culinary equipment and table manners, people announce to the world that they are like – or unlike – members of particular groups. These announcements may be silent, but they are phenomenally effective and have real-world impacts. Habits as seemingly minor as bite size and eating speed mark a person as upper-class or working-class, masculine or feminine, and both social and economic opportunities rest on aspirants' abilities to eat in culturally competent fashions (Bourdieu, 1984; Russell, 2009).

Of course, practical limitations constrain people's ability to use food in order to express their desired identities. Notably, you cannot eat resources you cannot acquire: poor people can't regularly purchase caviar and imported cheeses, and desert-dwellers can't live off fresh fish and clam chowder. Archaeologists must always be alert to the effects of local ecologies and personal or group finances on dietary choices (DeFrance, 2009; Pavao-Zuckerman and Loren, 2012; Peres, 2017).

It is also important to recognize that the various aspects of a person's identity aren't like individual strands in a braid, woven together but easily separated for analysis. They are more like bodily organs, recognizably different yet mutually reliant, with each shaping how the others work. A person is not American on one front, and a woman on another, and Muslim on a third: that person's identity, who she believes herself to be and how she interacts with the world (and, for archaeological purposes, with material culture), is of an American Muslim woman. The ways in which she expresses her femininity are shaped by her upbringing and her faith;

how she practices her faith is shaped by the fact that she's American and female; and her gender and her religion affect her citizenship experience and actions. Her ancestry, employment, residential area, family structure, physical abilities, and more are similarly permeating. (The technical term for this idea is "overdetermination," which Voss [2008a:5] explains as "a theory of irreducibility, in which a given phenomenon is conceptualized as an effect produced by a potentially infinite number of other contributing and interacting phenomena.")

This chapter nonetheless treats different components of identity as functionally separable. This is the norm in the archaeological food litera-ture, a large majority of which focuses on one or two elements of identity at a time.[1] (When two elements are considered, one is almost always gender.) I attribute this not to a widespread lack of theoretical awareness but to the fact that most archaeological data sets either reflect multiple people's foodways or are limited in size. Middens and street dumps, for example, commingle leftovers, tools, and tableware from adults and children, men and women, healthy people and invalids, popular characters and awkward wallflowers. Meanwhile, it takes a lot of skeletal stable isotope or dental calculus samples – all from the same time period and area – to be able to explore the dietary effects of multifaceted identities. Few archaeologists, and probably no prehistorians, have data that permit them to assess how complex, overdetermined identities related to food.

Ethnicity

Ethnicity is linked to genes and heritage in that people whose ancestors have long lived in a particular region tend to resemble each other genetic-ally and culturally more than others whose ancestors derive from more distant regions – but like other aspects of identity, ethnicity requires establishment and maintenance. It is not fixed; it is not intrinsic; it is,

---

[1] How archaeologists study identity today is not how they've studied it in the past, and even today there's ongoing debate about what identity is, how it's negotiated, and how it's expressed. Few archaeologists still see identities as predetermined or stable, but various authors present them as (a) shaped through human interactions, (b) formed of multiple interrelating strands (e.g., overdetermined), (c) things that people *do* rather than things that people *are*, and (d) perhaps irrelevant or even non-existent in past cultures. Approaches (a)–(d) entered the archaeological literature in that order (see Casella and Fowler, 2005; Insoll, 2007; Meskell, 2002). Be sure to note the date on any archaeology-of-identity study you read!

rather, pushed and pulled into shape as people negotiate between what they call themselves and what others call them (Voss, 2008a:1).

Ethnicities are thus unstable phenomena. They come into being (Voss, 2005, 2008a), the characteristics assigned to them change, and their boundaries expand and contract as societies alter their perceptions and regulations. The instability of ethnicity means that not only can people affiliate themselves with particular ethnicities via their dress, their speech, their manners, and of course their foodways, but they can also change those ethnicities by partially adhering to expectations and partially not.

Individuals and groups may thus affirm or challenge ethnic labels applied to them by others, and people may shift their ethnic affiliations as they shift social contexts. In the eighteenth-century colonial Presidio of San Francisco, for example, many individuals shifted castes when they got married, moved, altered their appearances, went to court, or simply asserted a change; the same parents registered various of their offspring as different castes; and soldiers changed caste status in order to facilitate their promotions (Voss, 2005:463–464). Then, by the early nineteenth century, presidio-dwellers let the old caste system lapse and embraced a new, shared ethnicity as "Californianos" (Voss, 2005).

They had been downplaying caste differences for at least a couple of decades already: late eighteenth-century households throughout El Presidio de San Francisco devoted zero perceptible energy to differentiating themselves through dress or food. Everyone cooked the same foods in the same ways, making beef and bean stews and wheat and corn porridges. The only ethnic difference anyone worried about appears to have been Colonial Resident vs. Native American: even when there were shortages, no one at the San Francisco Presidio incorporated either Native foods or Native cooking equipment into his or her repertoire (Voss, 2005).

Presidio residents were thus using food to distinguish themselves from local subjugated populations. This is not a rare practice among colonialists. Archaeology shows that colonizers have used food to emphasize ethnic distinctions on multiple continents and in multiple eras – and that they've done this deliberately, not simply translocating old culinary habits but developing new ones that highlighted how special the arriving population was in contrast to the indigenous locals. When the Norman French conquered England in 1066, they ratcheted up their already-notable enthusiasm for hunting and developed complex post-hunt butchery ceremonies at which specific cuts of meat were ceremonially allotted out (Sykes, 2005). These bloody performances reinforced Norman machismo (a core element of Norman identity); Norman speech (French terminology dominated the hunt); and Norman etiquette (in contrast to older, simpler Saxon hunting traditions). (See Chapter 4 for more on Norman foodways.)

Ethnicities don't only differentiate themselves via food and foodways. They also interact through food: its production, its sale, its donation, its sharing. In nineteenth-century Mono Mills, California, residents of the Chinatown neighborhood relied on stoneware vessels traditionally used to store soy sauce, peanut oil, and black vinegar: items classically associated with being Chinese (Sunseri, 2015). One household, though, also stored parched pine nuts – a food of the local Paiute[2], who may also have mentored the Chinese in how to knap their small glass and obsidian flakes for cutting food (Sunseri, 2015). The influence was mutual, as Chinese-made ceramics (notably, a porcelain spoon) were found in the Paiute neighborhood. Interaction between the two groups was leading to small-scale deviations from historical patterns.

Such deviations were, without doubt, often strategic. Archaeologists can see this by examining how members of a single ethnic group adjusted their foodways in different situations. Chinese diaspora communities like those at Mono Mills offer an excellent opportunity to do this, because during the nineteenth century Chinese workers spread across the United States. Archaeologists have identified Overseas Chinese habitations in cities, towns and campsites, in the mountains, and in forests and on the coast. (An important side note here: archaeologists need to be sure that they grasp a group's starting point *or points* when they explore the impacts of culture contact. Consider that while "Chinese-American" can be seen as a single ethnicity, many ethnic groups call China home. Archaeologists have documented variation in how Chinese people cooked and ate dating back thousands of years. In the Bronze Age, for example, different Zhou communities used different sizes of cooking vessels, dissimilar serving utensils, and varied recipes [Jaffe et al., 2017]. Fortunately for archaeologists, most nineteenth century Chinese immigrants to the USA came from the Pearl River Delta, with a shared Cantonese food culture [Voss et al., 2018].)

Comparing faunal remains from southern-Chinese-dominated railroad worksites, rural settlements, and urban neighborhoods reveals that everyone was adapting traditional Chinese cuisine, but in different ways. Urban and

---

[2] Determining foods' ethnic affiliations can be difficult or even inappropriate. In historic Florida, for example, Spanish colonizers brought up eating plenty of seafood may have viewed some local species as tasting of home, while "European" sheep and goats would have been familiar foods for free and enslaved Africans (Voss, 2008b). Awareness of such complexities greatly improves culture contact studies.

rural residents chopped some of their meat into bits with cleavers, as was done in China, and ate plenty of familiar meats such as duck, chicken, turtle, fish, and pork. But much, sometimes most, of their meat was non-traditional beef, butchered in Anglo-American fashion (Kennedy, 2015). Railroad and timber workers had fewer choices (and left fewer identifiable animal bones behind for study), but they too balanced a taste for fresh and dried fish and pork with reliance on European-American beef (Kennedy, 2015).

Within these broad patterns, though, we can see considerable variation in how Chinese immigrants adapted their foodways to local opportunities and constraints. In Riverside, California, Chinatown residents ate cleaver-butchered pork as well as emphatically non-Anglo meats such as cat and rat. In Sandpoint, Idaho, where most Chinese people worked in restaurants, they ate mostly beef – perhaps because they could take it home from work, saving themselves both money and time (Kennedy, 2015). Food choices differed by socioeconomic situation, too. In Sacramento, Chinese merchants savored mostly pork, as they might have done in the old country; boardinghouse residents ate beef instead (Kennedy, 2015). In San Francisco, Chinatown tenement dwellers ate a broader range of plant foods than merchants did. Perhaps restaurant and grocery store workers were bringing surplus food home, or perhaps tenement residents were more interested than wealthier merchants in saving money by experimenting with a wider variety of foods (Cummings et al., 2014). Across the United States, Chinese immigrants and their American-born children shared foodways that mixed traditions and tastes from southern China with those from Europe and North America, but specifics varied depending on where they went and the economic and environmental circumstances in which they found themselves.

It is deeply unsurprising that the Chinese diaspora shaped both immigrant and indigenous cuisines in the increasingly multiethnic communities of nineteenth century United States. It is satisfying that we can use specific developments in foodways to investigate economic and social relations in these communities. And it is intriguing to learn that the diaspora had fairly rapid impacts on foodways back in China as well. Nineteenth-century deposits in Guangdong Province, China, contain ceramic dishes that are identical to tableware found in California and across the American West. Some are traditional Chinese pieces (used by the emigrants to establish a sense of home and cultural continuity in new lands), but others are items that were manufactured specifically for global export, and a few are fragments of American and British make (Voss et al., 2018). Intensifying internationalism meant that both homeland and emigrant Chinese were setting their tables with new dishes (Voss et al., 2018).

Not all aspects of a people's foodways are equally subject to alteration when two ethnicities come into contact. However, archaeology complicates any simple expectation that routine sustenance is relatively easily adjusted, and ritually or symbolically important foods and feasts unalterable except in the face of significant pressure.

We can stay in historic California for a case study that illustrates why this common assumption is not a rule. During the end of the eighteenth and early nineteenth centuries, Native peoples in the Los Angeles Basin ate as they never had before, swiftly and dramatically changing their diets as the effects of Spanish colonization resonated across coastal southern California (Reddy, 2015). Spanish livestock, agriculture, and land management systems altered regional vegetation and traditional food procurement methods. Native American converts moved into missions, transforming their diets. People of European and Native descent came into contact at pueblos and ranches, in villages and in fields.

Prior to the Spaniards' arrival, the Gabrieliño/Tongva had lived in the Los Angeles Basin as village-dwelling, food-storing hunter-gatherers. They ate wild grasses, legumes, and other small-seeded plants; few nuts crossed their lips (Reddy, 2015). Then, during the Mission Period (1771–1834 CE), they expanded their plant diet to include assorted European domesticates. Paleoethnobotanical remains from a Gabrieliño/Tongva village complex include fragments of chickpeas and garden peas, oats, barley, wheat, and corn (Reddy, 2015). These remains are not equally distributed across the Gabrieliño/Tongva settlement – but they are found in burials, among the traces of mourning ceremonies, and in deposits identified as the remains of domestic feasts. Wild grasses are dominant in all of these contexts, but the introduced plants are consistently present. The Mission Period Gabrieliño/Tongva were incorporating European foods into their sacred rituals and their communal celebrations, not just into their everyday meals. (This contradicts ethnographic reporting that the Gabrieliño/Tongva abhorred others' foods to the point that they secretly buried gifted foods and believed that if consumed, such foods would make them sick [Kroeber, 1925:631]). The archaeological evidence thus tells a complex story of general adherence to traditional foodways, modulated by the incorporation of small amounts of foods that appear to have been neither prestige enhancers (as in Mills, 2008) nor transgressive statements of "outsider" identity, but simply appreciated resources (Reddy, 2015).

At this point I've claimed that when two ethnicities come into contact, (a) not all aspects of a people's foodways are equally subject to alteration and (b) ritually important foodways aren't necessarily shielded from modification. What other factors do archaeologists think make particular ethnic food practices more or less open to change?

One repeatedly cited factor is the extent to which new foods and new habits echo existing ones. Faunal remains from eighteenth-century New France and the Illinois Country (roughly today's northeastern USA and Quebec) indicate that French settlers were much more open than Britons to eating American birds, beavers, and bears (the last of which the *hommes d'élites* at Fort Pentagoet appreciated as "very delicate and white as … veal") (Scott, 2007:246). British households ate game they knew from home – hares and rabbits, geese and ducks, fish and grouse – but avoided unfamiliar meats and overall consumed far less wild flesh than their French counterparts.

Some of the disparity is plausibly attributable to religious differences. The Pope had classified beaver theologically as "four-legged fish," edible on fast days when terrestrial meat was forbidden, so Catholics of French descent had an incentive to eat beavers that Protestant Britons lacked (Scott, 2007:249). This might well be why, when British replaced French residents in one of the houses at Fort Michilimackinac in Michigan, the proportion of beaver bones in that house's midden dropped by more than half, from 7.1 to 2.8 percent of faunal biomass (Scott, 2007). Religious differences cannot, however, account for French people, but not Britons, splitting bear heads for presentation at feasts or consuming twice as much game as domesticated meat.

What may account for these distinctions is a French tradition of appreciating wild game, and of associating it with elite dining (Scott, 2007). French colonists may have come to the New World thinking of hunting and fishing as prestigious activities, and so been happy to seize upon the ample opportunities afforded them in American rivers and forests. In France, aristocrats dined on sandhill crane and trumpeter swans; now in Michigan and the Mississippi Valley, French folks of lesser means might do the same (Scott, 2007). English colonists had similar opportunities, but their cookbooks and cuisine eschewed wild meat instead of elevating it. A group readily adopts new foods *when those foods slot easily into group traditions*: when (a) the novelties fit readily into an existing category of foods (e.g. for the French, "game birds"), and (b) that category is considered desirable to eat.

The categories into which the newly adopted foods slot are not necessarily those in which their original consumers would place them. Today
Americans gulp cola as a casual soft drink; rural Kenyans sip it as a
prestige beverage; Haitians assign it the power to revive the dead; rural
Mexicans drink Pepsi as a wine replacement during Mass (Dietler, 2007;
Pilcher, 2002). Maize, saturated with ritual significance in Aztec Mexico,
lost its ideological power as it entered European diets (Morán, 2016: 82;
see Chapter 7), and acquired entirely new associations upon arriving in
West Africa, becoming to various peoples a totem, a symbol of military
power, and a mysterious character in folktales (McCann, 2001:252). As
foods enter new cultures, they inevitably acquire new meanings and new
uses. Sometimes the change is drastic and should be relatively easy to spot
archaeologically, as when Spaniards stripped chocolate of its spiritual
weight and reclassified it as medicine and then as recreation (Coe and
Coe, 2007:126). Sometimes alterations are subtler or even archaeologically imperceptible: surely newly adopted domesticates were appreciated
somewhat differently in Neolithic villages across Anatolia (Arbuckle, 2013;
Arbuckle et al., 2014), but at least for now the details of those differences
remain uncertain.

Much of the archaeological food and ethnicity literature focuses on
historical eras, in which people can investigate interactions between groups
whose relationships are newsworthy today, and whose historical relationships have modern relevance. However, scholars do discuss ethnicity and
foodways in peri- and prehistoric contexts as well. No one, for example,
would argue that the nature of relations between southern Mesopotamian
Uruk immigrants and southeastern Anatolian locals in the fourth millennium BCE is directly relevant to ethnic interactions in the modern Middle
East. Stein's (2012) paper on foodways at the Turkish Bronze Age site of
Hacınebi is motivated, rather, by a broader interest in how ethnically
distinct groups negotiate long-term stays in settlements outside their homelands. Stein argues that the residents of Hacınebi's "Uruktown" maintained
peaceful relations with their Anatolian neighbors by intermarrying with
them. This created multiethnic households, in which most of the domestic
cookware was Anatolian in style but the vessels used in public looked
Mesopotamian (Stein, 2012).

One very interesting discussion in the archaeology of food and ethnicity
is the case of the Philistines and the Israelites, the pig-lovers and the pig-
haters (after Hesse, 1990). Pork avoidance is a tenet of both the Jewish and
the Muslim faiths, and for many believers it originated as a divine com-
mandment. Curious researchers of all faiths, however, have wondered for

centuries *why* pig-eating is banned. Was it a health issue? An economic one? An environmental necessity that morphed into a religious require-ment? Was the ban a byproduct of broader ideological concerns – not a goal in and of itself, but a side effect of an overarching concern with purity? Or was it, perhaps, a way of establishing firm ethnic boundaries between invaders and invaded? (See discussions in Faust and Lev-Tov, 2011; Hesse, 1990; Hesse and Wapnish, 1997, 1998).

It's clear from the faunal record that many Philistines enjoyed eating pork: in some (though not all!) of their cities pig bones constitute more than 20 percent of excavated animal remains. It's equally clear that the Philistines and the Israelites had what one might term a contentious relationship (2 Samuel 21:15: "There was war *again* between the Philistines and Israel. . ." [italics mine]). Some researchers have argued, therefore, that the Israelites' desire to define themselves against the Philistines led them to ban a favored Philistine food: "The Philistines eat pork. We're *not* Philis-tines; we do not eat pork." Others see a more complicated story, noting that the Philistines ate variable amounts of pig – it was hardly a signature food – and that for cultural more than ecological reasons Israelites probably weren't eating much pig meat even before the Philistines arrived. Indeed, the Israelites lived during an era when many Levantines, even those in communities well away from Philistia, ate little if any pork (Hesse and Wapnish, 1997, 1998). The question for these researchers is how and when pork avoidance became *important* to Israelites: when the food rule became central to Israelite identity, and ultimately acquired the weight of divine regulation.

Some scholars posit that the change occurred when Jews returned home from their exile in Babylon and needed ways to bind both returning and never-exiled Judeans into a single, unified community (Hesse and Wapn-ish, 1998). Others argue that the avoidance became very important to the Israelites when they acquired Philistine "arch enemies who consumed this meat as a regular practice" (Faust and Lev-Tov, 2011:18). These latter authors believe, moreover, that the Philistines mirrored the Israelites in adopting pork-eating as an ethnic signature. As interactions between Phil-istines and Israelites intensified, the Israelites assigned new significance to their avoidance of pork – and the Philistines began to eat more of it (Faust and Lev-Tov, 2011). Pig-loving and pig-hating became paired markers of ethnic identity, the two sides of a single coin.

All agree, ultimately, that pork avoidance was not only a religious proscription, but also a core element of secular identity. Hesse and Wapn-ish (1998:131) note that in passages such as 2 Maccabees 7:1 ("It happened also that seven brothers and their mother were arrested and were being compelled by the king, under torture ... to partake of unlawful swine's flesh"), pig meat consumption is not a matter between a person and his or her God; it's a point of contention between Jews and non-Jews, between members of one group and outsiders. As the Iron Age progressed, Jewish homes might adopt Philistine cooking pots (Ben-Shlomo et al., 2008), but never Philistine pork.

Race

Race and ethnicity are not the same thing. Yes, "race" is a cultural phenomenon, like ethnicity. Yes, "race" changes, just as ethnicity does. And yes, race and ethnicity are tied to each other, sometimes to the point that one virtually determines the other. But race, unlike ethnicity, refers to bodily distinctions: perceived variations in color and shape that members of a particular culture associate with specific social traits and values (Voss, 2008a:28, cf. Orser, 2007:8; Scott, 2001b). Race is, for many people, unforgettable and un-ignorable: no matter their dress, language, or demeanor, they are slotted into a particular racial category the moment they walk into a room. Such people don't need food to establish their racial bona fides.

The archaeology of food and race is, therefore, mostly not about how people have used food to establish racial distinctions. Nor is it about people transgressing racial categories. What characterizes the literature on food and race is an interest in people trying to build the best version of their racial identity they can: taking pride in shared traditions, shielding themselves from racist hurts, and rejecting negative stereotypes placed on them by others (e.g., Mrozowski et al., 2008; Scott, 2001a; Warner, 2015). Archaeologists are particularly concerned with how people assigned to races perceived as "inferior" – most notably, Americans of African descent – used food to improve their lives. McKee (1999) and Lev-Tov (2004) explore how enslaved black Americans used various strategies to improve their food security, reducing slaveowners' power to punish them by withholding food and demonstrating their own ability to act autonomously. Mullins (1999) documents nineteenth-century black Americans' preference for relatively expensive national brands that could be purchased by mail. Buying via the mails allowed black Americans to avoid non-black shopkeepers' racist slurs and cheats, and buying national brands expressed their participation in the lifestyle shown in brand advertisements. Urbanites also decreased their fish consumption post-Reconstruction, disassociating themselves from racist caricatures of countrified fishing and poor black fish-sellers (Mullins, 1999).

Warner (2015:2) argues that nineteenth- to early twentieth-century black Americans sought "to assert their aspirations, values, and personal stories in ways that satisfied their sense of dignity and worth yet would not arouse the ire of an oppressive white society . . . [Their] food choices . . . served as a relatively safe way to express a unique outlook and history, as well as to offer a subtle, yet persistent, commentary on the racist stereotypes and violence that surrounded them." Black families in Maryland faced both legal harassment and social persecution. At various times legislators denied them voting rights, school funds, land access, and other resources; police arrested and juries convicted dark-skinned people on little evidence; the Ku Klux Klan attempted to intimidate them. At least twenty-eight people died in mob lynchings between 1882 and 1931 (Warner, 2015:16). Public discourse was saturated with nastily derogatory caricatures of black people, despite African-American scholars and ministers speaking powerfully in opposition to racism (Warner, 2015:28).

Many black Marylanders nonetheless earned economic stability and respectable, if tenuous, middle-class status. They had money to spend on food, including costly items for special meals (Warner, 2015). Yet in Annapolis, the black Maynard and Burgess families produced much of their food themselves, raising chickens and turkeys in their city backyard, fishing in local waterways, and probably bartering with or buying from local black vendors. Fish and poultry were both available at the market, but the Maynard and Burgess faunal assemblage includes only shallow-water local fish, none of the bluefish or sea trout that dominated commerce, and it includes the remains of a lame turkey that would have been deemed unfit for market (Warner, 2015). Household food production relieved the families from having to cope with racist shopkeepers, and trading with fellow African-Americans helped maintain the social networks that eased life in an oppressive society (Warner, 2015:82).

A fascinating strand of the food-and-race literature explores how a shared ethnicity may be built by diverse people who share only a racial assignation. Consider that in Virginia during the eighteenth century, slave trading brought "Africans from Senegambia, Sierra Leone, the Gold Coast, Bight of Biafra, Bight of Benin, and the west coast of Central Africa . . . to the Tidewater, where they mixed with American-born blacks, mulattos, and black Indians" (Franklin, 2001:91). These many and varied peoples were commonly forced into working as tobacco plantation field hands, enslaved simply because they were collectively assigned to a single, dark-skinned race.

The mix of African- and American-born people enslaved on the Rich Neck Plantation in the 1740s were surely traumatized and terrified by the dehumanization and exploitation they suffered (Franklin, 2001). The African-born were probably also confounded and at times demoralized by their isolation from anyone who shared their histories, languages, or beliefs. But the archaeological record reveals that the heterogeneous blacks of Rich Neck didn't merely collaborate to survive: together they forged a new, shared identity. Supplementing farmed foods with wild game and foraged nuts and berries, they ate stews whose compositions were influenced by African cuisines and baked African yams in the ashes of their fires. They dry-roasted game, however, as the English liked to do (Franklin, 2001). The enslaved Afro-Virginians of Rich Neck Plantation created a new cuisine, one that featured ingredients originating on three continents – European pork and American opossum, American maize and African yams – and recipes borrowing from two and modulated for the third. As they developed this cuisine, the enslaved residents of Rich Neck developed themselves into a community, with norms and tastes distinct from those of white Virginians (Franklin, 2001).

These norms and tastes shifted through time. People began to eat more raccoon and less opossum, for example, and added rabbit to their roster of meats (Franklin, 2001). Such changes, which don't appear rooted in either ecological or economic necessity, prove that Afro-Virginian cuisine was shaped by more than poverty and hunger. So too do warm recollections of specific foods by ex-slaves such as Anthony Dawson, who noted that he loved opossum but raccoon meat was more delicate (Franklin, 2001). Afro-Virginian culinary traditions arose in part from need, but need did not dictate their final form.

Gender

> [Inca] wives did not sit at the table, although they all ate together; the woman sat behind her husband's back, facing the other way, so that they sat back to back; and she had the pottage in their pans and served them to her husband, and gave him to drink when he asked for it, while she ate at the same time; and in this manner they would sit and eat in their homes and at the public banquets of the people.
>
> Cobo 1963 [1653]:174

An Old School essentialization of gender dominated archaeological research on ancient foodways for much of the twentieth century (Brumbach and Jarvenpa [2006], Crabtree [2006], and Peterson [2006] provide interesting overviews of assumptions about gender in the archaeological literature on food production; see Graff 2018 for assumptions about gender and food preparation). Famously, *Man the Hunter* (Lee and Devore, 1968) roamed the landscape in pursuit of bloodshed, while Woman the Gatherer stayed peacefully close to home (Washburn and Lancaster, 1968). Participants at the famous and hugely influential "Man the Hunter" symposium kept this binary division of labor tidy by narrowing "hunting" to focus on chasing large, mobile animals, and expanding "gathering" to include small animals and shellfish (Brumbach and Jarvenpa, 2006). Brumbach and Jarvenpa (2006) argue that the selective definitions adopted by the participants at the "Man the Hunter" symposium – as well as their apparent willingness to ignore ethnographic evidence that didn't accord with their model – neatly shouldered women out of the conversation about hunting, at a time when hunting was considered to be at the root of what made us human. Until the 1990s, attempts to demonstrate the importance of women's contributions to the diet failed to change the underlying assumption that motherhood "immobilize[s]," keeping both gathering and farming women close to home as their men roamed (Conkey and Spector, 1984: 8).

Today archaeologists, like other anthropologists, generally describe gender as related to anatomical sex but not the same thing. Your gender is established by how you present yourself (your appearance and your demeanor), how you behave (your activities and your ways of interacting with others), and what you and others believe about your sex's abilities and tendencies. The extent to which your gender is premised on your physique depends on your culture. Some cultures find it entirely acceptable for two people with the same genitalia to profess different genders; some find that wholly unacceptable. Either situation, nonetheless, requires that archaeologists be alert to the fact that gender is culturally constructed.

Three facts in particular must always be kept in mind. First, archaeologists cannot assume that the culture they study recognized only men and women as gender options. Seventeenth-century Inka referred to young children and very old adults in gender-neutral terms; classical Greeks and Romans fully gendered only free adult citizens, leaving slaves, children, and foreigners sexed (as animals are sexed) but not men or women in social terms (Costin, 2016; Dupont, 2015). The ethnohistoric Zuni and Chumash recognized multiple genders, between which some people shifted over time (Joyce, 2008:58). In other Native North American groups, people often acquired new, non-binary gender identities when they pursued craftwork traditionally associated with their "opposite sex" – when a boy chose to spend his time weaving baskets like a woman, for example (Hollimon, 2006).

Second, even cultures that recognize only Men and Women hold varying beliefs about what each gender can and should do (and about the relative values of those activities). Consider the Spanish-colonial Americas, where people not only espoused but also enforced a gender binary. Transgressors – convicted, if need be, by inspections of their genitalia – were "severely punished" and forced to behave in accordance with gender norms "perceived to be congruent with their genitalia" (Voss, 2008a:92). What these norms were, however, varied, and disagreements existed as to their parameters. Does a lazy man retain full patriarchal privileges? Ought a good woman participate in craft production? Can committing rape confer honor on a man? The answers to such questions shift through time, between speakers, and with respect to different segments of the population (Gifford-Gonzalez, 2008; Voss, 2008a:297–299).

Third, people vary within genders. Some women are very "girly," others reject that style wholeheartedly; some are pre-menopausal and others post-menopausal; some are heterosexual, and others are not. We nonetheless accept them all as women. Archaeologists shouldn't assume that in the past people sharing a gender led basically similar lives either (Alberti, 2006; Joyce, 2008). Avoiding this can be a very tricky proposition, as for most cultures and eras we rely on human remains and art to evaluate gender: male vs. female skeletons' pathologies and mortuary treatments, the activities and aesthetics of images with and without breasts. We thus rely on *sex* data to investigate *gender*. Because only a very small percentage of people have bodies that aren't anatomically either male or female, we're almost always trying to use binary data (male vs. female) to investigate what may have been trinary, quaternary, or theoretically even duodenary (12-part) gender systems. Archaeologists, especially those lacking good historical or ethnographic information about gender in the culture we're studying, thus end up framing our studies in terms of two or at most three (*very rarely* four) genders. This is certainly true of the gender-and-food readings discussed here. Astute readers may, however, note that dietary variation within a sex could arise from any number of factors – including, perhaps, the existence of multiple genders.

Access to Food

Access to specific foods is not simply about relative status: one gender getting the "good stuff" and one not, revealing to us which gender outranked the other. Specific foods have specific social roles and meanings (e.g., Hastorf, 1991; Moss, 1993). Access to religiously significant foods is linked to participation and presence in ritual activities. Access to politically important foods relates to access to power. If archaeologists discover that Gender X had limited access to a symbolically or politically important food, then we can reasonably infer that Gender X had limited involvement in at least some aspects of ritual or political life.

Therefore, when Hastorf (1991, 2001) determines that under Inka rule men of the Sausa were consuming more meat and maize than Sausa women, she doesn't simply say that Sausa men outranked women. She argues that the differences reflect men's participation in public political networking and payment of labor taxes. Public politicking involved eating meat and drinking maize beer at various rituals and gatherings. In addition, the Inka demanded that their subject populations periodically work for the state, most commonly via agricultural labor and military service. In return for this work, the Inka state fed its laborers meat, maize, and beer. When archaeologists see the differences between Sausa male and Sausa female stable carbon and nitrogen isotopic signatures, therefore, what they are looking at are differences in how men and women participated in the public sphere, especially its political and symbolic realms (Hastorf, 1991).

White (2005) reports a similar distinction between men's and women's diets among high-ranked Maya, and stresses the distinction's ritual as well as political impact. Food was a key element of Mayan religious lives: the rituals that people had to complete in order to keep the supernatural world content required food, usually feasting. Stable nitrogen and carbon isotope values from multiple sites suggest that for centuries prior to the Spanish Conquest, Maya males consistently ate more meat than Maya females (White, 2005). In most cases, men were also eating more C_4 foods than women were: not just maize itself, but also C_4-fed animals and marine taxa.

Among these foods it's reasonable to think that deer and dogs were featured. Both were commonly eaten at feasts and in rituals, and those intended for such use were fed up on maize ahead of time. (According to White and colleagues [2001], the Maya have at least nine words for dogs, which symbolized fire and the hearth, and whose remains are found in both domestic and ritual contexts. Preclassic Maya dog remains found in special contexts such as wall caches and sub-floor deposits have stable carbon isotope values that are very different from dog bones found in prosaic contexts such as middens. The ritual dogs were fed maize – a food that was religiously as well as economically central to the Maya[3] – for most of their lives, perhaps in part as a way to make them "human" for sacrifice.) If such C4-fed animals were largely reserved for ritual feasts, then ancient Maya men were more prominent at these feasts then Maya women were. At least they *ate* more at the feasts; women did the cooking for them (White, 2005). This suggests that ancient Maya women lacked men's access to the supernatural, and to the power and authority it could confer (White, 2005). Even if Maya men's meat and maize weren't primarily eaten at ritual feasts, elite men were eating more of prestigious and religiously significant foods than their wives, daughters, and sisters were.

Gender shapes not only what people eat, but also how they eat, where, with whom, and from what vessels. As a result, members of different genders may have different opportunities to deploy food for economic, political, or ideological reasons. Monroe and Janzen's (2014) study of political feasting in Dahomey (in the modern Republic of Bénin) illustrates how women and men may separately use food in order to benefit themselves. In the seventeenth to nineteenth centuries CE, Dahomean kings hosted public feasts as part of their strategies for attracting and holding political followers, demonstrating the king's wealth and asserting his power. These public feasts took place outside and in the courtyards of royal palaces. Royal women and children, meanwhile, resided inside the palaces' most private spaces, which were inaccessible to virtually all men. Palace women, who worked as soldiers, bureaucrats, artisans, and brewers, sought power in their spheres just as the men did in theirs. Deep inside the walls of the Cana-Agouna palace, archaeologists found pottery and animal bones that match Dahomean feast norms (Monroe and Janzen, 2014). The royal men and the royal women of Cana-Agouna both used food to gain power; the men did so publicly and the women privately.

Labor

A core element of gender archaeology is how gender plays into household and societal labor organization. To what extent was there a division between men's work and women's work? For which tasks were members of different genders responsible? How much work – how much time, and how much energy – did those tasks require? Were they conducted in the

---

[3] And to other central American peoples: see Chapter 7 for a discussion of maize in Aztec thought.

public eye, or were they concealed inside the privacy of homes or other institutions? Cooking, not surprisingly, is at the core of many of these investigations, as few if any areas of labor are more heavily gendered in our own societies.[4]

Archaeology has proven that, as one would expect, the amount of work it took to prepare meals in the past was quite different from the amount of work it takes today. Indeed, food preparation could be so onerous that it literally damaged people's skeletons. At prehistoric Abu Hureyra in Syria, for instance, the hours cooks spent kneeling in front of stone mortars and querns damaged their spines, legs, and feet (Figure 6.1). Bracing themselves with their toes as they knelt and pushed their tools forward and back, women (the injuries are concentrated on female skeletons) ground their families' grain as they hyperflexed their big toes, damaged their vertebral disks, and enlarged their knee joints (Molleson, 1994). "These are the repetitive stress injuries of the Neolithic" (Molleson, 1994:73) – and they were caused by food.

Such food-related stress injuries are documented elsewhere in the world as well. In Mesoamerica, the bioarchaeological evidence for women's cooking labor is enriched by ethnohistoric documents and art that allow us to picture women's days more fully. Brumfiel (1991) reports that in the sixteenth century, Aztec mothers and daughters spent hours upon hours preparing maize for eating (Figure 6.2). Once they had raw shell maize in hand, they would boil it in a pot with water and lime, then allow the mix to cool and rest. This softened the maize and loosened the hulls from the kernels even as it improved the grain's nutritional value. After several hours, they would drain and rinse the softened maize. They could then begin to grind it into dough – and grind, and grind, and grind. Aztec women spent up to eight hours a day grinding maize into usability (Brumfiel, 1991, see also Rodríguez-Alegría, 2012). Dough finally in hand, Aztec women could then pat it into thin disks that they would lay on ceramic griddles over the hearths. This last stage alone, turning the dough into tortillas, could take two or three additional hours per day: Brumfiel (1991:238) speculates that the larger tortillas pictured in the *Codex Mendoza* might reflect women's

---

[4] Table manners and tastes are gendered as well as labor, of course. Texts and iconography provide archaeologists' insights into these: few prehistorians can say anything about mealtime conduct norms for anyone, let alone for members of different genders. Yet accounts such as the one at the start of this section, written by Spanish missionary Bernabé Cobo in 1653, demonstrate that gender's impact on how past peoples ate was often profound in archaeologically invisible ways.

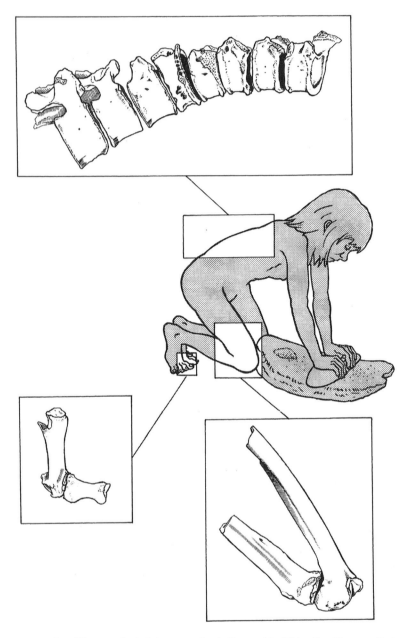

FIGURE 6.1. The osteological impacts of grinding at Neolithic Abu Hureyra, Syria. Reproduced from Molleson (2000:fig. 11.8, p. 315), by permission of Oxford University Press, USA (www.oup.com).

FIGURE 6.2. Aztec mother teaching her daughter to make tortillas. In the bottom right of the image a jar holds soaked corn and a griddle sits on the hearth (the ringed circle surrounded by three smaller circles representing stones), ready to have a tortilla placed on it to cook. Redrawn from the Codex Mendoza, Folio 60r, by Sarah T. Mincer.

desire to save themselves work by producing fewer, bigger tortillas instead of many small thin ones. (Men weren't going to help. They had plenty of work to do themselves, but also tortilla-making was simply women's work: into the twentieth century; even carrying corn to a mill would humiliate a man [Bauer, 1990].)

Astonishingly, tamales represented even more work than tortillas. Tamale dough required lengthy beating before cooking, and each tamale had to be wrapped and cooked in its own corn husk (Brumfiel, 1991). Peasants ate tamales only on special occasions, for which female work parties frequently stayed up throughout the night to finish the cooking.

Such gendered cooking obligations shaped ancient economies. Time that women spent cooking was time that they could not dedicate to other tasks. Samuel (2010) estimates that Pharaonic Egyptian households' flour needs required that someone relatively young and strong spend three hours per day in front of a saddle quern. (The task could, of course, be divided among multiple women *if* the household included more than one grown, fit female.) Not until the introduction of easier-to-use quern emplacements in the mid-first millennium BCE were older and weaker women able to help grind. This means that across dynasties, flour-making cost Egyptian households three hours a day of a healthy adult's labor: physically wearing labor, no less, which presumably left women depleted for other tasks.

Three hours a day adds up to more than one thousand hours, roughly 130 workdays, over the course of a year. This is more time than ethnographically documented Greek farmers would spend producing the same amount of grain (ca. 800 kg): that includes their work manually tilling, sowing, harvesting, and readying the crop for storage *combined* (Halstead, 2014:182). (Never forget to include processing when you estimate the labor costs of various subsistence strategies!) Halstead (2014:183) points out that tying up women's labor to that extent could have limited domestic production on multiple fronts, including agriculture itself: if you lose three hours of women's time daily then the harvest season becomes even more dramatically time-crunched, and farmers have an even harder time recovering their crops before weather, animals, or other humans get to them. (See also Chapter 3.)

Archaeologists working on multiple continents have used the traces of ancient food work to infer women being pulled back from the public sphere into enforced domesticity. In both prehispanic Peru and Pre-Pottery Neolithic southwest Asia, food preparation gradually stopped being done where everyone could see it and where cooks could socialize with all and sundry; cooking spaces became increasingly constrained and separated from the rest of settlement life. Scholars aver that changes in the spatial distribution of plant remains and grinding equipment testify to shifts in gender norms.

These shifts can be linked to broader social changes. In Wanka II (1300–1460 CE) Peru, political control was dispersed among thousands of local groups. In the Wanka III period (1460–1532 CE), the Inka state held control, having conquered the local Sausa and incorporated their lands into the Empire. Examining the spatial distribution of domesticated plant remains from neighboring Wanka II and Wanka III sites reveals that at Wanka II Tunánmarca, crop byproducts are widespread across a domestic compound. Maize remains in a patio area suggest group participation in food processing and/or eating, in a space used by a wide variety of people for tool-making, trash dumping, and myriad other uses (Hastorf, 1991). At Wanka III Marca, in contrast, crop remains are clustered up against a compound's patio walls. Women's work – for crop processing was women's work in the Andes – became increasingly circumscribed after the Inka conquest (Hastorf, 1991).[5]

Wright (2000) infers similar circumscription ten thousand years earlier and oceans away. During the Pre-Pottery Neolithic (ca. 9700–6700 BCE), southern Levantine grain-grinders gradually ceased working outdoors in communally visible areas, pulling farther and farther back into their stone houses. Archaeologists find Early Neolithic food storage and preparation facilities both inside and outside houses. Grinding slabs and hearths, heavy mortars and pounding tools occur in houses and just outside them. Later Neolithic milling and cooking facilities, in contrast, sit in private rooms and spaces, away from general view. Wright (2000: 117) suggests that such spatial shifts reflect probably-female cooks' movement from "open social setting[s]" to "relatively cloistered settings." (In Greece too, Early Neolithic people placed their hearths outdoors whereas Late Neolithic people cooked in private yards or inside. Human stable isotopes and lipid residues inside vessels also suggest Late Neolithic household dietary independence and inequality, but people probably still ate communally on some occasions [Halstead, 2015:38–41].)

Peterson (2006:551–552) challenges the security of Wright's conclusions. She notes that many of the houses Wright studied had upper stories that are now lost: who knows what people might have done on their roofs, in full view of their neighbors? More fundamentally, Peterson argues that Wright's idea that *women's* activities were increasingly circumscribed rests on the unstated assumption that men were working elsewhere: that they remained out in public and circulating freely. Peterson finally questions Wright's assumption that indoors was a problematic place to be, suggesting that what we see as tiny, dark, and cramped spaces might originally have been high-value locations.

Peterson's critiques are themselves open for discussion. Many Neolithic people had to be out in public: there's no other way they could have tended their fields or herded their livestock. (The genders and ages of such people are unascertained.) Perhaps Neolithic villages considered their homes' deepest recesses to be of great value indeed: does that necessarily mean that people working there were similarly valued? Or that esteemed people

---

[5] A fascinating literature on women's role in *chicha* – beer – production in the Andes falls outside the scope of this book. *Chicha* was hugely important in Andean political play, and women were commonly the ones tasked with making it, while men were at times the ones privileged to drink it. I encourage readers to find works by Hastorf (1991) and Jennings and Chatfield (2009) in particular in order to learn more about drink, gender, and power in the ancient Andes.

are inevitably empowered people? Peterson nonetheless highlights an important fact: there are important complexities to cooking-based "women subjugated" narratives even in prehistoric contexts.

For one thing, not all women are necessarily equally affected by a culture's gendered food obligations. In Epiclassic (ca. 650–900 CE) Mexico, the distribution of food preparation equipment suggests that urban elite women avoided the exhausting tedium of maize grinding (Turkon, 2007). Their homes contained serving and dining vessels but little evidence of food preparation. Rural elite women, in contrast, prepared food in addition to eating it. Turkon (2007) infers that urban elite women distanced themselves from maize preparation in ways that rural elites could not.

For another, members of a gender may have similar culinary responsibilities but otherwise very different experiences and identities. In nineteenth-century eastern Africa, concubines and freewomen may have cooked together, but at the resultant meals they sat separately, and concubines spent the rest of each day as enslaved women, required to provide their owners with sexual relations and lacking freewomens' legal and traditional rights (Croucher, 2011). Graff (2018) is probably right that the shared cooking time provided a bridge of some kind between freewomen and slaves, but the chasm between the two surely remained vast.

One final point on this front: in some cultures both males and females bear responsibility for food preparation as well as production. Skeletal pathologies suggest that in the Tiwanaku state (500–1100 CE in the south-central Andes) both sexes farmed, herded, processed maize, and very possibly walked on small potatoes in order to process them for freeze-drying (Becker, 2013). Terracotta figurines depict both men and women kneading dough and preparing food two and a half millennia ago in central Greece (Picazo, 2008). Today in northeastern India, Galo women cook daily meals but men cook meat for festivals, and in Fiji Lauan women prepare most of each day's food but oven houses are "the realm[s] of men," who bake yams and taro, leaf-wrapped packets of meat mixed with coconut cream, and sweet puddings for Sunday meals and special events (Deori, 2016; Jones, 2009:59–61). It is common across cultures for women to be the primary food preparers, but we mustn't assume that this was always the case, or that if women were the primary cooks that men were entirely uninvolved.

Another stream of research discusses how gendered labor played into the construction and negotiation of other aspects of social life. Gendered food politics is a particular theme. We hear, for example, that women's food labor was "essential" to the Inka Empire (Bray, 2003a:22; see also Gose,

2000). The Inka collected girls from throughout their empire to serve as "chosen women" (*aclla*). The *aclla* worked for the state spinning, weaving, brewing, and preparing special foods until they were either doled out by the king as wives for his subjects or sacrificed (Bray, 2003a). Their textiles, beer, and food were so important to the imperial enterprise that preparing a residence for the *aclla* was one of the first things the Inka state did when it conquered new territory (Bray, 2003a). The chosen women cooked special foods for vitally important religious ceremonies, but their value extended beyond the ritual sphere. *Aclla*–produced food and drink advertised the Inka state's benevolent superiority, fed its laboring subjects, and obligated them to repay the state's hospitality with further labor (Bray, 2003a; Gero, 1992; Gose, 2000).

Women's food labor was a core part of Andean political life long before the Inka came to power. At the Early Intermediate Period (200 BCE–600 CE) site of Queyash Alto in Peru, archaeologists uncovered a high-status household with large quantities of beautifully made dishes, copper *tupu* pins for fastening women's clothing, and a deposit of large quantities of butchered llama remains: meaty ribs and vertebrae, split-open long bones and mandibles (Gero, 1992). In another area of the site, numerous charcoal and ash-rich pits dotted an open plaza. These pits, which ranged up to a meter wide and a meter deep, held llama limb bone fragments and the shattered remains of drinking vessels. Jars, ceramic ladles, and two llama cranium "dippers" reinforce the idea that people drank copiously in this plaza, and knives and other cutting tools suggest that they dined well on llama meat as they did so (Gero, 1992). Abundant panpipe fragments complete the image of a feast rich in food and drink, set to music and highly visible to everyone in the vicinity (Gero, 1992).

Gero believes that the feasts held in this plaza were formal events sponsored by wealthy kin groups in order to improve their political standing. Women were present at the festivities: they left their copper *tupu*s among the plaza's ceramic and food remains (Gero, 1992). They may have attended as guests, but they also probably played centrally important roles in the ceremonies. Ceramic vessels from the same valley but later in the Early Intermediate Period depict both women and men holding decorated cups; some also show women holding food or cups near men who are not doing the same. The high-status women who lived at Queyash Alto were probably key parts of their kin groups' political negotiations, as the women prepared food and drink and served them to attendees at family-hosted feasts. How much power this gave the women themselves is unclear, but Gero (1992) proposes that the existence of powerful and fierce female deities in the Early Intermediate Period demonstrates that people were capable of seeing women as both potent and autonomous. Women may or may not have derived much individual power from their contributions to their kin groups' feasts, but they were highly visible participants, and the feasts could not have gone forward without their support.

Small but growing numbers of food archaeologists discuss genders other than "adult women" (e.g., Peres, 2017). For example, Lyons (2014) ethnoarchaeologically documents food labor's role in establishing both masculinity and femininity among the Tigray in Ethiopia. Men plow with oxen and avoid even entering kitchens, lest they be deemed effeminate or hermaphroditic. Women cook, but never plow – even if single and facing economic ruin due to untilled fields (Lyons, 2014). Men produce food and butcher animals outside of village compounds; women build stoves and granaries and prepare food inside compound walls. Both women potters, who trespass against Tigrayan gender norms by working outside compounds with heavy tools, and male blacksmiths, who violate expectations by pounding, grinding, and "cooking" metal at indoor hearths, pay harsh social penalties for their actions (Lyons, 2014). Lyons's study stands out among food studies in its discussion not only of normative men and women, but also of people who transgress gender norms. As an ethnoarchaeologist, Lyons has access to oceans of data unavailable to people who study past cultures, of course. Still, the gendered activities she reports have clear material signatures, and hope needn't be lost.

Gendered food labor has become an element of conversations about good archaeological practice as well (e.g., Brumbach and Jarvenpa, 2006). In 1993, Diane Gifford-Gonzalez argued that modern perspectives on the value of women's work[6] were damaging archaeological research. Gifford-Gonzalez's argument was that twentieth-century Western archaeologists belonged to a culture that devalued women's work: they saw cooking, sewing, and other forms of domestic labor as necessary but not evolutionarily, culturally, or historically important. Archaeologists naturally tend to investigate topics that strike us as important. Combine those two realities, and what you get is archaeologists paying little if any attention to food preparation. Graff (2018) reports routine discard of "crud ware" (i.e., cooking wares) on Pueblo sites and elsewhere, and Gifford-Gonzalez (1993) argues that researchers misinterpreted evidence that they did

---

[6] This can be seen as an archaeological twist on the hypothesis that gender values affect food values: some cultures value women-produced foods highly and some don't (Hastorf, 2016:187–188).

recover. Such oversights compromised our inferences of the lives and material impacts of the majority of humanity – women and children and many men, too.

In what ways might overlooking cooking lead people to misinterpret the archaeological record? Gifford-Gonzalez gave the example of animal bones left by modern African Dassanetch people in their pastoral camps. Approximately one-third of these long bones have jagged breaks across their shafts, a fracture type unfamiliar to Africanist archaeologists of the time. This unfamiliarity is striking, as by 1990 archaeologists had published numerous studies of bone fracture patterns. Yet virtually all of these studies focused on how uncooked bones break. Might boiled or roasted bones break differently? The answer was that . . . no one knew, because as of 1993, the necessary research hadn't been done (Gifford-Gonzalez, 1993:183–184).

Nor had people adequately explored the differences between marks left by cutting raw meat off the bone and those left by cutting cooked bone-in meat, or the impacts that cooking technologies and styles can have on bone transport (Gifford-Gonzalez, 1993). Imagine yourself standing by the carcass of a newly slain deer, considering how you want to butcher it and what parts of it you want to haul back home for dinner. The answers to your questions depend to a great extent on how you picture "dinner." Do you picture joints of meat roasting over an open fire? Do you intend to make a stew? Do you want boneless meat strips that you can grill, stir-fry, or dry for future snacking? The cuisine you picture shapes: (a) how you butcher the carcass; (b) which parts of that carcass you haul home; and (c) how those parts get further chopped, cracked, sliced, boiled, burned, or otherwise modified once they arrive at your destination (Gifford-Gonzalez, 1993). "To the extent that we underplay [cooking] tasks because we think of them as routine, simple, passive, or fundamentally unproductive (in our culture's gender paradigm, female), we undermine our understandings of processes forming the archaeological record" (Gifford-Gonzalez, 1993:199).

Sandra Montón Subías took up this argument at the dawn of the twenty-first century, asserting that outside of the dedicated subfield of gender archaeology, archaeology in 2002 remained largely oblivious of historical, sociological, economic, and ethnographic literature on the social and symbolic importance of cooking. Montón Subías attributed the oversight to the strong association between women and cooking, noting that ritual meals – theoretically or actually conducted by men – had received much of the attention spent on food (Montón Subías, 2002). She outlined why such ignorance is unacceptable, explaining that cooking influences archaeological settlement patterns, labor organization, technology, preservation, and more, adding that in many sites "elements employed or resulting from food processing are the most common ones" (Montón Subías, 2002:8).

Since 2002, this problem has been redressed to a considerable degree. In addition to numerous journal articles – notably Graff (2018) – archaeologists have been publishing books such as Klarich's (ed.) *Inside Ancient Kitchens: New Directions in the Study of Daily Meals and Feasts* (2010) and Graff and Rodríguez-Alegría's (ed.) *The Menial Art of Cooking: Archaeological Studies of Cooking and Food Preparation* (Graff and Rodríguez-Alegría, 2012). Not all researchers may be alerted to the importance of cooking, but certainly gender biases no longer render archaeology blind to its importance. Limitations remain – Graff (2018:6) cites a continuing reliance on a binary view of gender as one issue – but overall she characterizes the archaeology of cooking as "poised to contribute to" more complex and anthropologically-up-to-date discussions.

The archaeology of food is a field in which both researchers' and subjects' identities have been important points of discussion. Today we have, in my opinion, largely surmounted the obstacles imposed by pre-feminist ignorance of cooking's social (and biological) significance. Our greatest challenges at present lie in the stunning complexity of identity. Now that we no longer think of individual facets of identity as personally intrinsic, stable, and mutually unrelated, it can be extremely difficult to link particular food practices to ancient identities. There is no one way to succeed in doing so, and archaeologists working in different areas and time periods are developing varied strategies. All require considerable amounts of data. One cannot explore complex phenomena with limited information; the noise will overwhelm the signal. That commonality aside, the diversity of these strategies proves that no one data set is necessary in order to explore how people used food – that great shaper and expresser of identity – to affiliate themselves with, and distance themselves from, each other.

CHAPTER 7

Food, Ritual, and Religion

> *[Aztec] gods ate gods, humans ate gods, gods ate humans, children*
> *in the underworld suckled from divine trees, and adults in the*
> *underworld ate rotten tamales!*
>
> Carrasco, 1995: 434

This chapter is about food's involvement with people's beliefs: religious beliefs in particular, but also cultural assumptions and ideologies not directly related to doctrine or theology. These are messy and potentially confusing topics, especially as archaeologists (like other anthropologists) don't agree what religion is, what ritual is, or how the two of them relate to each other. To the extent that people agree on a definition of ritual, it is as repetitive behavior that has a purpose and conveys meaning. Some archaeologists view ritual as religious belief put into action; others see ritual practices as shaping what people believe. There is also no archaeological consensus about why ritual and/or religion matter. Some authors are interested in ritual/religion's adaptive importance; others concern themselves with its social functions (notably, how ritual activities relate to political maneuvering); still others with the sensory and emotional impacts of ritual observances.

I see ritual and religion as dance partners, moving in response to each other even in situations where one (say, religious doctrine) is ostensibly in charge. Rituals are conducted following "scripts" (Morris, 2018) that are often provided by religion. But putting these scripts into practice entails innumerable choices – about music, for example, or paraphernalia, or participants, or the strictness of script adherence – and in making these choices, people create, maintain, and modify religious norms and beliefs as well as other social realities. Even when a particular ritual practice endures over long stretches of time, its meaning and social impact vary (Hastorf, 2015:270; Insoll, 2011:2–3).

Rituals are often intertwined with food activities: consumption, sacrifice, offering, donation, and abstention are all widespread elements of ritual observance. The archaeological record is full of the bones of sacrificed animals and the residues of festal beer and wine; in certain areas and time periods it's empty of, or at least sparse in, tabooed species. "Rituals and beliefs [. . .] are put into operation by symbols. . ." (Hicks, 2010:xiv): food makes a phenomenally powerful symbol since we are biologically required to involve ourselves with it every day, and its use culminates in our literally incorporating it into our own bodies (Dietler, 2011). That so much of how we experience food is via smell may also be relevant, because smell is closely tied to memory, and to emotionally charged memory at that (Sutton, 2001:88–90). Indeed, food's sensory power might make it a particularly potent element of rituals, which have been described as "heightening or stimulating sensory experience to instill . . . values" (Sutton, 2010:209).

The symbolic power and meanings of foods are further enhanced by the fact that those meanings don't stay confined inside the rituals where they're put into play. People commonly eat the same foods at both mundane meals and religious ceremonies – which means that they ingest religious paraphernalia during family dinners, and family staples during religious worship. The everyday and the extraordinary reinforce and extend each other's messages and associations, knotting people into a culture-wide web of meaning (Douglas, 1975; Madgwick and Livarda, 2018; Sutton, 2001:20).

Archaeologists try to identify which traces of the past testify to ancient rituals or beliefs. This is a major challenge, much discussed in the archaeological literature (e.g., Brady and Peterson, 2008; Fowles, 2008; Madgwick and Livarda, 2018; Swenson, 2015; Verhoeven, 2011). Many researchers link food remains to ritual on the basis of their findspots. It is common practice to interpret bones, seeds, and other organic materials deriving from contexts saturated with symbolic meaning (graves, temples, sometimes even entire sites) as dedicated to ritual activities. Ancient people may have been skeptical or agnostic about the meanings or values of their ritual actions (Taylor, 2011:95, 99), just as modern people can be. Still, deposits found in symbolically important locations provide good information about what people *did* in ritual/religious situations, and actions are linked to (although not identical with) beliefs.

Of course, ritual activities and religious belief saturate human existence and shape people's actions well outside the narrow confines of tombs, temples, and similarly set-aside places. Archaeologists hoping to explore the breadth of ancient belief must figure out how to identify ritual and religious patterning in all sorts of contexts and areas, including those with clear signs of domestic habitation and day-in, day-out economic labor.

Reconstructing Religious Activities: Feasting, Fasting, Offering, Sacrifice, Almsgiving

Some archaeologists reconstruct religious activities in order to learn about ancient beliefs. More commonly, archaeologists seek insight into other aspects of social life that were entwined with religious observance: political systems, for example (see Chapter 5), or gender norms (see Chapter 6). Researchers often have multiple forms of activity available for analysis, since food and religious life interweave in a wide variety of ways. Feasting, fasting, almsgiving, offering; Christians take Communion, Hindus eschew beef, Mormons store a year's supply of food, Jains do not cook or eat in the dark, Theravada Buddhist monks carry alms bowls, Wari' ate their dead (Conklin, 1995; MacClancy, 1993:35).

One can broadly divide this tremendous variety of practices into (a) food use in religious rites and (b) religiously motivated food practices in daily life. Beginning with the former, many religions not only involve food in their observances, they give it a starring role. Communion – the consumption of Jesus's body in the (literal or metaphorical) form of bread[1] and wine – is one of only two sacraments recognized by most Protestants, and one of seven enumerated by the Roman Catholic and Eastern Orthodox churches.

Archaeologists find a variety of foods featuring in past religious obser-vances, from rare delicacies to everyday staples. At El Yaral in southern Peru, for example, researchers discovered sacrificed domestic guinea pigs, llamas, and alpacas – all standard sources of meat in the prehispanic Andes – that eight hundred years previously Chiribaya people had buried beneath the floors of their homes. (Rofes [2004] provides photos of several sacrificed guinea pigs, some with offerings carefully balanced on their small corpses and one with coca leaves stuffed into its mouth). Because the sacrificed rodents and camelids mummified naturally in the dry soils of El Yaral, excavators were able to tell that the Chiribaya color-matched the camelids and rodents that they would bury together. They sacrificed

---

[1] Crackers and cut-up hot dog buns are theologically acceptable for many Christians. The Vatican, in contrast, requires that Catholics consume fresh, unleavened, pure wheat wafers that are not 100 percent gluten-free (*Circular letter to Bishops on the bread and wine for the Eucharist*, July 2017).

brown, cream, gray, orange, and white guinea pigs, but no black ones. (Rofes wonders if the black ones were being saved for medical use, as in Andean ethnography black guinea pig meat has healing properties.) Ninety percent of the interred guinea pigs were young and 60 percent were infants. This suggests that the villagers preferred to sacrifice the smallest rodents and save their older, larger relatives for human consumption (Rofes, 2004). Chiribaya religious life involved careful selection of food animals for sacrifice.

The foods served at a feast held inside a third-century AD temple of Mithras in Belgium expand our understanding of Mithraic practice. Temples scattered throughout the Roman Empire testify to the fact that the cult of Mithras was widespread and popular, but historians can tell little about it because cult members kept their teachings and practices strictly secret. Art from Mithraic temples reveals stories from the god's life, such as a dinner shared with the Sun atop a bull's hide, and highlights the importance of subsidiary deities associated with the rising and the setting sun (Lentacker et al., 2004). But what did Mithras worship actually involve?

A large pit found by a Mithraic temple at Tienen, Belgium, sheds light on this question. The pit contained hundreds of cooking, eating, and drinking dishes, as well as nearly fourteen thousand animal bone specimens, all deposited together around the time of the summer solstice (Lentacker et al., 2004). Of these bones, 7,615 are from domestic chickens; nearly two thousand more are unidentifiable bird bones that probably derive from poultry as well. Butchery and burning marks as well as body part representation data indicate that Tienen's cooks beheaded the chickens and then sometimes cut their feet off before grilling, frying, or broiling them for Mithras worshippers to consume together. Fish, lamb, pork, and beef were also served, but chicken was clearly the dominant meat at the Mithraic meal. Poultry bones are also unusually plentiful at Roman sanctuaries to Mithras in Germany, France, Switzerland, Austria, and Hungary – and not at most temples dedicated to Jupiter, Hera, Mercury, or any of the other deities in the standard Greco-Roman pantheon (Gál and Kunst, 2014; Koch et al., 2018; Lentacker et al., 2004). Chicken bones were secreted into walls, benches, and floors and collected in pits and pots at various *mithraea* too (Lentacker et al., 2004).

All of Tienen's measurable poultry bones come from more or less the same-sized birds. Hens and roosters are different sizes, and the Tienen birds' measurements match those of contemporary roosters from France. This suggests that all of the adult fowl in the Tienen assemblage – around 286 individual birds – were roosters (Lentacker et al., 2004). All sixty-seven measurable bones from a Mithras temple in Germany also come from roosters, and although it's not a universal pattern, other *mithraea* seem to have male-dominated assemblages as well (Lentacker et al., 2004). Roosters, of course, are famous for announcing the rising of the sun. Art and myth show the sun as centrally important in Mithraic doctrine. It appears that when it came time to celebrate the longest day of the year, Mithras worshippers feasted on roosters for their solar symbolism (Lentacker et al., 2004).[2]

Only some archaeologists are as lucky as those studying the Tienen temple, with its plethora of food remains that are clearly linked to religious activities. It is often difficult to determine what ancient people ate specifically as part of ritual activities. Plant and animal leftovers were rarely left in place on temple dishes or braziers for archaeologists to pick through millennia later, and many foods would have been destroyed during consumption anyway. We commonly have better luck finding the remains of offerings made to gods and spirits than the remains of human foods. With the former we can often recover at least the provisions that supplicants didn't later take away to eat themselves (a widespread norm) and the vessels in which those dishes were served (e.g., Hamilakis and Konsolaki, 2004; Nelson, 2003; Otto, 2015:218).

Generally speaking, archaeologists rely primarily on iconography, on texts, and on ethnography to identify ritual consumption of specific foods. We may be sure that ancient people were eating a food (wheat, for example), but linking its consumption to religious ceremonialism is tenuous without documentary or iconographic help. Archaeologists don't even assume that repeated consumption of human flesh was ideologically motivated. Ethnographic and ethnohistoric evidence inform strong conclusions that people ate people ritually, as opposed to when they simply needed the nutrients or wanted to make a political point (e.g., Coe, 1994:160; Jones et al., 2015).

The challenges multiply when we recall that while people's actions during religious rites were related to what they believed, people did not necessarily follow the prescriptions of their faiths without questions, doubts, and/or personal agendas. Reconstructing ritual practice is the easy part: determining what that practice may have *meant* to its participants is challenging enough that many archaeologists declare it inappropriate to

---

[2] In contrast, people worshipping Magna Mater (Cybele) sacrificed laying hens to their goddess. Koch and colleagues (2018) cite a rule that female deities got female sacrifices; gender shapes what you eat even when you're a deity.

even try. The people willing to make that leap tend to work in historical
time periods or in areas with rich ethnographic or ethnohistoric documen-
tation of culturally affiliated communities. These sources provide archaeologists with a relative wealth of information to contextualize and interpret
what they find.

Eating with the Gods and Ancestors

We've previously established that feasting and daily commensality are
intertwined, and that ritual is not necessarily in opposition to the secular.
People thus share both home-cooked meals and feasts with supernatural
beings as well as with each other. For example, ethnographic accounts
describe Andeans overeating at feasts in order to feed the dead: the living
stuff themselves so that they may share the excess with those not physically
present (Hastorf, 2015). Such sharing may have practical as well as spiritual
motivations. As Hastorf (2016:229) notes, gifts establish obligations, so eating
with the gods creates obligations for deities as well as people.

The archaeological record has evidence in multiple places and times for
people eating with supernatural beings. In Late Bronze Age Mesopotamia,
for example, laypeople as well as temple workers shared their daily foods
with deities and ancestors. Plant and animal remains, artifacts, and features
inside thirty burned houses at Tall Bazi in northern Syria reveal homes
wherein families sat together on furs and benches to eat barley bread and
groats (Otto, 2015). They held their plates and bowls on their laps, not
having any dining tables in the main rooms where they ate. However, they
did have altars and cultic vessels in these rooms: finds in various houses
included one vessel depicting the storm god, four shaped partially like
animals, and several more unusually shaped vessels. One house had a
small covered libation jar installed beside its altar, thirteen had cooking
pots near theirs, and five houses had the remains of bulls' heads near theirs
(Otto, 2015). These remains show us people feeding their houses' gods and
ancestors, placing (as dictated in contemporary texts) "the ritual portion of
beef, the ritual portion of mutton, the head of the ox, the head of the ram
before the gods" (*Emar* 369:28; Sallaberger, 2015:189).

The word "portion" there is key, indicating as it does that deities were
only one of the groups partaking of an animal's meat. At Tall Bazi,
excavators found the remains of a single sheep or goat in three locations
within one house. Some bones lay near the altar; others were near a hearth
in that same room; still others sat in a cooking pot in an entirely different
room (Otto, 2015). Humans, gods, and ancestors shared not only the same

FIGURE 7.1. Ritual grain server (*gui*) with masks and dragons. Late Shang Dynasty, ca. twelth- to eleventh-century BCE. Bronze, 5½ x 8⅜". Image courtesy of the Freer Gallery of Art and Arthur M. Sackler Gallery, Smithsonian Institution, Washington DC: Purchase – Charles Lang Freer Endowment, F.1941.8.

dining spaces but also the same food sources. Sometimes, at least, humans and deities even shared literally the same food. Cuneiform texts from Emar, 60 km away from Tall Bazi, state that offerings made to the gods in temples were later consumed by the people who donated them and by city elites (Sallaberger, 2015).

Mesopotamian human–divine commensality was not, however, necessarily viewed as commensality by those who participated in it. Texts indicate that human diners ate divine "leftovers"; the gods themselves remained aloof (Oppenheim, 1997: 189–191). In contrast, ancient Chinese mourners feasted explicitly with the dead beside their newly dug graves. In the Late Shang Dynasty (ca. 1200–1045 BCE), family members feasted with the recently departed in order to convert them into new ancestral spirits (Nelson, 2003). Such ancestors could bless their descendants with health, wealth, and good fortune, and, as inscriptions on Shang oracle bones and bronze vessels attest, they cared deeply about being fed. The living with the ability to do so therefore invested heavily in ancestor creation, leaving sizable collections of elaborate food and drink containers in the tombs of those whom they wished to transform. (Figure 7.1 shows an elaborately decorated Late Shang *gui*, or ritual grain server.)

The grave of Lady Hao, for example, in the Shang cemetery at Yin Xu, contained 195 bronze vessels including a used cooking stove and three grain steamers, a wide variety of meat serving dishes (some in matched sets), and 144 drinking vessels (one weighing 118 kg) (Nelson, 2003). The drinking vessels were arranged in the queen's inner coffin, and the meat containers between the inner and outer coffins. Two jade bowls and three eating utensils lay atop the coffins: Nelson (2003:85) speculates that perhaps the queen's spouse and two children "share[d] one final course with Lady Hao, as she became an ancestor."

Yet were humans and ancestors both actually eating at this shared feast? Or might the dishes in the tomb represent offerings rather than food-sharing?[3] It seems clear that human beings ate and drank beside Lady Hao's grave. Soot on her stove's legs testifies to its previous use, and cost-saving was clearly not a priority for her mourners: she was buried with 1600 kg of elaborate bronzes as well as jade, ivory, bone, stone, shell, and ceramic artifacts (Linduff, 2001; Nelson, 2003). Furthermore, many of Lady Hao's bronze vessels appear to have been washed and then wrapped up in fine cloth before being deposited with her. (Nelson [2003] remarks that it must have taken many servants to cook and clean for Lady Hao's graveside banquet: the meat and grain required preparation, the millet ale needed heating and pouring, and everything then had to be cleaned!)

Did Lady Hao herself eat? That the dead did partake is illustrated by another tomb, in which a plate of mutton and beef was laid near the deceased's mouth (Nelson, 2003). Lady Hao, however, seems to have dined on the "essences" of food and drink rather than on their substances (Nelson, 2003:87). Vessels went into her tomb cleaned rather than full, she apparently having supped on their aromas while more corporeal family members enjoyed their tastes.

Food-sharing practices can illuminate ancient worldviews about non-human beings (Bray, 2015). Ethnohistoric Andeans understood *huacas* as powerful beings that participated in human society despite their physical manifestation as stones, trees, and mountains (Bray, 2015). Building on the standard premise that eating together maintains and builds social bonds, Bray sought out feast remains found in close proximity to pre-Columbian *huacas*. Having identified them at several sites, she argues that such deposits reflect humans socializing with non-humans – that is to say, recognizing them as people. Bray thus uses archaeological feasting evidence to argue that in the Andes humans and non-humans shared person-hood. Here ancient foodways testify to a worldview fundamentally different from our own (Bray, 2015).

---

[3] A thousand years later, Chinese people were offering food not just to the newly dead but also to underground nature spirits who might have been offended by the tomb-digging. Feeding these spirits kept construction workers, mourners, and the deceased free from supernatural harm (Selbitschka, 2018).

It's worth stressing here that eating isn't necessarily the most ritually important food activity. McNeil (2010), for example, suggests that when it came to ancient Maya ancestor veneration, the process of making the food for rites may have been more important than the final products were. Cooking for the ancestors – religious cookery in general – is often ritually important in and of itself, saturated with meaning and with emotion (McNeil, 2010). Consider the various foods deposited in Early Classic (ca. 400–600 CE) royal tombs at Copan. Cooks used cacao, turkey, fish, and maize to make tamales, pinole, and more, always adding some blood-colored cinnabar or valuable hematite as a final touch. Cinnabar contains toxic mercury. Both hematite and cinnabar would have made the dishes unpleasantly grainy. As McNeil (2010:306) notes, "one hopes" that living people weren't eating such dishes! And there is no evidence that they were: people burned some of the food offerings and let others decay, merely moving them aside if they needed space within the tomb for additional ceremonies. Such examples remind us that all food activities, from gardening to cooking to kitchen cleaning, can carry great ideological weight.

Ritual Beliefs and Human Interactions

Most archaeologists reconstruct the many food-related rituals and beliefs of ancient religions and cultures with an eye to how such rituals may have affected humans' relationships with each other and not just with the divine. A particularly fascinating example of food cosmology shaping how humans interacted with each other is the ancient Aztecs, who sacrificed their finest community members in order to keep the gods fed, offering up the blood and hearts of strong warriors, admired maidens, and beloved children to keep the deities happy enough to allow the maize to grow. Humans fed each other to the gods so that the gods would feed the humans (Carrasco, 1995).

This was a fair exchange, as in Aztec eyes human beings *were* maize (Figure 7.2). Fetuses were implanted by Tezcatlipoca, to grow inside their mothers in exactly the same way as plants grow in the earth (Clendinnen, 1995[1991]:180). Children were to be tended as cultivated plants were tended, both requiring adult help to grow and ripen into maturity. Babies were "maize blossoms," young girls "tender green ears," mature warriors "Lord Corn Cob[s]" (Pilcher, 1998:17). Only the finest human beings were in danger of sacrifice, as subpar offerings such as barbarians ("old and stale tortillas" [León-Portilla, 1963:163]) would displease the gods. Human bones

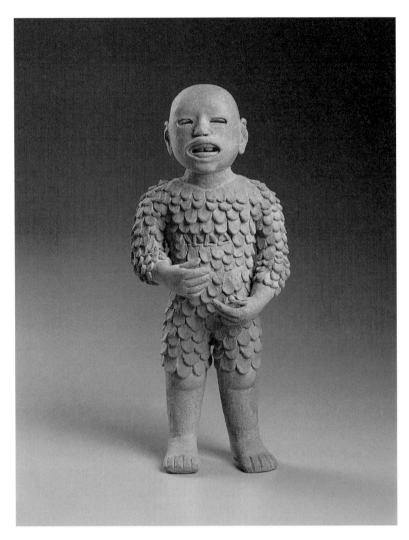

FIGURE 7.2. Ceramic sculpture of an Aztec priest in costume as the agricultural god Xipe Totec, ca. 900–1200 CE The costume consists of the flayed skin of a human sacrifice, and its wearer represents a living seed encased in a dried husk. Image courtesy of the Kimbell Art Museum, Forth Worth, TX (AP 1979.39, 15¾ × 6⅝ × 3⅞").

were seeds, blood vessels were reeds, blood was "most precious water" (Clendinnen, 1995[1991]:183).

Blood was "most precious" because water was precious. Water enabled plants to grow, keeping humanity fed as well as watered. Tlaloc, god of rain, was "He who caused the trees, the grasses, the maize ... to grow;" when his rains faltered, his sister, Sustenance Woman, would be depicted as dried-out, dying maize (Clendinnen, 1995[1991]:182). At the end of each year's dry season, the Aztecs sacrificed maize-wearing children, "precious blood sacrifices ... so that thus indeed rain was asked for, rain was requested" (Arnold, 1991:221; Tate, 2010).[4]

During the festival that marked the coming of the winter rains and the season of harvest and war, a woman was beheaded at the pyramid of the Maize Lord and her skin cut off her body. A priest then donned most of this skin to impersonate the earth deity Toci, "Our Grandmother," but the skin of one thigh was made into a face-mask for Toci's son, the Young Lord Maize Cob, whose impersonator also wore a cap signifying the frost that kills growing maize. The Toci impersonator sacrificed four captives (her priests slew more) before leading Lord Maize Cob – "The Man of War" – to the skull rack in the main temple precinct, where warriors awaited Maize Cob and his thigh-skin mask, which they would carry as they set off to fight the enemy. Parades, dances, and songs lasted through the night, until the priests of Sustenance Woman, wearing additional flayed human skins, emerged from their temple to scatter maize kernels and squash seeds for the gods as well as over the scrambling people below. Meanwhile, next year's seed corn – the sacred kernels intended for future planting – was placed inside the temple of Sustenance Woman (Clendinnen, 1995 [1991]:200–203). Maize wore human skin as it sent warriors off to battle, and it wore human skin as it tossed sustenance onto crowds of its supplicants.

Human sacrifices were thus harvests, giving the ever-hungry gods their maize to eat. The gods, in their turn, provided the rain and the crops that fed humanity. "The human body, cherished as it might be, was no more than one stage in a vegetable cycle of transformations, and human society a human arrangement to help sustain that essential cycle" (Clendinnen, 1995 [1991]:262). Death was a prerequisite for new life, and everyone – even the gods, dying and being reborn and becoming various foodstuffs in myth after myth – eventually became food (Tate, 2010).

The Aztecs' example of ideologically determined food behavior shaping human interactions is, of course, a spectacularly dramatic one. It is not,

---

[4] *"And the little noble children ... their tears signify it, the rain ... indeed already it will arise the rain, indeed already we will be rained on."* Both this and the quote in the text are from Arnold's (1991:223) translation of a Nahuatl account of the ceremony, recorded in the Florentine Codex, Book 2, chapter 20.

however, unique, in terms of the impact of ideology and food on ancient social relations. Archaeologists have evidence across continents and through millennia of ritually motivated food activities bringing people together as well as setting people apart. Researchers discuss which segments of society were strategically included in or excluded from rites, ceremonies, and ritualized feasts (e.g., Halstead and Isaakidou, 2011; Hamilakis and Konsolaki, 2004); which had access to ritually important resources (e.g., Marom and Zuckerman, 2012); and which were interred with particular foods (e.g,. Aranda Jiménez and Montón Subías, 2011).

Since ritual and symbolism focus people's attention and emotions, the social effects of religious activities involving food may have been particularly strong. Consider that during the mid-third millennium BCE, people journeyed across much of Britain to participate in immense feasts at Durrington Walls on the Salisbury Plain. Only 2.8 km away from Stonehenge, Durrington Walls must once have been near-equally impressive. During the Late Neolithic period, its ditch and a bank encircled a space well over 200 m in diameter, in which two timber circles echoed Stonehenge's ring of stones. Even before the monumental earthworks were built, Durrington Walls was a place of considerable activity. Occupation layers underneath the earthworks contain houses and a public building; middens and pits full of rapidly accumulated animal bones, ceramics, and other food debris testify to large-scale feasting (Craig et al., 2015).

These deposits are contemporaneous with the main phase of construction at Stonehenge, when its immense sarsens and gate-like trilithons were being hauled into place. Ceremonial avenues from each site to the river Avon reveal travel between Durrington Walls and Stonehenge, and each site is full of what the other lacks. Durrington Walls has virtually no burials; Stonehenge has more than one hundred and possibly more than two hundred. Stonehenge is short on houses and food debris; Durrington Walls is rich in both (Craig et al., 2015). Excavators believe that Durrington Walls and Stonehenge were complementary locations within a massive ritual complex on the Neolithic Salisbury Plain. The people who erected Stonehenge did so while living at Durrington Walls.

That these people came from all over Britain to do so we first learned not from their remains. (As recently as 2016, archaeologists publicly deemed none of the human bones or teeth dating to this period at Stonehenge suitable for strontium isotopic analysis; such an analysis was published in 2018, but with a note that at least some of the people buried at the site were brought there as already-cremated remains [Chan et al., 2016; Snoeck et al., 2018].) We learned it rather from the resources that they brought with them, notably their food. Most materials found at Stonehenge and Durrington Walls were available within a few kilometers of the site. The pottery is made of local clays; the lithics (apart from the massive sarsens) are local flints and chalk (Chan et al., 2016). Some construction timbers may have come from as far as 10 km away (Chan et al., 2016). However, only two of thirteen (construction-era) Durrington Walls cattle teeth subjected to strontium isotopic analysis come from animals that could have been raised less than 30 km away from the site (Viner et al., 2010). Four of the teeth belonged to animals raised 90 km away or more. (That is 90 km away as the crow flies; the actual distances traveled would have been higher as people moved their cattle across and around water, over hills and through valleys [Viner et al., 2010].) Archaeologists have reason to believe that Durrington Walls's cattle weren't trade goods but came to the site with their owners as travel provisions (Chan et al., 2016). Their origins, therefore, reveal the places from which Durrington Walls's people traveled to come feast, camp, and build Stonehenge.

Durrington Walls's food remains further inform us about when these gatherings took place and about some elements of what occurred. The residents of Durrington Walls ate ample quantities of roasted pork (Albarella and Serjeantson, 2002; Craig et al., 2015). A dearth of small piglet remains indicates that people weren't raising this meat on site, but bringing it in from other locations (Wright et al., 2014). A few of the bones have broken-off arrowhead tips embedded in them and other traces of damage from projectile weapons. That such damage appears on bones from varied parts of the animals' bodies may mean that people weren't executing these domesticates at point-blank range, but "hunting" them or otherwise shooting them from a distance (Parker Pearson et al., 2011).

Pig tooth eruption and wear stages reveal that a majority of the pigs in a large feasting midden were slaughtered before they completed their first year, in autumn and winter (Wright et al., 2014). These animals had not yet reached their maximum meat weight, so their slaughter was economically sub-optimal. However, midwinter was a ritually important time at Durrington Walls and Stonehenge, as was midsummer (Wright et al., 2014). Durrington Walls's timber circles were aligned to the midwinter sunrise, and its ceremonial avenue to the midsummer sunset; Stonehenge's circle and avenue are aligned with the midwinter sunset and the midsummer sunrise (Parker Pearson et al., 2007).

Food remains thus tell us that four and half thousand years ago people were traveling from across Britain to the Salisbury Plain, where in the middle of winter they feasted on roasted pork as well as beef from animals they had brought with them on their journeys. Although residing at Durrington Walls, they labored as well at Stonehenge, moving massive boulders into positions that we all recognize today.

Food Symbolism in Daily Life

Food's ideological importance was not, of course, limited to special occasions or certain days and times. Symbolism saturates everyday foods and food activities. In the Andes, culinary freeze-drying echoes mortuary treatments (Hastorf, 2016:96); among the West African Jola, spirit-shrines supervise labor in the fields (Davidson, 2016:92); in Japan rice has a soul, and consuming it rejuvenates humans and communities (Ohnuki-Tierney, 1993:55–56). Many of us say a prayer before meals and/or select our foods in accordance with religious proscriptions.

Archaeological evidence confirms that everyday foods and food-related activities were symbolically laden in the past as well. Some peoples, for example, drew links between the storage of food and the storage of humans. An excellent example comes from Israel, where archaeologists have found Chalcolithic ossuary jars with shapes akin to those of grain silos, human burials inside actual silos, and a painted clay silo model as well as two rich burials inside a large storage facility (Rosenberg et al., 2017). Depositing grain into storage and withdrawing it later must have been ideologically weighty actions, plausibly requiring ritual accompaniment (Rosenberg et al., 2017).

In some cultures, discarding leftovers entailed attention to ritual regulations of one kind or another. (I'm not talking about ritual deposition at "special" sites or of ritually significant feasts, but about quotidian leavings from everyday meals.) Past Torres Strait Islanders discarded the remains of dugong[5] meals in a variety of locations: dugong bone mounds consist almost entirely (97–98 percent) of dugong cranial bones and ribs, while more generalized middens contain a range of species and dugong body parts, tossed in un-arranged (McNiven, 2013:574). The bone mounds clearly reflect ritual activities, with carefully arranged rows of ribs and skull bones and dugong ear bones (hunting charms for modern Torres Strait

[5] Dugongs are large marine mammals that look similar to their close relatives, manatees. For photos of hunted dugongs and dugong bones, descriptions of dugong hunting rituals, explanations of why you have to stay silent when trying to harpoon them, and a statement that – contrary to what those of us whose mental images of the animals may have been shaped a little too much by *Sam the Sea Cow* might imagine – dugong hunting could be quite dangerous; see McNiven and Feldman (2003).

Islanders) arranged in pairs behind dugong crania (McNiven, 2013:567). The middens are also consistent with discard done with attention to ritual, however. Why do they contain dugong limb bones and vertebrae? These near-valueless elements rarely make it into either modern or very, very old Torres Strait middens: modern hunters toss them into the sea as soon as they've butchered their catch. McNiven (2013:574) speculates that people deposited them in middens in order to emphasize the difference between these deposits of daily meal remains and the formally arranged dugong bone mounds. Islanders also deliberately shaped the middens into low-elevation circular or linear mounds in and around the village: "living architecture," over and around which people ate, slept, and lived (McNiven, 2013:581). Their curated contents were on constant display, announcing to all and sundry the activities and assets of those who contributed to them. Cosmology and politics shaped middens' contents and their construction.

Ritual and symbolism are also widely intertwined with hunting, with gathering, with cultivation, with dining, with grain-grinding, and with myriad other food activities. I have highlighted food storage and discard simply because they are two forms of food behavior whose ideological importance is unfamiliar to many. Virtually any food activity can have symbolic resonance, especially since everyday and sacred food activities intertwine (e.g., Luby and Gruber, 2009; Otto, 2015).

Piety and Religious Observance

Did ancient people follow the rules of their faiths? If so, how strictly? Historically, Judaism, Christianity, and Islam have all required that their followers eat (and not eat) according to certain rules. Most famously, observant Jews and Muslims have been required to eschew pork. This should, on the whole, lead to a distinct lack of pig bones in Jewish and Muslim settlements and neighborhoods. Jewish neighborhoods should also lack hunted prey (only ritually slaughtered animals may be kosher); scale- or finless sea creatures (no eels or catfish); and non-kosher animal body parts (no hind leg bones, at least in Ashkenazi Jewish areas). Muslim areas should be short on alcohol consumption debris. Such well-known faith-based proscriptions offer archaeologists opportunities to link assemblages of food remains with major religious groups (Cool, 2006; Grau-Sologestoa, 2017; Greenfield and Bouchnik, 2011; Insoll, 1999:94–100; Valenzuela-Lamas et al., 2014). Thus, for example, when scholars wanted to confirm or refute the location of a Jewish community in Hungary's medieval royal capital of Buda, L. Daróczi-Szabó (2004) turned to the animal bones found inside a deep well in the Buda Castle district. He hypothesized that the lower fills of the well would be associated with Jewish consumers, whereas its upper fills, dating to the years after King Louis the Great (temporarily) expelled the town's Jews, would reflect Christian eating habits. And indeed, Daróczi-Szabó found subtle differences between the well's upper and lower fills: 97 pig bones in the upper fills (4.4 percent of mammal bones) versus only three small ones in the lower fills (0.4 percent of mammal bones, and two of the three may actually date to the post-expulsion era); proportionally fewer hind limb bones in the lower fills; and a non-kosher catfish bone in the upper fills (Daróczi-Szabó, 2004).

Simple identifications of particular assemblages as "Jewish" or "Muslim" (or Christian, or Hindu, etc.) are rarely the goal, however. Normally, archaeologists are far more interested in trying to use food remains to learn something about a religion or a religious tradition: its origins, for example, or how its rites varied across communities, or how strictly people adhered to its rules. Staying with the Judeo-Muslim pork ban, we see multiple articles investigating when and where it arose, why it became religiously important, and the extent to which community members obeyed the ban (Hesse, 1990; Hesse and Wapnish, 1998; London, 2008; Zeder, 1998). The ethnic components of this literature were described in the previous chapter, but a couple of additional points are worth revisiting here.

The distribution of pig remains in prehistoric and early historic southwest Asia at first glance appears consistent with religious expectations. Zooarchaeological evidence reveals that pig meat was a standard food in southwest Asia up through the Early Bronze Age. In the areas that would come under Israelite sway, its consumption ebbed in the later Bronze Age and bottomed out in the late Iron Age (some settlements still kept pigs, but only a few). Pig-eating rebounded strongly in Hellenistic, Roman, and Byzantine eras, then declined again as Islam expanded throughout the region. Unfortunately for anyone expecting a clean "polytheistic and Christian settlements contain pig bones; Jewish and Muslim settlements do not," however, the broad chronological patterning that initially seems to match this expectation is complicated by where the bones appear in each era. Some Philistine settlements lack pig bones; some have plenty during certain eras but not in others (Faust and Lev-Tov, 2011; Hesse, 1990; Hesse and Wapnish, 1998). Iron Age polities well outside Israel and Judah joined their Jewish neighbors in eschewing pork. What was going on? What might have motivated people to ban pig-eating in the first place, and why do we see pig avoidance among polytheists as well as Jews and Muslims?

The answer is not simply that people living in pig-friendly habitats ate pork and those living in pig-unsuitable environments didn't. This idea is disproven handily by the fact that proportions of pig bones fluctuate within individual sites. At Tell Halif, for example, pork-eating was relatively common in the Early Bronze Age I but rare in the Early Bronze Age III, up again in the Late Bronze Age then down again in the Iron Age (Zeder, 1998). Ecological factors undoubtedly constrained pig-raising (you can't raise pigs in arid environments), but they didn't determine it. Similarly limited in impact were agricultural production methods, nomadic contributions to the local economy, and concerns re the health implications of eating pork (Hesse, 1990; Zeder, 1998).

Instead, archaeological data support the idea that what would become globally relevant religious proscriptions originated at least in part in political and economic maneuvering. Ancient southwest Asian authorities had an incentive to discourage pig-eating because the animals undermined elite control over the populace. Urban households raising pigs (which produce no easily taxable products such as wool) were more independent from centralized economic control than were their non-pig-eating neighbors; such independence naturally earned authorities' displeasure. At Tell Halif, pig bones are scarce in eras when its citizens were integrated into a tightly coordinated regional economy, and more common in periods when regional control faltered (Zeder, 1998).

Often the story is not about a religion itself or its history, but about how its observance interacted with other aspects of people's social and economic lives. (This is part of archaeologists' deep interest in how food and belief intertwine with other aspects of society, as described earlier in this chapter.) For example, historical archaeologist Elizabeth M. Scott (1996) found no evidence that an eighteenth-century German-Jewish trader and his family kept kosher during their first decade of residence in Fort Michilimackinac, Michigan. In fact, pork was the most important domestic meat in the Solomon family's diet – 27 percent of animal biomass! – and they ate non-kosher wild animals too. As the household became wealthier and more secure in local society, however, its members dramatically decreased their consumption of non-kosher pork (to 9 percent of remains) and wild game. Scott infers that when poor, Ezekiel Solomon ate to "fit in" with his non-Jewish (and sometimes anti-Semitic) neighbors; once rich, he could buy things other than food to express his neighborly solidarity and eat according to his religious conscience. (Said conscience didn't prevent him from eating some pork, but considerably less than he once did.)

Multiple studies have also identified Christians being variably strict about adhering to the expectations of their faiths, often for socioeconomic reasons. For example, instruction booklets for Byzantine monks prescribed a relatively ascetic diet, commonly two vegetarian meals per day plus water or wine. Meat was a costly luxury whose consumption was associated with immorality and depravity – officially, monks were only permitted to eat meat if they were ill – and non-meat animal foods such as dairy and eggs were expensive (Gregoricka and Sheridan, 2013). It's hard not to wonder, therefore, if the abbot of huge, wealthy St. Stephen's Monastery in Jerusalem was bothered by the apparent fact that members of his community were eating animal protein. Gregoricka and Sheridan (2013) suggest that St. Stephen's affluence and urban location may have enabled some of its monks to minimize their asceticism and eat meat, cheese, or other expensive animal foods. Not all monks did so: only 30 percent of the fifty-five people studied had elevated $\delta^{15}N$ ratios in their leg bones. The variation is plausibly related to differences in status (Gregoricka and Sheridan, 2013).

Excavations at Moreaucourt Priory in France testify to laxity among medieval Benedictine Sisters of Christ as well. The Rule of Benedict dictates that only the sick and very weak should eat the meat of four-footed animals, but the sisters deposited plenty of pig, cattle, and sheep bones in their kitchen's well. As Jones (2007:253) comments, "whether or not a large number of the priory's communion qualified as being 'very weak,' it is perfectly clear from the food remains on a wide variety of monastic sites across Europe that holy men and women found enough latitude in Benedict's rule to adjust his prescription quite considerably."

These were adjustments, though, not wholesale rejections of the precepts of their faith. Moreaucourt's kitchen discards include numerous pig, sheep, and cattle bones, but also the remains of many Benedict-acceptable fish, geese, chickens, and shellfish (Clavel, 2001; Jones, 2007:254). Moreover, the floor of the kitchen was strewn with tiny bone fragments. Heavily concentrated around a central hearth platform, 90 percent of these fragments derive from fish: primarily herring and some eel. All parts of the fish body are represented. Jones (2007:256) combines these data with the charcoal evidence (large chunks of oak and beech; slivers of willow and hazel) and describes "herrings and eels threaded onto thin wands of hazel and willow, and suspended above a fire to be infused with the smoke of beech and oakwood." The room was a smokery, producing a steady supply of religiously acceptable fish.

These studies illustrate the fact that just as modern people vary with respect to their levels and forms of religious observance, so too did people in the past. Archaeologists don't expect perfect adherence to religious dictates, because (as emphasized throughout this book) people's food habits are the end results of many different streams of influence. Moreover, archaeologists recognize that it's the variation in religious practice that makes things interesting. Ezekiel Solomon's family became more dietarily observant with time? Some but not all Byzantine monks regularly ate forbidden foods? Provincial Romans didn't worship in quite the same way as citizens living in Rome itself? At least a few sixteenth-century Italian nuns owned satirical, penis-decorated bowls – even as the Catholic Reformation required them to lead lives so chaste that even eye contact with non-nuns was to be avoided (Librenti et al., 2017)? Those stories are intriguing, and more than that they offer much better insights into past realities than simple "they were or weren't observant" tests ever could.

Since the extent to which people follow a religion's dictates is, in part, a function of their commitment to that religion, archaeological food data allow us to track changes in religious belief. Take the case of early medieval England, where prior to the rise of Christianity people occasionally ate horses. Thirty percent of Early Saxon settlements contain butchered horse bones (Poole, 2013). Then Christianity filtered through society. The bishops abhorred hippophagy as a pagan habit, condemned by the Pope as "a filthy and abominable practice" that should be firmly suppressed (*The Letters of Boniface* ca. 732 AD; Poole, 2013:321). Horsemeat consumption dropped: fewer than 20 percent of Middle and Late Saxon sites contain butchered horse bones. Horses may have become famine foods, eaten only when people were desperately hungry. It is also possible, however, that throughout the Anglo-Saxon period horses were feasting foods, eaten by people adhering to at least some pagan beliefs (Poole, 2013). The fact that Middle Saxon horse-eaters were, for the most part, relatively low in status does not permit us to choose between these alternatives (Poole, 2013). Low-status people are often more vulnerable to hunger than their better-off compatriots. In England they might also have offered the strongest resistance to religious change. Elites were England's earliest converts, and even non-believers had economic and political reasons to avoid blatant defiance of church proscriptions (Poole, 2013).

Horse-eating persisted in England for centuries after the missionary monk Augustine arrived in 597 CE. But archaeology reveals that hippophagy also changed as Catholicism took hold. Fewer people ate horsemeat, and those who did were plausibly either (a) pushed to do so by sheer hunger or (b) adhering to old beliefs and symbolism. Moreover, the pace of ideological change varied across society. Elites adopted Christian precepts faster than did peasants, for example, and people of Scandinavian heritage (whose progenitors placed special value on ritual horseflesh consumption) seem to have held out the longest (Poole, 2013).

The Economic Implications of Religious Foodways

What people believe shapes what they do with food. In some cases, beliefs require people to produce extra food, unusual cooking or serving vessels, or architecturally distinctive settings for cooking and eating. Beliefs also lead people to go out of their way to acquire rare or psychoactive foods (mushrooms, peyote), to produce and prepare foods in special ways (kosher/halal slaughter), to limit the people allowed to be farmers, slaughterers, and/or cooks (caste proscriptions), and to acquaint themselves with unfamiliar foods and cuisines (pilgrimage supplies and new encounters). Thus, what people believe plays a huge part in shaping their food economy, potentially affecting everything from the scale and focus of their food production to the organization of their labor supply to the extent of their private ownership of resources. This doesn't mean that people have a "regular" secular economy, on top of which they add the requirements of their own particular belief system like icing is layered on top of a cake. Belief systems permeate people's lives, and they're not an optional element of society as icing is optional on a cake. Beliefs are more like leavening: an integral component of the cake itself, and one that determines its ultimate elevation and shape.

Archaeologists all over the world find evidence of the economic relevance of belief systems. In the Middle East, for example, carbon and nitrogen stable isotopes in 2000-year-old sheep and goat bones reveal large-scale trade networks aimed at provisioning Jewish pilgrims to Jerusalem: people were raising animals in the deserts to sell to hungry believers in the city (Hartman et al., 2013). In Europe, animal remains suggest that the builders of Stonehenge came together from all over western Britain, bringing with them the pigs and cattle that they would share in communal feasts (Craig et al., 2015). In North America, a millennium ago Anasazi people spatially and symbolically linked *kivas*, in which men conducted secret rituals, with "mealing rooms," in which women worked grinding maize (Mobley-Tanaka, 1997). And in Mesoamerica, texts and images reveal that ancient Maya elites sponsored innumerable rituals accompanied by feasts. Births, initiations, betrothals, weddings, deaths, ancestral/lineage commemorations, calendrical passages, accessions to politico-ritual positions, architectural dedications, and deity celebrations all occasioned feasts (Foias, 2007). Supplying these politically as well as ritually vital events required producing not only the foods that humans would share and those intended as offerings to the deities, but also the containers to store, cook, and serve these foods; the costumes, incense burners, and other ritual paraphernalia that would feature at the celebrations; and the facilities in which everything would take place (Foias, 2007:171–172). The costs of the feasts might well have been increased still further by ritual breakage of the pottery involved and by hosts' giving valuable foods and other gifts to guests, as historic and modern Maya have done (Foias, 2007:174).

Let us briefly revisit Moreaucourt Priory and its fish smokery. Moreaucourt was only one of many medieval communities following Catholic dietary ordinances. Laypeople weren't expected to eschew four-footed-animals' meat completely, but many monastic communities were, and even laypeople followed a liturgical calendar punctuated by numerous fasts and days of abstention from red meat. Europe's Christians, particularly those in religious orders, needed fish. Nature couldn't necessarily keep pace with the demand. In northern France, fish bones found at inland monasteries testify to rising reliance on marine imports as local freshwater fisheries failed to meet needs (Jones, 2007:257). Medieval faunal assemblages confirm fish transport and trading as well as production, earthworks testify to the digging of fish ponds, and texts recount fish donations and fishery allocations (Jones, 2007:256–257). Throughout Europe, Catholic religious demands shaped economic activity.

Many archaeologists argue that beliefs can either spur or delay seismically important economic changes. Hayden's argument that feasting drove plant and animal domestication was discussed in Chapter 3. Fuller and Castillo (2016) describe how cosmologies may propel agricultural diversification. They note the ritual and symbolic importance of sticky foods in East and Southeast Asia, corral paleoethnobotanical and genetic data indicating that ancient people in these regions bred rice and other grains to be increasingly sticky, and conclude that ancient ideologies contributed to the development of modern rice diversity. Dietler (2007) has argued that feasts are ideal venues for incorporating new foods into people's diets; that includes overtly religious as well as merely ritualized celebrations.

Missionary expansions have contributed and even propelled culinary revolutions. Notably, Columbus, Cortes, and their fellow Europeans changed global foodways as they pursued their and their sponsors' political, economic, and religious aims. Some of the changes were even explicitly religious in motivation. Catholic friars in Mexico, for example, issued a ban on amaranth cultivation due to its "idolatrous" uses: Aztecs ritually baked and ate amaranth dough images of Chicomecoatl, Huitzilopochtli, and other indigenous deities (Morán, 2016:89; Pilcher, 1998:35). A millennium earlier, Christianity and bread wheat spread across western Europe in a tag team of spirituality and foodways. (Jones [2007:270] refers to "the evangelism of cross, book and plough.") As a result, at the end of the first millennium CE, western Europeans ate the pale bread wheat that in church became the literal body of Christ[6], while eastern Europeans ate rye, a sheaf of which the pagan deity Jaryla, god of the fields, held in his hand as he rode on his white horse, annually aging, dying, and being reborn (Jones, 2007:262).

Beliefs can also limit people's willingness to change their foodways. Arbuckle (2013), for example, has argued that in Neolithic Anatolia a thousand-year-long delay in some people's acceptance of domesticated cattle stemmed from the symbolic importance of wild cattle in their culture. Herded cows provide foods that wild ones don't (milk! cheese!), but that didn't convince the ancient inhabitants of Çatalhöyük and other central Anatolian Neolithic sites that they were worth keeping. In general, archaeologists accept that faith doesn't necessarily push cultures toward either adopting or rejecting new foods and foodways. It shapes cultures' reactions to economic opportunities and challenges, but not in a uniform fashion.

The archaeology of thus sheds light not just on ancient rituals and belief systems, but also on how those rituals and beliefs influenced people's economies, politics, travels, and personal interactions. This last of this book's topical chapters highlights the extent to which they are all entangled. I hope that in teasing their different subjects apart for the purposes of discussion I have not masked the interreliance of economics, politics, identity, and ideology; I could shift virtually every archaeological case study I've discussed so far to a different chapter and it would still be relevant. The studies I discuss next, however, have a special role. Let us turn now to how archaeology of food can reveal and even improve life in the twenty-first century.

---

[6] Remember the first footnote in this chapter, where I noted that the Vatican requires Catholics to consume pure wheat wafers? The Holy Roman Church has deemed wheat the only acceptable grain for the Holy Eucharist since the eleventh century CE. Spanish missionaries didn't just introduce wheat to the New World; they actively pushed it on Native Americans who thought it tasted terrible (Pilcher, 1998:35).

CHAPTER 8

Archaeology, Food, and the Future

Food is omnipresent in our lives. It plays a prominent role in our economics and our politics, our faiths and our traditions, our private existences and our public events, our routines and our celebrations. It is physically ubiquitous, leaving traces in buildings and on campsites, in our bodies and on our landscapes. A wide variety of archaeological methods allow us, therefore, to study an even wider range of aspects of life in the past. We can study human remains to examine ancient social inequalities (Chapter 4); animal bones to reconstruct ethnic distinctions (Chapter 6); ruined buildings to assess economic strategies (Chapter 3); ceramic scatters and burnt seeds to investigate political power (Chapter 5).

In 2016, Hastorf called for food archaeology to be recognized as its own subdiscipline, of value not just to those of us who are interested in past cultures but also to anyone who wants insights into how humans interact with food. Archaeology allows us to examine foodways through time and across space in a way that no other discipline can. How do we eat? How do we farm? What happens if we farm this way as opposed to that way? History gives us only partial answers to these questions, and the modern world still less insight. If we want to comprehend the range of ways in which we humans can eat, as well as the consequences of choosing certain options, then we have no choice: we must look to archaeology.

Fortunately, plenty of archaeological information already exists about past foodways, and tremendous potential exists for gathering more. Analytical methods are developing rapidly (e.g., Colonese et al., 2017; Hendy et al., 2018b; Jaouen and Pons, 2016; Makarewicz and Sealy, 2015). The world is full of remains as yet unstudied: not only those that remain unrecovered, but also those that lie in museum basements and storage facilities, examined (if at all) using decades-old techniques and without food-related questions in mind. I believe, therefore, that food archaeology is both intellectually valuable and likely to grow in the years to come.

I even believe that the archaeological study of food can make the world a better place. Thinking about food in the past can help us better our own diets; we can use archaeological methods to address serious problems facing the world today. Let us consider a few ways in which the archaeological study of food and foodways might prove useful as we move through the twenty-first century.

Sustainable Food

Archaeologists have long been investigating the ecological impacts of ancient production and consumption strategies. Discoveries about resource use in the past can provide insight into the range of situations in which sustainability is feasible, and help us identify approaches that in the past have led to or mitigated serious environmental degradation (e.g., Altaweel, 2013; Bogaard et al., 2017; Lambrides and Weisler, 2016; Whitaker and Hildebrandt, 2011). In recent years, archaeologists with an interest in the social aspects of food have shown us how political aspirations can drive ecologically inappropriate food production (e.g., Zori et al., 2013), that gender norms and marital status can propel the transplantation of wild resources (Hildebrand, 2003:167–176), and that the symbolic values of various foods can shape whether and how people choose to produce them (e.g., Russell, 2012; Sykes, 2014a).

Archaeology allows us to view human actions and their effects through a uniquely long-term lens. As Frazier (2007) notes, we need such a lens if we are to gauge the sustainability of human resource use: year- or decade-long fluctuations in temperature, rainfall, storm winds, etc. mustn't be mistaken for long-term phenomena. Using archaeological methods, we can evaluate the environmental impacts of human food habits over the course of centuries and even millennia. We can reconstruct the choices that communities made about which foods to eat and how to acquire them; the timing and pace of dietary changes; preceding and ensuing changes in local environments; and, in some cases, the social divisions and pressures that precipitated ecological crises. Such a long-term perspective is an important contribution to the efforts of conservation biologists and ecologists, who historically based their conclusions and recommendations on data covering a decade or less and overlooked the extent to which ancient human dietary urges shaped modern ecosystems (Boivin et al., 2016; Frazier, 2007). Thousands of years ago people were clearing forests to grow their crops, hunting or gathering selected foods into extinction, importing delicacies (and their diseases) into new areas and habitats, allowing domesticates to interbreed with their wild species-mates, and more (Boivin et al., 2016; Grayson, 2001; Hofman and Rick, 2018; Iriarte et al., 2012; Levis et al., 2017; Rick and Erlandson, 2008). From California[1] to Cyprus[2] to Canberra[3] to the Caribbean[4], 'natural' environments are, and long have been, impacted by how we eat.

Food archaeology also helps clarify the origins and development of ongoing ecological challenges. Archaeological data demonstrate that many taxa now seen as environmentally destructive and undesirable were once considered important food sources; many are, in fact, invasive species imported into new areas specifically for eating. Reductions in biodiversity have stemmed from people's desire to protect their foods from competitors and from predators. In England, for example, medieval elites eradicated the bears, wolves, and lynxes that preyed on their valuable deer (see Chapter 4; Sykes, 2017).

As yet, a minority of archaeologists discuss the sustainability of dietary habits in terms of culturally specific food traditions and tastes. One who does is Kitty Emery (2007, 2008), who in multiple papers assesses the extent to which the ancient Maya over-hunted various animal species, and the likelihood that such overhunting contributed to the Classic Maya "collapse" in the ninth century CE. The question isn't whether the Maya drove their preferred species to extinction – they didn't – but whether they altered

[1] American "wild boars" are the feral descendants of pigs brought to the Americas by Spanish conquistadors who wanted a nice supply of pork for their travels.

[2] Fallow deer were extirpated on Cyprus in the sixteenth century CE, saddening many. Should we be cheered by the fact that deer weren't native to the island? They were shipped in roughly ten thousand years ago, by hunters willing to haul them over at least 70 km of open ocean in order to stock their home with venison (Vigne et al., 2014, 2016). They probably brought wild boars over even earlier, more than 12,500 years ago (Vigne et al., 2014).

[3] Captain Cook referred to Australia as 'this continent of smoke' due to the scale of Aboriginal fire use at the time of European contact, and explorer Ernest Giles wrote that Aborigines "were about, burning, burning, ever burning; one would think that they … lived on fire instead of water" (Flannery, 1994:217). Aborigines' "fire-stick farming" created a landscape that was a mosaic of savannas, open woodlands, and denser forests, supporting a variety of animal populations – some of which proved vulnerable to extirpation when the firestick ecologies ended (Bliege Bird et al., 2008; Flannery, 1994; Murphy and Bowman, 2007).

[4] You may not want to eat an opossum, but a millennium or so ago other people did, and they stocked their islands accordingly (Giovas, 2019).

animal distributions and local ecologies to the point that they disrupted their food supply, undermining the stability of their political system and propelling a massive restructuring of their society.

Assuming that hunters generally prefer to concentrate on a few large animal species rather than to scramble after a wide variety of smaller ones, Emery (2007) studied the proportions of large animals (especially white-tailed deer) in Maya zooarchaeological assemblages from different time periods. She found that the proportion of large animals declined slightly during the peak of Classic Maya civilization (i.e., the Late Classic), and then, after the "collapse," (in the Terminal/Postclassic) plummeted. Focusing more tightly on white-tailed deer, she identified a rise in deer consumption during the Late Classic, but again a plunge in the Terminal/Postclassic.

Emery suggests that the Late Classic rise in deer eating may at least in part be attributable to forest clearance for plant food production. During the apogee of the Classic Maya, their large, densely populated settlements were supported by fields and gardens that had once been covered by neotropical forest. White-tailed deer love woodland margins and field edges: they are likely to have appreciated the environments that the Maya were creating near their settlements. Meanwhile, Maya elites (especially those at politically complex sites) clamored for status-enhancing large game. This demand encouraged people not just to intensify their hunting but also to maintain a reliable supply of venison in the form of captive deer herds (Emery, 2007, 2008).

At some sites, the emphasis on large game ended when the Late Classic did (Emery, 2007). At others, people kept eating the same species throughout the "collapse" and afterwards (Emery, 2008). Overall, Maya hunters caused no extinctions nor any regional reduction in biodiversity, and they emphatically did not bring their civilization to an end by overexploiting their meat supply (Emery, 2008; Emery and Brown, 2012).

However, the Classic Maya did depress deer populations living near some sites, relegating themselves to hunting other game. This was particularly the case at the biggest settlements, which relied more heavily on white-tailed deer than smaller settlements did. Perhaps deer were simply more available near big sites, surrounded as they were by particularly large tracts of deforested land and attractive deer habitats (Emery, 2008). At least as likely, though, is that urbanites sought deer out more enthusiastically than villagers did, for political reasons. Looking at changes in faunal data through time, Emery (2008) found that (a) deer consumption peaked during eras of intense political activity and (b) elites' rubbish contained higher proportions of deer than did the trash of lower-class people. The logical inference is that deer were a high-value food, and that eating them was part of how people jockeyed for status. The more people there were jockeying, the greater the pressure they placed on local deer populations. Across the region, varying levels of political activity meant varying human impact on white-tailed deer populations (Emery 2008).

Emery and Brown (2012) add that Maya beliefs about hunting may have helped preserve regional animal populations. Modern highland Maya believe in a supernatural Animal Guardian who protects and oversees wild animals. Hunters conduct ceremonies before and after expeditions and at auspicious dates, often at dedicated hunting shrines. Hunters bring offerings and curated animal parts to the Animal Guardian; the spirit allows them hunting success and recycles the curated bones' life force, regenerating forest populations. Only when the Animal Guardian is content do animals present themselves to hunters as prey, and hunts cannot succeed without such animal participation (Emery and Brown, 2012). Ethnographic, historical, and archaeological evidence all suggest that the ancient Maya may also have believed in an Animal Guardian, whose interests humans must serve if meat is to be made available.

This does not mean that the Classic Maya's ability to avoid overhunting was rooted in conscious attention to hunting sustainably. In conversations, some but not all modern Maya hunters argue that the Animal Guardian sets hunting levels: the spirit world, not the human one, attends to the health of animal populations (Emery and Brown, 2012). Emery and Brown stress that intent is not required for an activity to be sustainable. Hunters don't need to see themselves as primarily responsible for animal populations' wellbeing in order to hunt in ways that maintain it (Emery and Brown, 2012; see also Alvard, 1998). Culture shapes how people eat, and how people eat shapes their environmental impact; whether that impact is largely positive, negative, or mixed depends not on their intentions but on their actions.

Modern Foodways

Archaeological research is also contributing to ongoing conversations about the sustainability of modern foodways. Take, for example, the issue of the environmental impact of meat consumption. Most Westerners today know that meat is ecologically costly to produce. Globally the food system contributes between 19 and 29 percent of greenhouse gas emissions, and in high-income nations roughly 70 percent of those emissions are attributable to animal foods (Behrens et al., 2017). Countries with enthusiastically carnivorous populations contribute disproportionately to global emissions, as do those that enjoy grass-fed as opposed to grain-fed beef: Australia's food-related emissions are more than 200 percent higher than those of similarly wealthy countries, and the USA and Canada's emissions are 40 percent higher (Behrens et al., 2017). Meateating has similarly problematic impacts on eutrophication (abnormal algae growth that disrupts aquatic ecosystems) and on land use (agricultural production occupies approximately one-third of the earth's ice-free land) (Behrens et al., 2017).

A core concern for many meateaters is protein consumption. Indeed, many English-speakers use "protein" when they mean "meat" (frustrating nutritionists, who scream to the winds that the two are not synonyms [e.g., Nestle, 2012]). Men have been particularly invested in eating lots of protein, as modern mass media present protein consumption as a hallmark of modern masculinity (Parasecoli, 2005). Many American men would, in fact, benefit from eating less red meat and less protein in general (US Department of Health and Human Services and US Department of Agriculture, 2015–2020: *Dietary Guidelines for Americans*), but gender norms as well as tastes indicate that access to proteinaceous foods is likely to remain of concern to well-off Westerners as well as needier people around the globe.

How might archaeology help us resolve this concern? Sykes (2017) points out that the study of food in the past may contribute to global food security by encouraging us to reconsider our assumptions about what constitutes food. Around the ancient world we see people eating mice, insects, horses, lizards, dogs, and various plant species that Westerners commonly see as "weeds" (e.g., Fritz, 2007; Hadjikoumis, 2016; Sianto et al., 2012; Sutton, 1995). The handful of grain crops and few domesticated animals that supply the overwhelming bulk of most Westerners' diets represents only a tiny fraction of what people can eat and have eaten.

Broadening our definition of "food" to include more species helps us identify options for feeding the planet that extend beyond the short list of domesticates that at present sustain most of us. As an example, let's consider the autumn of 1848, when "ravaging hordes of crickets" descended on the fields of Mormon settlers in Nevada, plunging them into a struggle against destitution (Madsen and Madsen, 1987). Settlers beat tin pans to scare the insects away; they pulled ropes across the tops of the grain to unseat them; they beat at the cricket-covered plants with everything they could lay their hands on; they deployed fire as well as water to try and protect their crops.

Nothing availed. Settlers described the insects as hideous little beasts, with "an eagle-eyed staring appearance ... [that] suggests ... that it may be the habitation of a vindictive little demon," or as "dumpy, black, swollen-headed ... a cross of the spider on the buffalo" (Call, 1847 and Kane, 1847, cited in Madsen and Madsen, 1987:172). They were nothing but relieved when birds arrived to eat the marauding insects, eventually declaring a "Miracle of the Gulls." Today a monument stands on the grounds of the Mormon temple in Salt Lake City, its inscription reading "Seagull Monument: Erected in Grateful Remembrance of the Mercy of God to the Mormon Pioneers" (Figure 8.1; Madsen and Madsen, 1987).

The settlers' Native neighbors, meanwhile, ate the crickets (Madsen and Madsen, 1987). They gathered the insects in the early morning when they were too chilled to flee, or drove them into baskets, purpose-built corrals, or ditches dug for this specific use. People might have nibbled a live cricket or two, but usually they roasted their catch, sometimes grinding the insects up and making them into cakes or mush, sometimes merely rubbing off the legs and wings before dining. (Nineteenth-century whites described the "fruitcake ... [of the] children of the desert," a sun-dried mix of crushed berries and ground-up grasshoppers." [Bryant, 1848:162]). The recipes were generally simple, but the results widely appreciated, even considered delicacies (Madsen and Kirkman, 1988). (Experimental ethnoarchaeologists have described the taste of a freshly roasted grasshopper as "desert lobster" [Madsen and Kirkman, 1988:596]).

Other kinds of insects have also proven acceptable foods to people living in a wide variety of areas and time periods. Archaeologists have found lice in human feces from Greenland, termites in Oregonian coprolites, and red harvester ants baked into seedcakes in Wyoming (Sutton, 1995). Traces of bogong moths remain on some Australian grinding stones; the largest hearth at a Californian caterpillar procurement site measured 4 by 6 m (Sutton, 1995). Elsewhere archaeologists have identified flies, beetles, ants, lice, moths, caterpillars, and more in contexts that suggest that people were not only eating the insects, they were doing so deliberately (Sutton, 1995).

Insects require far less land and water to raise than mammals (van Huis and Oonincx, 2017). They can live off extremely low-quality food (e.g., chicken manure), which they convert into high-quality edible flesh. As cold-blooded animals, they don't expend energy on maintaining their body temperatures and thus convert their food into flesh far more efficiently than warm-blooded animals do. Insect farming produces far fewer greenhouse gas emissions than standard livestock production. We are surrounded by

(a)   (b)

FIGURE 8.1. Material evidence of varying approaches to insects in the American West. (a) Deposits at Lakeside Cave, UT. Excavated, these ~4500-year-old sediments proved to contain thousands upon thousands of grasshopper remains as well as human feces containing grasshopper parts. From Madsen and Kirkman 1988: fig. 3. © Society for American Archaeology 1988, published by Cambridge University Press. (b) Seagull Monument, Temple Square, Salt Lake City, Utah. Photo by Rich JJ/Wikimedia Commons/CC-BY-SA-3.0.

sustainable food options that also happen to be rich in protein and often vitamins and minerals as well (Sutton, 1995).

Of course, if we want to broaden our diets in service of the planet we needn't immediately leap into entomophagy. (Please don't let me discourage you if you would like to do so, though. As Sutton [1995] cheerfully points out, Westerners have no trouble at all enjoying bee vomitus [honey], and non-insectoid arthropods such as crabs and lobsters fetch high prices at the market. Why not try a cricket or two? You can find cricket chips, ant lollipops, and other potentially delicious options online. Just be wary of wild-caught specimens: you don't want to eat any toxins they may have picked up, and some species are threatened by pollution, pesticides, or overexploitation [van Huis and Oonincx, 2017].)

We can also expand our dietary horizons by consuming a broader range of *parts* of animals and more varied *sources* of animals. For example, many non-vegetarian Westerners eat no animal body tissues other than muscle meat. Rocky Mountain oysters (bull testicles) are a dare or a joke for most urbanites. Few North American or European supermarket meat cases display eyeballs or noses or lungs. Archaeology, like many other disciplines, demonstrates that a wide variety of body parts – even bones, if small or strategically processed – can be consumed (e.g., Arnold and Lyons, 2016; Munro and Bar-Oz, 2005; Reinhard et al., 2007).

Going further, archaeology helps us check our assumptions about what body parts – and what kinds of food more broadly – are to be valued. Going back to Chapter 4, recall that Reitz and colleagues (2006) found that pork, ham, bacon, and spare ribs featured on the tables of historic Charleston's working classes as well as those of its elites. Pig feet and heads could also be found throughout the city, savored by both the upper crust and the lower. In general, researchers could find no consistent differences between the pig remains found at high-status homes and low-status homes. This study reminds us that culinary elegance does not necessarily feature the foods that we appreciate today: that not just the foods that we eat, but also the values that we attach to them, have the potential to change. We needn't begin our quest for more sustainable diets by eating foods that currently strike us as distasteful or even repulsive. We can, instead, rejigger our thinking about which of the foods that we currently eat might be worthy of a more prominent place on our tables.

As for animal sources, a minority of North Americans and Britons eat wild mammals. Why not? Doing so doesn't simply provide us with new sources of food; it might also help protect the foods on which we currently rely. English wild deer cause millions of dollars of damage to crops and forests every year even as Britons import venison from New Zealand (Sykes, 2017). These costs are defrayed at least partly by the sale of hunted venison, but prices are kept limited by the prevalence of farmed and imported venison as well as the general British reliance on other meats (Macmillan and Phillip, 2008). Rabbits are a greater problem, causing in 2008 approximately 115 million pounds in crop damage – an amount roughly one hundred times greater than the value of rabbits in the British human and captive animal food supply (Macmillan and Phillip, 2008; see also B. Potter [1902], *The Tale of Peter Rabbit*). Rabbits – not native to Britain – were a luxury meat in the medieval era, and a thousand years before that Romans living in southern England imported and ate rabbits from southern Europe (Sykes and Curl, 2010). Today Britons eat little wild or domesticated rabbit meat. Adjusting English diets to include more wild venison and rabbit might help protect English agriculture and forestry (Sykes, 2017).

Dietary adjustments are not necessarily easy. How might we encourage people to change their foodways, in service to the planet? Food archaeology, which can track the situations in which past peoples have adjusted their diets as well as those in which they have not, may provide a modicum of insight (e.g., Dietler, 2007; see Chapter 6).

Business and Health

It has been more than 40 years since the archaeologists of the University of Arizona's Garbage Project began sampling modern trash, and by doing so revealing patterns in American food wastage. Chapter 4 summarized Garbage Project archaeologists' discovery that beef and sugar wastage skyrocketed during highly publicized shortages of these foods: panic-buying in bulk led to three times as much food being thrown away as happened normally (Rathje and Murphy, 1992:60–61). This was far from the only Garbage Project discovery with important social implications.

The Garbage Project also proved that what people say they consume on surveys differs pronouncedly from what they actually consume. This is a problem, because even today a preponderance of our knowledge about food wastage comes from consumer surveys that rely on people's ability and willingness to report what they do with a reasonable degree of accuracy. Do we eat as healthily as we claim we do? Not really: at a time when people saw cottage cheese as a classic health food, the amount of it that they ate totaled roughly one-third of what they reported (a difference of 311 percent [Rathje and Murphy, 1992:71]). Conversely, people reported eating far, far fewer potato chips than they actually did: they tallied only 19 percent of the amount represented by the bags in their trash. People *underreported* sugar consumption by 94 percent; bacon consumption by 80 percent; ice cream consumption by 63 percent. They *overreported* vegetable soup consumption by 94 percent, skim milk consumption by 57 percent, and high-fiber cereal by 55 percent (Rathje and Murphy, 1992:71). (Rathje calls this tendency to adjust reporting of unhealthy and healthy foods the "Lean Cuisine syndrome." "Good Provider Syndrome," meanwhile, is the tendency of people to overreport home cooking of fresh ingredients and underreport reliance on ready-to-eat foods. Both syndromes bear loud witness to the pressure that modern Americans feel to adhere to socially valued food behaviors.) There are obvious business implications to these findings: as Humes (2012:155) notes, the data suggest that "the focus groups and consumer preference surveys that so many business decisions are based on are practically worthless."

More serious are the health implications of our inability (or unwillingness) to report our actions with accuracy. How much alcohol do Americans drink? The Garbage Project found people generally underestimating their consumption by 40–60 percent on surveys; 75 percent of households reported no drinking during a typical week, but a check of people's trash revealed that 50 percent of households consumed at least eight beers a week. (These data aren't testifying to holiday drinking, which was apparently rampant in 1990s Tucson. A small study examining the garbage generated on various American holidays found ample drinking debris after every single one. One household's after-Halloween pickup included no food or candy debris but ninety-two beer cans, a bunch of cigarette butts, and nine grocery store bags. An after-President's Day pickup included so many Budweiser containers that it spurred the archaeologists to worry about "pathological alcohol consumption" and hypothesize "that in many American households, the excuse for feasting is that there is a surplus of cash, a day or two off work, and a thirst for ethyl alcohol" [Wilson and Rathje, 2001:413]). These are data of value to everyone interested in public health.

So are data about red meat consumption. Garbage Project archaeologists used the weights printed on discarded meat packaging, minus the fat and bone scraps in the same garbage, to estimate meat consumption in households in different neighborhoods. Comparing their calculations with survey data on meat-eating, they saw that almost everyone's recollections were inaccurate. Part of this was simple rounding-off of awkward numbers like "0.17 lbs." But the rounding was not random: people asked about their beef and pork habits adjusted their estimates in relation to their position in the socioeconomic hierarchy. People living in upscale neighborhoods rounded downwards, whereas lower-income people rounded up (Rathje and Murphy, 1992).

Archaeological food research may thus be useful to both the commercial sector and public health interests. Archaeologists provide information about who consumes what, how much, when, and under what circumstances. Combining our information with data from surveys, focus groups, store loyalty programs, and other sources of consumer behavior data can help researchers understand buying patterns and health vulnerabilities in the present as well as in the past.

Ecology and Garbology

> *In garbage ... there are no half-truths, no spin, no politics. The accrual of what a people ate will be there, master and slave, worker and lord alike, an honest tale of crusts, rinds, bones, and seeds.*
>
> Humes, 2012:146

The Garbage Project also clarified what happens to food after it is thrown away and ends up in a landfill. Digging into New York City's massive[5] Fresh Kills landfill with a 1300-pound bucket auger and a mobile derrick, Garbage Project archaeologists extracted samples of trash from as low as 97 feet below the surface of the landfill. Each dip of the auger – a toothed cylinder that drilled through everything from rotting food to a whole buried car (Humes, 2012:143) – brought the excavators hundreds of pounds of easily datable garbage. Team members took the temperature of each sample and recorded the depth from which it had emerged as well as its date of deposition, easily determined from contents such as legible newspapers or distinctive beer can pull tabs. (Coors, for example, used a particular shape of pull tab only from March 1974 to June 1977 [Rathje and Murphy, 1992:27]).

Every five or ten feet, team members would race over to the surfacing bucket with a plywood board, collecting its contents for more detailed analyses (Rathje and Murphy, 1992). Civil engineers and microbiologists ran in as well, taking samples and placing them in airtight containers so

---

[5] Now closed down, it remains the highest geographic feature on the eastern US seaboard from Florida to Maine. Five hundred and five feet thick in its center, roughly 2.8 by 3.8 miles in area, it is twenty-five times as large as the Great Pyramid at Giza and forty times as large as the Temple of the Sun at Teotihuacan (Rathje and Murphy, 1992:4).

that anaerobic bacteria would survive until they could be analyzed in the lab. Some archaeologists shoveled the still-steaming garbage onto wire mesh screens; some scooped whatever fell through the mesh into bags or canisters; some sorted and bagged the remains that remained on top of the screens; some hurried to get every container safely labeled. No more than twelve minutes after the derrick had hauled the bucket of garbage to the surface, it sat roughly sorted and labeled and ready for transport to various analytical facilities (Rathje and Murphy, 1992).

Garbage Project archaeologists took forty-four such samples at Fresh Kills[6], recording significant differences between deposits excavated at different depths inside the landfill. Samples from the top 35 feet of the mound – up to roughly twenty years in age – remained relatively dry. Hot dogs and bread were easily recognizable, and researchers had no trouble reading lurid headlines in the newspapers they found (Rathje and Murphy [1992:8] cite "Woman Butchered – Ex-Hubby Held" as a gory example). Humes (2012:144) reports that when the auger dumped out a quarter-century-old heap of trash, project leader William Rathje poked his finger into some bright green chunky paste and yelled out "Hey! I think it's guacamole!" Twenty-five years after being thrown out, its avocado slices remained unrotted, "fresher in appearance than it would have looked after just a few days sitting in Rathje's kitchen sink" (Humes, 2012:144).

Decomposition in landfills, it turned out, was no rapid process. In landfills from Arizona to New York, organic remains sat undegraded for decades, their volume staying as high as one-third to two-thirds of the remains in decades-old landfill samples (Rathje and Murphy, 1992:114). After twenty years, a third to a half of discarded food and yard waste remained recognizable. (Rathje apparently enjoyed showing people a decades-old, easily identifiable hot dog [Schiffer, 2017:205].) Those twenty years, moreover, were when that waste had been biodegrading with maximum efficiency; below eight feet deep in a landfill a lack of oxygen means that few efficient microorganisms survive (Rathje and Murphy, 1992:115–117). The slow pace of decomposition was good news in terms of the pace at which toxic substances leach out of landfills – they're "basically just sitting there" (Humes, 2012:158) – but bad news in terms of how long even biodegradable food remains can sit in landfills, filling desperately needed space.

---

[6] They also excavated at more than ten other landfills in the United States and Canada.

The Garbage Project's discoveries about the volume of food in landfills led to another of their key findings: that Americans waste astounding amounts of edible food. The sheer quantity of food in American landfills is shocking. Rathje's team tallied 17 percent of garbage by weight as food, much of it once-edible portions (Humes, 2012:159). In 2012, the Environmental Protection Agency estimated that despite years of efforts to encourage composting, food waste still totaled 14 percent of landfill contents by weight (Humes, 2012:161). Our dumps are full not only of eggshells and coffee grounds, but also of whole Kaiser rolls and expired hamburger meat. According to Rathje, "it was typical for the households we looked at to waste 15 percent of the food they bought" (Humes, 2012:160). The amount of food we waste is no longer news, but the Garbage Project called attention to the problem fifteen years before it became a widespread topic of conversation (Humes, 2012:16).

The Garbage Project also shed light on which *kinds* of food were wasted in higher or lower proportions. Halloween candy? Rarely wasted: our early November garbage is full of empty candy wrappers. Valentine's candy? February garbage includes lots of unopened heart-shaped boxes and pink and red candy packages (Rathje and Murphy, 1992:64). Cultural norms encourage us to give our lovers chocolates, our friends little boxes of slogan-bearing hearts, but the candy's primary value is its social meaning. The food itself often goes straight into the dump.

More broadly, the proportion of food you waste is related to the diversity of your diet. The Garbage Project named this the First Principle of Food Waste: "The more repetitive your diet – the more you eat the same things day after day – the less food you waste" (Rathje and Murphy, 1992:62). Culinary novelty (exotic ingredients, unfamiliar cuts of meat) and culinary specificity (items with singular uses such as hot dog buns and Kaiser rolls) promote food wastage. Those buns get thrown out 30–60 percent of the time! As Schiffer (2017:203) says, "variety may be the spice of life, but in the case of food it comes at a price."

More than 70 percent of US garbage winds up in landfills, but the contents and development of these massive earthworks remained poorly understood until toward the end of the twentieth century. Much of the improved understanding can be attributed to archaeologists. Widespread media attention paid to Rathje and Murphy's 1992 *Rubbish!* led to more civic conversations about landfill alternatives and waste management strategies more broadly (Zimring, 2015). The US Navy, Environmental Protection Agency, and Department of Agriculture funded Garbage Project research to provide information about trash at sea as well as on land

(Harrison, 2012). By the time Rathje died in 2012, the field that he had guided had become a global and interdisciplinary enterprise (Zimring, 2015).

There remains, however, plenty of room for more archaeological research into modern garbage, research that can have concrete impacts not just on how we manage our waste but also on how much waste we generate. It is only by understanding the patterns of our wastage that we can build strategies for combating it. American dining and discard habits have changed since the Garbage Project archaeologists began their well-known work. We no longer eat as we did in the 1990s, let alone the 1970s or the 1950s. More of us care deeply about recycling (not even an option for most people during the decades studied by the Garbage Project), and more of us compost our food scraps. How have the changes in our food habits changed our dumps and landfills? What stories might be told of landfills and household rubbish dumps around the world, in rural as well as urban communities, in rich and poor areas? Engineers, sociologists, biologists, and more study these questions (e.g., Zimring and Rathje, 2012), but an archaeological perspective is necessary if we want to study the deposits themselves and how they change through time.

One recent study is that of Lehmann (2015), who decided to explore Australian food wastage using a Garbage Project approach. Waste audits and surveys have estimated that food comprises roughly 40 percent of household garbage in New South Wales and Victoria, meaning that the average household annually wastes more than a thousand dollars of food. In New South Wales alone, roughly 800,000 tons of food waste enters landfills every year.

Lehmann wanted to know what kinds of food were being wasted. She worked on a small scale: three samples, from three towns in the Grampians region. She found that even if townspeople were composting or feeding scraps to their chickens, food waste still comprised nearly half (46 percent) of their garbage. Food packaging was another 19 percent. On average, households threw out more than ten pounds of food and more than three pounds of recyclable food packaging per week (Lehmann, 2015). Pasta sauce and baby food jars lay next to yogurt containers, soup cans, and cereal boxes, many – especially large glass jars and recyclable plastic containers – still containing food that had passed its sell-by date. (If people were trying to save money by buying their food in larger packages that sold for fewer dollars per pound than smaller packages, their efforts didn't always pan out well [Lehmann, 2015].) Food packaging deposited in recycling bins was far cleaner, and fewer containers had passed their "best by" dates.

The Garbage Project itself is ended, its archaeologists scattered. But archaeological investigations of food discard continue, helping shape how children as well as adults treat our food. When the head of the Columbus Solid Waste Authority wanted to educate kids about waste, he contacted Dr. Sheli Smith, who decades earlier had been one of the first archaeology students to participate in Garbage Project research. Smith devised a school project wherein children would study the food waste in their cafeteria as well as their own trash, and tour the local landfill. One hundred high schoolers participated in a pilot study. They were shocked to discover that their cafeteria was wasting sixty-five pounds of edible food a day, so much that it would take twenty thousand household composters to process it all. According to Smith, "it changed their behavior. They stopped wasting so much food. They demanded the school stop wasting so much" (Humes, 2012:166). Columbus schools expanded the project to other schools in the district, then classrooms all over Ohio took it up, with children as young as eight developing plans to minimize the amount of food they waste (Humes, 2012). Today you can find garbology projects for kids all over the internet and garbology programs at various colleges (e.g., Camp 2010).

The archaeology of garbage reveals to us the realities and the consequences of our actions. In doing so it enables us, young and old, to improve our economies and our environments.

Wildlife Conservation

The above statement is as true in other countries as it is in our own, and for the same reason: unlike interviewees, garbage neither misremembers nor tries to present itself in a positive light. We can, therefore, analyze garbage around the world in order to investigate a wide variety of ecologically as well as socially and/or legally undesirable behaviors. For example, archaeological investigations of what modern people eat can contribute to the global battle against illegal bushmeat hunting.

Bushmeat – meat from wild animals – is immensely important in many areas of the world. According to Brashares et al. (2014), wild taxa support 15 percent of the global population, and more than a billion people depend on wild-caught meat as their main source of animal protein. Harvesting wildlife produces more than $400 billion dollars annually (Brashares et al., 2014). Sadly, even as wild animals sustain many of the globe's poorest people, their populations are declining.

These declines have terrible consequences not just for animal biodiversity or regional environments. Researchers link wildlife depletion to human-on-human violence, vigilantism, regional destabilization, and even terrorism. When wildlife populations drop, hunters and fishers striving to maintain yields acquire trafficked workers – children as well as adults. Forced labor (slavery) becomes increasingly common. According to the United Nations Office on Drugs and Crime (2011), men sold to fishing boats off the coast of Thailand work 18- to 20-hour days without pay, often starving or physically abused and sometimes murdered. Child labor enables West African communities to hunt farther and farther from their wildlife-depopulated homelands (Brashares et al., 2014). Criminal and terrorist organizations traffic in looted wildlife (as well as looted artifacts) as they pursue profits (Brashares et al., 2014; Campbell, 2013; Danti, 2015). Armed conflicts ensue, as criminals, governments, and civilian vigilantes attempt to exploit and/or protect wildlife populations (Brashares et al., 2014).

Many of the most famous endangered species – elephants, gorillas, black rhinoceroses – are hunted for reasons other than their meat, but a significant number of species are pursued specifically so that they may be eaten. Surveys about bushmeat hunting encounter many of the problems documented by Rathje and the Garbage Project forty years ago, from inaccurate memories (Golden et al., 2013) to concern about social costs and even legal liabilities (Borgerson, 2015; Borgerson et al., 2018). Archaeology can help clarify the frequencies with which these animals are hunted (Is bushmeat hunting a regular occurrence or a rare event? Does the answer vary by species?); the timing of their pursuit (Is it year-round? Is it during seasons when food is otherwise scarce? Is it focused around religious festivals or other special events?); and who hunts and who eats them (the poor? the wealthy? the Westernized, or the un-Westernized? those with large families to feed, those whose jobs put them in close proximity with wild animals, those who view bushmeat hunting as their job and sell it to others?).

Schmitt and Lupo (2008), curious about the relationship between food and socioeconomic status, tallied the faunal remains in modern Central African garbage deposits in order to investigate whether or not wealthier and higher-status farming households eat more meat and a greater diversity of species. They traveled to a pair of small villages nestled on the edge of the Ngotto Forest Reserve in the Central African Republic, where farmers grow manioc, peanuts, maize, and yams and raise a scattering of chickens. Some keep goats and a few raise ducks, but these animals are rarely eaten: most of the villagers' meat is bushmeat, bought or traded from forest-dwelling foragers, with some also caught in illegal snares that the farmers set up near their fields (Schmitt and Lupo, 2008). Common prey include duikers, giant pouched rats, guenon monkeys, brush-tailed porcupines, and other small animals. Some regularly eaten animals, such as tree pangolins, are currently listed as *Vulnerable* on the International Union for Conservation of Nature's Red List of Threatened Species, due in significant part to bushmeat hunting pressure (IUCN, 2017). (Chimpanzees are "rarely taken" and gorillas "uncommon," but neither is completely off the menu [Schmitt and Lupo, 2008:318]).

Schmitt and Lupo selected twelve households' middens for study. In these middens they identified twenty-two different animal species, including duikers, monkeys, rats, porcupines, and forest hogs. They compared the bones discarded by different households to find that the wealthiest villagers ate the most meat and the greatest variety of animals: the village chief's garbage included a bigger and more diverse assemblage of animal bones than that of any other household. Contrary to what we might expect, though, the chief's family didn't eat more large-bodied game or "high-quality" cuts of meat than other people. (Once again, we food archaeologists are reminded to check our assumptions about what foods people value.) Rather, people chose their meats according to personal taste. "Some individuals prefer stewed pouched rat with a side of manioc, others prefer roasted porcupine, and the Ndele pastor informed us that his favorite meal is civet cooked in oil" (Schmitt and Lupo, 2008:321). In addition, two households weren't notably wealthy but ate considerable meat from varied animal species: hunters lived in these households, producing meat that fed their families and that got sold to other families in the local markets. For some villagers bushmeat hunting is a full-time job.

Schmitt and Lupo conducted their research with an eye to classic archaeological questions about the relationships among status, wealth, and what people eat. These are excellent questions, and their findings along those lines are fascinating. We can, however, also look at their work with an eye to modern conservation issues. What if any endangered taxa are eaten in these two villages, and in what numbers? What social group(s) drive the bushmeat hunting?

Schmitt and Lupo reported no endangered species' remains in any of the middens they analyzed. This suggests that pangolin meat isn't regularly consumed in these two villages. Many bones could not be assigned to specific species, however, so it's very possible that endangered animals were in the samples without the archaeologists' knowledge. Medium-sized duikers' and medium monkeys' bones were in every single household's trash, and larger duikers and monkeys were also recovered (Schmitt and Lupo, 2008). Given local hunting norms, some of these bones surely derive

(a)   (b)

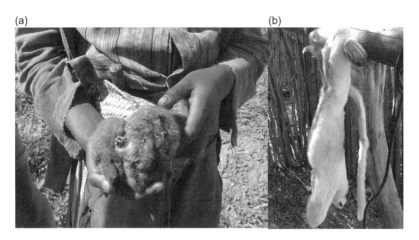

FIGURE 8.2. Malagasy bushmeat. (a) A child holds mouse lemur (*Microcebus rufus*) carcasses. Photo courtesy of K. Kling. (b) A Verreaux's sifaka (*Propithecus verreauxi*) carcass. Photo courtesy of E. Rakotomalala. In the summer of 2018, the IUCN classified mouse lemurs as *Vulnerable* and sifakas as *Endangered*.

from Bay and Yellow-Backed duikers, both of which are classified *Near Threatened* on the IUCN Red List; some of the monkey bones might likewise derive from species of concern to the IUCN. As for who's responsible for the hunting, Schmitt and Lupo clearly show that the wealthy are bushmeat's primary consumers, but they're neither its primary producers nor associated with the consumption of any particular species.

A similar study, but one focused explicitly on wildlife conservation as well as human health, is underway in Madagascar. Doctoral student Katharine Thompson is using archaeological methods in combination with survey data to investigate bushmeat hunting outside Kirindy Mitea National Park. Rural Malagasy people eat a range of vulnerable and endangered species, including lemurs, fosa, and bats (Figure 8.2; Borgerson, 2015; Razafimanahaka et al., 2012). Excavations of household middens reveal which species are targeted and by whom. Survey data enrich these findings, allowing Thompson to explore how economics (poverty, employment status, ownership of domestic animals), ideology (belief in traditional Malagasy taboos), gender (rural Malagasy norms dictate female cooks and male hunters), family structure (number of children), and health (nutritional or disease stresses) shape people's consumption of endangered species. Results are not yet in, but when they are, much more will be known about who consumes lemurs and why, enabling wildlife conservationists to target their efforts more effectively.

In Conclusion

Food archaeology offers us perspective. It alerts us to our assumptions and our biases – about what constitutes food, about the places in which we might find it, and about what we might do with it when we have it. It illuminates life in the past, and it reveals to us the possible consequences of actions we might take in the present.

Today, some archaeologists are making concrete efforts to improve modern foodways. Take, for example, the members of the Food Evolutions project (www.foodevolutions.org). This project, a collaboration between researchers at University College Dublin and Washington College (Maryland) as well as Irish company Odaios Foods, presents itself as "a natural extension of experimental archaeology." The project's researchers plan to use ancient techniques and recipes to enhance modern eating, increasing the nutritional value of prepared foods and encouraging us to eat sustainably. Their position is that ancient technologies were designed to "increase the density and bioavailability of nutrients:" why not deploy them today? Ancient people commonly consumed their milk fermented rather than fresh, as yogurt or cheese or kefir. They foraged for edible wild plants and ate varieties of grain that feature on few modern tables. Members of the Food Evolutions project make cheese and taste carefully harvested seaweed as they try to fuse modern and ancient foodways. They argue that doing so connects people more closely with their food supply, encouraging them to eat in ways that are healthy, sustainable, and, importantly, enjoyable.

Most of us who study the archaeology of food have no such intentions. We seek to illuminate what happened long ago rather than to alter what we do now, although we believe that our discoveries help us understand ourselves and to make informed decisions for the future. On a day-to-day basis, however, we do the research that we do because we love figuring out how people fed themselves and their loved ones, and why they made the choices that they did. We study past foodways because we're fascinated by how competitors struggled for power and how allies strove for peace; how families celebrated and how communities mourned; how ethnicities developed and how faiths worshiped. The archaeology of food is, in many ways, an archaeology of life, complex and colorful and fascinating. Welcome to the field: grab a trowel and dig in.

References

Adams, J. L., 2014. Ground stone use-wear analysis: A review of terminology and experimental methods. *Journal of Archaeological Science* 48, 129–138.

Adler, C. J., Dobney, K., Weyrich, L. S., Kaidonis, J., Walker, A. W., Haak, W., Bradshaw, C. J. A., Townsend, G., Soltysiak, A., Alt, K. W., Parkhill, J., and Cooper, A., 2013. Sequencing ancient calcified dental plaque shows changes in oral microbiota with dietary shifts of the Neolithic and Industrial revolutions. *Nature Genetics* 45, 450–455.

Albarella, U., and Serjeantson, D., 2002. A passion for pork: Meat consumption at the British Late Neolithic site of Durrington Walls. In Miracle, P., and Milner, N., (eds.), *Consuming Passions and Patterns of Consumption*. McDonald Institute for Archaeological Research, Cambridge, pp. 33–49.

Albarella, U., and Thomas, R., 2002. They dined on crane: Bird consumption, wild fowling, and status in medieval England. *Acta Zoologica Cracoviensia* 45, 23–38.

Alberti, B., 2006. Archaeology, men, and masculinities. In Nelson, S. M., (ed.), *Handbook of Gender in Archaeology*. Altamira, Lanham, MD, pp. 401–434.

Allen, J., Cosgrove, R., and Garvey, J., 2016. Optimality models and the food quest in Pleistocene Tasmania. *Journal of Anthropological Archaeology* 44, 206–215.

Allen, M. W., 2016. Food, fighting, and fortifications in pre-European New Zealand: Beyond the ecological model of Maori warfare. In VanDerwarker, A. M., and Wilson, G. D., (eds.), *The Archaeology of Food and Warfare: Food Insecurity in Prehistory*. Springer, New York, pp. 41–59.

Allison, A., 1991. Japanese mothers and Obentos: The lunch box as ideological state apparatus. *Anthropological Quarterly* 64, 195–208.

Altaweel, M., 2013. Simulating the effects of salinization on irrigation agriculture in Southern Mesopotamia. In Wilkinson, T. J., Gibson, M., Christiansen, J., and Widell, M., (eds.), *How Small-Scale Processes Contributed to the Growth of Early Civilizations*. Archaeopress, Oxford, pp. 219–239.

Alvard, M. S., 1998. Evolutionary ecology and resource conservation. *Evolutionary Anthropology: Issues, News, and Reviews* 7, 62–74.

Ambrose, S. H., Buikstra, J. E., and Krueger, H. W., 2003. Status and gender differences in diet at Mound 72, Cahokia, revealed by isotopic analysis of bone. *Journal of Anthropological Archaeology* 22, 217–226.

Andrefsky, W., Jr., 2005. *Lithics: Macroscopic Approaches to Analysis*, 2nd ed. Cambridge University Press, New York.

Andrefsky W., Jr., 2009. The analysis of stone tool procurement, production, and maintenance. *Journal of Archaeological Research* 17, 65–103.

Aranda Jiménez, G., and Montón-Subías, S., 2011. Feasting Death: Funerary rituals in the Bronze Age societies of South-Eastern Iberia. In Aranda Jiménez, G., Montón-Subías, S., and Sánchez-Romero, M., (eds.), *Guess Who's Coming to Dinner: Feasting Rituals in the Prehistoric Societies of Europe and the Near East*. Oxbow, Oxford, pp. 130–157.

Arbuckle, B., 2013. The late adoption of cattle and pig husbandry in Neolithic Central Turkey. *Journal of Archaeological Science* 40, 1805–1815.

Arbuckle, B. S., Kansa, S. W., Kansa, E., Orton, D., Çakırlar, C., Gourichon, L., Atıcı, L., Galik, A., Marciniak, A., Mulville, J., Buitenhuis, H., Carruthers, D., Cupere, B. D., Demirergi, A., Frame, S., Helmer, D., Martin, L., Peters, J., Pöllath, N., Pawłowska, K., Russell, N., Twiss, K., and Würtenberger, D., 2014. Data sharing reveals complexity in the westward spread of domestic animals across Neolithic Turkey. *PLOS ONE* 9, e99845.

Armelagos, G. J., Sirak, K., Werkema, T., and Turner, B. L., 2014. Analysis of nutritional disease in prehistory: the search for scurvy in antiquity and today. *International Journal of Paleopathology* 5, 9–17.

Arnold, E. R., and Lyons, D., 2016. Ethnozooarchaeology of professional butchering in the Mahas region, Sudan. In Broderick, L. G., (ed.), *People with Animals: Perspectives and Studies in Ethnozooarchaeology*. Oxbow, Oxford, pp. 78–86.

Arnold, P. P., 1991. Eating landscape: Human sacrifice and sustenance in Aztec Mexico. In Carrasco, D., (ed.), *To Change Place: Aztec Ceremonial Landscapes*. University of Colorado Press, Boulder, CO, pp. 219–231.

Ashby, S. P., 2002. The role of zooarchaeology in the interpretation of socioeconomic status: A discussion with reference to Medieval Europe. *Archaeological Review from Cambridge* 18, 37–59.

Atalay, S., and Hastorf, C. A., 2006. Food, meals, and daily activities: Food *habitus* at Neolithic Çatalhöyük. *American Antiquity* 71, 283–319.

Bakels, C., 1996. Growing grain for others or how to detect surplus production? *Journal of European Archaeology* 4, 329–336.

Bar-Yosef, O., and Khazanov, A., (eds.), 1992. *Pastoralism in the Levant: Archaeological Materials in Anthropological Perspectives*. Prehistory Press, Madison.

Barrett, J. H., Locker, A. M., and Roberts, C. M., 2004. 'Dark Age Economics' revisited: The English fish bone evidence AD 600–1600. *Antiquity* 78, 618–636.

Barton, H., and Torrence, R., 2015. Cooking up recipes for ancient starch: Assessing current methodologies and looking to the future. *Journal of Archaeological Science* 56, 194–201.

Bauer, A. J., 1990. Millers and grinders: technology and household economy in Meso-America. *Agricultural History* 64, 1–17.

Baumann, T. E., 2009. The web of cultural identity: a case study of African-American identity and "soul food". *Tennessee Archaeology* 4, 66–93.

Bayliss-Smith, T. P., and Hviding, E., 2015. Landesque capital as an alternative to food storage in Melanesia: irrigated taro terraces in New Georgia, Solomon Islands. *Environmental Archaeology* 20, 425–436.

Beard, M., 2008. *The Fires of Vesuvius: Pompeii Lost and Found*. Harvard University Press, Cambridge, MA.

Beard, M., 2015. *SPQR: A History of Ancient Rome*. Liveright, New York.

Beaudry, M., 2013. Feasting on broken glass: Making a meal of seeds, bones, and sherds. *Northeast Historical Archaeology* 42, 184–200.

Beaudry, M. C., 2010. Privy to the feast: 'Eighty to supper tonight'. In Symonds, J., (ed.), *Table Settings: The Material Culture and Social Context of Dining, AD 1700–1900*. Oxbow, Oxford, pp. 62–79.

Beaumont, J., Montgomery, J., Buckberry, J., and Jay, M., 2015. Infant mortality and isotopic complexity: new approaches to stress, maternal health, and weaning. *American Journal of Physical Anthropology* 157, 441–457.

Becker, S. K., 2013. *Labor and the Rise of the Tiwanaku State (AD 500–1100): A Bioarchaeological Study of Activity Patterns*. Ph.D. thesis, Department of Anthropology, University of North Carolina, Chapel Hill, NC.

Beehr, D., and Ambrose, S. H., 2007. Investigating maize usage-patterns through stable isotope analysis of Mississippian pot-sherd residue. In Twiss, K. C., (ed.), *The Archaeology of Food and Identity*. Center for Archaeological Investigations, Southern Illinois University Carbondale, Occasional Paper no. 34. Center for Archaeological Investigations, Carbondale, IL, pp. 171–191.

Behrens, P., Kiefte-de Jong, J. C., Bosker, T., Rodrigues, J. F. D., de Koning, A., and Tukker, A., 2017. Evaluating the environmental impacts of dietary recommendations. *Proceedings of the National Academy of Sciences* 114, 13412–13417.

Ben-Shlomo, D., Hill, A. C., and Garfinkel, Y., 2009. Feasting between the revolutions: Evidence from Chalcolithic Tel Tsaf, Israel. *Journal of Mediterranean Archaeology* 22, 129–150.

Ben-Shlomo, D., Shai, I., Zukerman, A., and Maeir, A. M., 2008. Cooking identities: Aegean-style cooking jugs and cultural interaction in Iron Age Philistia and neighboring regions. *American Journal of Archaeology* 112, 225–246.

Bentley, R. A., 2006. Strontium isotopes from the earth to the archaeological skeleton: A review. *Journal of Archaeological Method and Theory* 13, 135–187.

Bentley, R. A., Wahl, J., Price, T. D., and Atkinson, T. C., 2008. Isotopic signatures and hereditary traits: Snapshot of a Neolithic community in Germany. *Antiquity* 82, 290–304.

Bettinger, R. L., 1991. *Hunter-Gatherers: Archaeological and Evolutionary Theory*. Plenum, New York.

Birch, T. E., 2015. Use-wear analysis, metal. In Metheny, K. B., and Beaudry, M., (eds.), *Archaeology of Food: An Encyclopedia*. Rowman & Littlefield, Lanham, MD, pp. 525–526.

Black, J. A., Cunningham, G., Fluckiger-Hawker, E., Robson, E., and Zólyomi, G., 1998-. A hymn to Ninkasi: Translation. *The Electronic Text Corpus of Sumerian Literature*. Oxford. www-etcsl.orient.ox.ac.uk/ (accessed July 18, 2017).

Bliege Bird, R., Bird, D. W., Codding, B. F., Parker, C. H., and Jones, J. H., 2008. The "fire stick farming" hypothesis: Australian Aboriginal foraging strategies, biodiversity, and anthropogenic fire mosaics. *Proceedings of the National Academy of Sciences* 105, 14796–14801.

Blitz, J. H., 1993. Big pots for big shots: Feasting and storage in a Mississippian community. *American Antiquity* 58, 80–96.

Bogaard, A., 2004. *Neolithic Farming in Central Europe: An Archaeobotanical Study of Crop Husbandry Practices*. Routledge, New York.

Bogaard, A., Charles, M. P., Twiss, K. C., Fairbairn, A. S., Yalman, E. N., Filipovic, D., Demirergi, G. A., Ertuğ, F., Russell, N., and Henecke, J., 2009. Private pantries and celebrated surplus: Saving and sharing food at Neolithic Çatal-höyük, central Anatolia. *Antiquity* 83, 649–668.

Bogaard, A., Evans, J., Henton, E. M., Twiss, K. C., Charles, M. P., Vaiglova, P., and Russell, N., 2014a. Locating land use at Neolithic Çatalhöyük, Turkey: The implications of $^{87}Sr/^{86}Sr$ signatures in plants and sheep tooth sequences. *Archaeometry* 56, 860–877.

Bogaard, A., Filipovic, D., Fairbairn, A., Green, L., Stroud, E., Fuller, D., and Charles, M., 2017. Agricultural innovation and resilience in a long-lived early farming community: The 1,500-year sequence at Neolithic to early Chalco-lithic Çatalhöyük, central Anatolia. *Anatolian Studies* 67, 1–28.

Bogaard, A., Krause, R., and Strien, H.-C., 2011. Towards a social geography of cultivation and plant use in an early farming community: Vaihingen an der Enz, south-west Germany. *Antiquity* 85, 395–416.

Bogaard, A., Ryan, P., Yalman, N., Asouti, E., Twiss, K. C., Mazzucato, C., and Farid, S., 2014b. Assessing outdoor activities and their social implications at Çatalhöyük. In Hodder, I., (ed.), *Integrating Çatalhöyük: Themes from the 2000–2008 Seasons*. Cotsen Institute of Archaeology UCLA, Los Angeles, pp. 123–148.

Boivin, N., Fuller, D. Q., and Crowther, A., 2012. Old World globalization and the Columbian exchange: Comparison and contrast. *World Archaeology* 44, 452–469.

Boivin, N., Fuller, D. Q., and Crowther, A., 2015. Old World globalization and food exchanges. In Metheny, K. B., and Beaudry, M., (eds.), *Archaeology of Food: An Encyclopedia*. Rowman & Littlefield, Lanham, MD, pp. 350–356.

Boivin, N. L., Zeder, M. A., Fuller, D. Q., Crowther, A., Larson, G., Erlandson, J. M., Denham, T., and Petraglia, M. D., 2016. Ecological consequences of human niche construction: Examining long-term anthropogenic shaping of global species distributions. *Proceedings of the National Academy of Sciences* 113, 6388–6396.

Bolender, D. J., 2015. From surplus land to surplus production in the Viking Age settlement of Iceland. In Morehart, C., and De Lucia, K., (eds.), *Surplus: The Politics of Production and the Strategies of Everyday Life*. University Press of Colorado, Boulder, CO, pp. 153–174.

Borgerson, C., 2015. Optimizing conservation policy: The importance of seasonal variation in hunting and meat consumption on the Masoala Peninsula of Madagascar. *Oryx* 50, 405–418.

Borgerson, C., Johnson, S. E., Louis, E. E., Holmes, S. M., Anjaranirina, E. J. G., Randriamady, H. J., and Golden, C. D., 2018. The use of natural resources to

improve income, health, and nutrition within the forests of Kianjavato, Madagascar. *Madagascar Conservation & Development* 13, 45–52.

Borgna, E., 2004. Social meanings of food and drink consumption at LMIII
Phaistos. In Halstead, P., and Barrett, J. C., (eds.), *Food, Cuisine, and Society
in Prehistoric Greece*. Oxbow, Oxford, pp. 174–195.

Bosi, G., Mercuri, A. M., Guarnieri, C., and Mazzanti, M. B., 2009. Luxury food
and ornamental plants at the 15th century A.D. Renaissance court of the Este
family (Ferrara, northern Italy). *Vegetation History and Archaeobotany* 18,
389–402.

Bottéro, J. (transl. Fagan, T. L.), 2004. *The Oldest Cuisine in the World: Cooking in
Mesopotamia*. University of Chicago Press, Chicago.

Bourdieu, P., 1984. *Distinction: A Social Critique of the Judgement of Taste*. Harvard
University Press, Cambridge.

Brady, J. E., and Peterson, P. A., 2008. Re-envisioning Ancient Maya ritual assemblages. In Fogelin, L., (ed.), *Religion, Archaeology, and the Material World*.
Center for Archaeological Investigations, Southern Illinois University Carbondale. Occasional Paper no. 36. Center for Archaeological Investigations, Carbondale, IL, pp. 78–96.

Braje, T. J., and Rick, T. C., 2013. From forest fires to fisheries management:
Anthropology, conservation biology, and historical ecology. *Evolutionary
Anthropology: Issues, News, and Reviews* 22, 303–311.

Brashares, J. S., Abrahms, B., Fiorella, K. J., Golden, C. D., Hojnowski, C. E.,
Marsh, R. A., McCauley, D. J., Nuñez, T. A., Seto, K., and Withey, L., 2014.
Wildlife decline and social conflict. *Science* 345, 376–378.

Bray, T., 2003a. Inka pottery as culinary equipment: Food, feasting, and gender in
Imperial state design. *Latin American Antiquity* 14, 3–28.

Bray, T., 2015. Ritual commensality between human and non-human persons:
Investigating native ontologies in the Late Pre-Columbian Andean world. In
Pollock, S., (ed.), *Between Feasts and Daily Meals: Towards an Archaeology of
Commensal Spaces*. Topoi, Berlin, pp. 225–241.

Bray, T. L., 2003b. The commensal politics of early states and empires. In Bray, T.
L., (ed.), *The Archaeology and Politics of Food and Feasting in Early States and
Empires*. Kluwer Academic/Plenum, New York, pp. 1–13.

Brettell, R., Montgomery, J., and Evans, J., 2012. Brewing and stewing: The effect of
culturally mediated behaviour on the oxygen isotope composition of ingested
fluids and the implications for human provenance studies. *Journal of Analytical Atomic Spectrometry* 27, 778–785.

Britton, K., Müldner, G., and Bell, M., 2008. Stable isotope evidence for salt-marsh
grazing in the Bronze Age Severn Estuary, UK: Implications for palaeodietary
analysis at coastal sites. *Journal of Archaeological Science* 35, 2111–2118.

Brown, J. A., and Kelly, J. E., 2015. Surplus labor, ceremonial feasting, and social
inequality at Cahokia: A study in social process. In Morehart, C. T., and De
Lucia, K., (eds.), *Surplus: The Politics of Production and the Strategies of Everyday
Life*. University Press of Colorado, Boulder, CO, pp. 221–244.

Brumbach, H. J., and Jarvenpa, R., 2006. Gender dynamics in hunter-gatherer
societies: Archaeological methods and perspectives. In Nelson, S. M., (ed.),
Handbook of Gender in Archaeology. Altamira, Lanham, MD, pp. 503–536.

Brumberg, J. J., 1988. *Fasting Girls: The Emergence of Anorexia Nervosa as a Modern Disease*. Harvard University Press, Cambridge, MA.

Brumfiel, E. M., 1991. Weaving and cooking: Women's production in Aztec Mexico. In Gero, J. M., and Conkey, M. W., (eds.), *Engendering Archaeology: Women and Prehistory*. Blackwell, Cambridge, MA, pp. 224–252.

Brumfiel, E. M., and Earle, T. K., 1987. Specialization, exchange, and complex societies: An introduction. In Brumfiel, E. M., and Earle, T. K., (eds.), *Specialization, Exchange, and Complex Societies*. Cambridge University Press, Cambridge, pp. 1–9.

Bruno, M. C., and Sayre, M. P., 2017. Social paleoethnobotany: New contributions to archaeological theory and practice. In Sayre, M. P., and Bruno, M. C., (eds.), *Social Perspectives on Ancient Lives from Paleoethnobotanical Data*. Springer, New York, pp. 1–13.

Bryant, E., 1848. *What I Saw in California: Being the Journal of a Tour by the Emigrant Route and South Pass of the Rocky Mountains, across the Continent of North America, The Great Desert Basin, and through California*. D. Appleton, New York.

Buckley, R., Morris, M., Appleby, J., King, T., O'Sullivan, D., and Foxhall, L., 2013. 'The king in the car park': New light on the death and burial of Richard III in the Grey Friars church, Leicester, in 1485. *Antiquity* 87, 519–538.

Burton, J. H., and Price, T. D., 2000. The use and abuse of trace elements for palaeodietary research. In Ambrose, S., and Katzenberg, M. A., (eds.), *Biogeochemical Approaches to Palaeodietary Analysis*. Kluwer Academic/Plenum, New York, pp. 159–171.

Bynum, C. W., 1987. *Holy Feast and Holy Fast: The Religious Significance of Food to Medieval Women*. University of California Press, Berkeley.

Camp, S. L., 2010. Teaching with trash: Archaeological insights on university waste management. *World Archaeology* 42, 430–442.

Campana, D. V., and Crabtree, P. J., 2006. The diet of Washington's soldiers at Valley Forge during the winter of 1777–1778. In Maltby, M., (ed.), *Integrating Zooarchaeology*. Oxbow, Oxford, pp. 27–32.

Campbell, P. B., 2013. The illicit antiquities trade as a transnational criminal network: Characterizing and anticipating trafficking of cultural heritage. *International Journal of Cultural Property* 20, 113–153.

Carrasco, D., 1995. Cosmic jaws: We eat the gods and the gods eat us. *Journal of the American Academy of Religion* 63, 429–463.

Casella, E. C., and Fowler, C., 2005. Beyond identification: An introduction, *The Archaeology of Plural and Changing Identities: Beyond Identification*. Springer, New York, pp. 1–8.

Castillo Butters, L. J., and Castillo, S. U., 2007. The Mochicas. In Silverman, H., and Isbell, W., (eds.), *Handbook of South American Archaeology*. Springer, New York, pp. 707–729.

Chan, B., Viner, S., Pearson, M. P., Albarella, U., and Ixer, R., 2016. Resourcing Stonehenge: Patterns of human, animal, and goods mobility in the late Neolithic. In Leary, J., and Kador, T., (eds.), *Moving on in Neolithic Studies: Understanding Mobile Lives*. Oxbow, Oxford, pp. 28–44.

Chase, B., Meiggs, D., Ajithprasad, P., and Slater, P. A., 2014. Pastoral land-use of the Indus Civilization in Gujarat: Faunal analyses and biogenic isotopes at Bagasra. *Journal of Archaeological Science* 50, 1–15.

Cheetham, D., 2010. Corn, colanders, and cooking: Early maize processing in the Maya lowlands and its implications. In Staller, J. E., and Carrasco, M. D., (eds.), *Pre-Columbian Foodways: Interdisciplinary Approaches to Food, Culture, and Markets in Mesoamerica*. Springer, New York, pp. 345–368.

Chevillot, C., 2007. La broche à rôtir articulée de Port-Sainte-Foy: Un instrument privilégié des banquets de la fin de l'Âge du Bronze sur la façade atlantique. In Burgess, C., Topping, P., and Lynch, F., (eds.), *Beyond Stonehenge: Essays on the Bronze Age in Honour of Colin Burgess*. Oxbow, Oxford, pp. 361–366.

Chicoine, D., 2011. Feasting landscapes and political economy at the Early Horizon center of Huambacho, Nepeña Valley, Peru. *Journal of Anthropological Archaeology* 30, 432–453.

Childe, V. G., 1928. *The Most Ancient East: The Oriental Prelude to European Prehistory*. Kegan, London.

Clavel, B., 2001. L'Animal dans l'alimentation médiévale et moderne en France du Nord (XIIe–XVIIe siècles). *Revue Archéologique de Picardie* 19, 1–204.

Clendinnen, I., 1995 [1991]. *Aztecs: An Interpretation*. Cambridge University Press, New York.

Cobo, B., 1963 [1653]. *History of the Inca Empire*. University of Texas Press, Austin.

Coe, S. D., 1994. *America's First Cuisines*. University of Texas Press, Austin.

Coe, S. D., and Coe, M. D., 2007. *The True History of Chocolate*. Thames & Hudson, London.

Collins, M. J., and Copeland, L., 2011. Ancient starch: Cooked or just old? *Proceedings of the National Academy of Sciences of the United States of America* 108, E145–E145.

Colonese, A. C., Hendy, J., Lucquin, A., Speller, C. F., Collins, M. J., Carrer, F., Gubler, R., Kühn, M., Fischer, R., and Craig, O. E., 2017. New criteria for the molecular identification of cereal grains associated with archaeological artefacts. *Scientific Reports* 7, 6633.

Conkey, M. W., and Spector, J., 1984. Archaeology and the study of gender. In Schiffer, M. B., (ed.), *Advances in Archaeological Method and Theory*, vol. 7. Academic Press, New York, pp. 1–38.

Conklin, B., 1995. "Thus are our bodies, thus was our custom": Mortuary cannibalism in an Amazonian society. *American Ethnologist* 22, 75–101.

Cool, H. E. M., 2006. *Eating and Drinking in Roman Britain*. Cambridge University Press, Cambridge.

Copeland, L., and Hardy, K., 2018. Archaeological starch. *Agronomy* 8, 4.

Costin, C. L., 2016. Who benefits? Structural change and lived experience in the late prehispanic Andes. In Hegmon, M., (ed.), *Archaeology of the Human Experience*. Archeological Papers No. 27. American Anthropological Association, Washington, DC, pp. 120–142.

Counihan, C. M., 1999. *The Anthropology of Food and Body: Gender, Meaning and Power*. Routledge, New York.

Coy, J., and Hamilton-Dyer, S., 2005. "Flesh, Fish, Biscuit and Beer": Victuals for the ship. In Gardiner, J., (ed.), *Before the Mast: Life and Death Aboard the Mary Rose*. Mary Rose Trust/Oxbow, Oxford, pp. 602–612.

Crabtree, P., 2006. Women, gender, and pastoralism. In Nelson, S. M., (ed.), *Handbook of Gender in Archaeology*. Altamira, Lanham, MD, pp. 571–592.

Crader, D. C., 1984. The zooarchaeology of the Storehouse and the Dry Well at Monticello. *American Antiquity* 49, 542–558.

Crader, D. C., 1990. Slave diet at Monticello. *American Antiquity* 55, 690–717.

Craig, O. E., Shillito, L.-M., Albarella, U., Viner-Daniels, S., Chan, B., Cleal, R., Ixer, R., Jay, M., Marshall, P., Simmons, E., Wright, E., and Pearson, M. P., 2015. Feeding Stonehenge: Cuisine and consumption at the Late Neolithic site of Durrington Walls. *Antiquity* 89, 1096–1109.

Croucher, S. K., 2011. 'A concubine is still a slave': Sexual relations and Omani colonial identities in nineteenth-century East Africa. In Voss, B. L., and Casella, E., (eds.), *The Archaeology of Colonialism: Intimate Encounters and Sexual Effects*. Cambridge University Press, Cambridge, pp. 67–84.

Crowther, A., Haslam, M., Oakden, N., Walde, D., and Mercader, J., 2014. Documenting contamination in ancient starch laboratories. *Journal of Archaeological Science* 49, 90–104.

Cuéllar, A. M., 2013. The archaeology of food and social inequality in the Andes. *Journal of Archaeological Research* 21, 123–174.

Cummings, L. S., Voss, B. L., Yu, C. Y., Kováčik, P., Puseman, K., Yost, C., Kennedy, R., and Kane, M. S., 2014. *Fan* and *Tsai*: Intracommunity variation in plant-based food consumption at the Market Street Chinatown, San Jose, California. *Historical Archaeology* 48, 143–172.

Curet, L. A., and Pestle, W. J., 2010. Identifying high-status foods in the archeological record. *Journal of Anthropological Archaeology* 29, 413–431.

Currie, T. E., Bogaard, A., Cesaretti, R., Edwards, N., Francois, P., Holden, P., Hoyer, D., Korotayev, A., Manning, J., Moreno Garcia, J. C., Oyebamiji, O. K., Petrie, C., Turchin, P., Whitehouse, H., and Williams, A., 2015. Agricultural productivity in past societies: Toward an empirically informed model for testing cultural evolutionary hypotheses. *Cliodynamics: The Journal of Quantitative History and Cultural Evolution* 6, 24–56.

D'Arms, J. H., 2004. The culinary reality of Roman upper-class convivia: Integrating texts and images. *Comparative Studies in Society and History* 46, 428–450.

Dahlin, B. H., Bair, D., Beach, T., Moriarty, M., and Terry, R., 2010. The dirt on food: Ancient feasts and markets among the Lowland Maya. In Staller, J. E., and Carrasco, M. D., (eds.), *Pre-Columbian Foodways: Interdisciplinary Approaches to Food, Culture, and Markets in Mesoamerica*. Springer, New York, pp. 191–232.

Danti, M. D., 2015. Ground-based observations of cultural heritage incidents in Syria and Iraq. *Near Eastern Archaeology* 78, 132–141.

Daróczi-Szabó, L., 2004. Animal bones as indicators of *kosher* food refuse from 14th century AD Buda, Hungary. In O'Day, S. J., van Neer, W., and Ervynck, A., (eds.), *Behaviour Behind Bones: The Zooarchaeology of Religion, Ritual, Status, and Identity*. Oxbow, Oxford, pp. 252–261.

Davidson, J., 2016. *Sacred Rice: An Ethnography of Identity, Environment, and Development in Rural West Africa.* Oxford University Press, New York.

DeFrance, S. D., 2009. Zooarchaeology in complex societies: Political economy, status, and ideology. *Journal of Archaeological Research* 17, 105–168.

DeFrance, S. D., 2014. The luxury of variety: Animals and social distinction at the Wari site of Cerro Baúl, Southern Peru. In Arbuckle, B. S., and McCarty, S. A., (eds.), *Animals and Inequality in the Ancient World.* University Press of Colorado, Boulder, CO, pp. 63–84.

Demirergi, A., Twiss, K., Bogaard, A., Green, L., Ryan, P., and Farid, S., 2014. Of bins, basins and banquets: Storing, handling, and sharing at Neolithic Çatalhöyük. In Hodder, I., (ed.), *Integrating Çatalhöyük: Themes from the 2000–2008 Seasons.* Cotsen Institute of Archaeology UCLA, Los Angeles, pp. 91–108.

Dennell, R. W., 1979. Prehistoric diet and nutrition: Some food for thought. *World Archaeology* 11, 121–135.

Deori, B. G., 2016. Indigenous foodways of the Galos: A challenge to archaeology. *Journal of Indo-Pacific Archaeology* 37, 59–63.

DeVault, M., 1991. *Feeding the Family.* University of Chicago Press, Chicago.

Dibble, H. L., Holdaway, S. J., Lin, S. C., Braun, D. R., Douglass, M. J., Iovita, R., McPherron, S. P., Olszewski, D. I., and Sandgathe, D., 2016. Major fallacies surrounding stone artifacts and assemblages. *Journal of Archaeological Method and Theory*, 1–39.

Dietler, M., 2001. Theorizing the feast: Rituals of consumption, commensal politics, and power in African contexts. In Dietler, M., and Hayden, B., (eds.), *Feasts: Archaeological and Ethnographic Perspectives on Food, Politics, and Power.* Smithsonian Institution Press, Washington, DC, pp. 65–114.

Dietler, M., 2003. Clearing the table: Some concluding reflections on commensal politics and imperial states. In Bray, T. L., (ed.), *The Archaeology and Politics of Food and Feasting in Early States and Empires.* Kluwer Academic/Plenum, New York, pp. 271–284.

Dietler, M., 2006. Alcohol: Anthropological/archaeological perspectives. *Annual Review of Anthropology* 35, 229–249.

Dietler, M., 2007. Culinary encounters: Food, identity, and colonialism. In Twiss, K. C., (ed.), *The Archaeology of Food and Identity.* Center for Archaeological Investigations, Southern Illinois University Carbondale, Occasional Paper no. 34. Center for Archaeological Investigations, Carbondale, IL, pp. 218–242.

Dietler, M., 2011. Feasting and fasting. In Insoll, T., (ed.), *The Oxford Handbook on the Archaeology of Ritual and Religion.* Oxbow, Oxford, pp. 179–194.

Dietler, M., and Hayden, B., (eds.), 2001. *Feasts: Archaeological and Ethnographic Perspectives on Food, Politics, and Power.* Smithsonian Institution Press, Washington, DC.

Dietler, M., and Herbich, I., 2001. Feasts and labor mobilization: Dissecting a fundamental economic practice. In Dietler, M., and Hayden, B., (eds.), *Feasts: Archaeological and Ethnographic Perspectives on Food, Politics, and Power.* Smithsonian Institution Press, Washington, D.C., pp. 240–264.

Diez-Martín, F., Sánchez, P., Domínguez-Rodrigo, M., Mabulla, A., and Barba, R., 2009. Were Olduvai Hominins making butchering tools or battering tools?

Analysis of a recently excavated lithic assemblage from BK (Bed II, Olduvai Gorge, Tanzania). *Journal of Anthropological Archaeology* 28, 274–289.

Diez-Martín, F., Sanchez Yustos, P., Domínguez-Rodrigo, M., Mabulla, A. Z. P., Bunn, H. T., Ashley, G. M., Barba, R., and Baquedano, E., 2010. New insights into hominin lithic activities at FLK North Bed I, Olduvai Gorge, Tanzania. *Quaternary Research* 74, 376–387.

Douglas, M., 1975. *Deciphering a Meal, Implicit Meanings: Essays in Anthropology*. Routledge & Paul, Boston, pp. 249–275.

Dubreuil, L., and Savage, D., 2014. Ground stones: A synthesis of the use-wear approach. *Journal of Archaeological Science* 48, 139–153.

Dupont, F., 2015. Food, gender, and sexuality. In Wilkins, J., and Nadeau, R., (eds.), *A Companion to Food in the Ancient World*. John Wiley and Sons, West Sussex, UK, pp. 76–84.

Dyer, C. C., 1988. Change in diet in the Late Middle Ages: The case of harvest workers. *Agricultural History Review* 36, 21–38.

Earle, T., and Christenson, A., (eds.), 1980. *Modeling Change in Prehistoric Subsistence Economies*. Academic Press, New York.

Ebeling, J. R., 2015. Tools/utensils, ground stone. In Metheny, K. B., and Beaudry, M., (eds.), *Archaeology of Food: An Encyclopedia*. Rowman & Littlefield, New York, pp. 506–508.

Ellis, S. J. R., 2004. The distribution of bars in Pompeii: Archaeological, spatial and viewshed analyses. *Journal of Roman Archaeology* 17, 371–384.

Elston, R. G., Zeanah, D. W., and Codding, B. F., 2014. Living outside the box: An updated perspective on diet breadth and sexual division of labor in the Prearchaic Great Basin. *Quaternary International* 352, 200–211.

Emerson, T. E., Hedman, K. M., Hargrave, E. A., Cobb, D. E., and Thompson, A. R., 2017. Paradigms lost: Reconfiguring Cahokia's Mound 72 beaded burial. *American Antiquity* 81, 405–425.

Emery, K. F., 2003. The noble beast: Status and differential access to animals in the Maya world. *World Archaeology* 34, 498–515.

Emery, K. F., 2007. Assessing the impact of ancient Maya animal use. *Journal for Nature Conservation* 15, 184–195.

Emery, K. F., 2008. A zooarchaeological test for dietary resource depression at the end of the Classic Period in the Petexbatun, Guatemala. *Human Ecology* 36, 617–634.

Emery, K. F., and Brown, L. A., 2012. Maya hunting sustainability: Perspectives from past and present. In Chacon, R. J., and Mendoza, R. G., (eds.), *The Ethics of Anthropology and Amerindian Research: Reporting on Environmental Degradation and Warfare*. Springer New York, New York, NY, pp. 79–116.

Ervynck, A., van Neer, W., Hüster-Plogmann, H., and Schibler, J., 2003. Beyond affluence: The zooarchaeology of luxury. *World Archaeology* 34, 428–441.

Evershed, R. P., 2008. Organic residue analysis in archaeology: The archaeological biomarker revolution. *Archaeometry* 50, 895–924.

Faccia, K., Waters-Rist, A., Lieverse, A. R., Bazaliiskii, V. I., Stock, J. T., and Katzenberg, M. A., 2016. Diffuse idiopathic skeletal hyperostosis (DISH) in a middle Holocene forager from Lake Baikal, Russia: Potential causes and the effect on quality of life. *Quaternary International* 405, 66–79.

Fales, F. M., and Rigo, M., 2014. Everyday life and food practices in Assyrian military encampments. In Milano, L., and Bertoldi, F., (eds.), *Paleonutrition and Food Practices in the Ancient Near East: Towards a Multidisciplinary Approach, History of the Ancient Near East Vol. 14.* S.A.R.G.O.N. Editrice e Libreria, Padova, pp. 413–437.

Faust, A., and Lev-Tov, J., 2011. The constitution of Philistine identity: Ethnic dynamics in twelfth to tenth century Philistia. *Oxford Journal of Archaeology* 30, 13–31.

Fitchen, J. M., 1998. Hunger, malnutrition, and poverty in the contemporary United States: Some observations on their social and cultural context. *Food and Foodways* 2, 309–333.

Fitzpatrick, S. M., (eds.), 2018. *Ancient Psychoactive Substances.* University Press of Florida, Gainesville, FL.

Flannery, T., 1994. *The Future Eaters: An Ecological History of the Australasian Lands and People.* Reed, Port Melbourne.

Fletcher, A., and Campbell, S., 2015. It is ritual, isn't it? Mortuary and feasting practices at Domuztepe. In Kerner, S., Chou, C., and Warmind, M., (eds.), *Commensality: From Everyday Food to Feast.* Bloomsbury, New York, pp. 109–124.

Flickema, T., 1981. The Siege of Cuzco. *Revista de Historia de América* 92, 17–47.

Foias, A. E., 2007. Ritual, politics, and pottery economies in the Classic Maya Southern Lowlands. In Wells, E. C., and Davis-Salazar, K. L., (eds.), *Meso-american Ritual Economy: Archaeological and Ethnological Perspectives.* University Press of Colorado, Boulder, CO, pp. 167–194.

Forbes, H., 1995. The identification of pastoralist sites within the context of estate-based agriculture in ancient Greece: Beyond the 'transhumance versus agro-pastoralism' debate. *Annual of the British School at Athens* 90, 325–338.

Forbes, H., 2016. Surplus, storage, and status in a rural Greek community. *World Archaeology*, 8–25.

Fowles, S., 2008. Steps toward an archaeology of taboo. In Fogelin, L., (ed.), *Religion, Archaeology, and the Material World.* Center for Archaeological Investigations, Southern Illinois University, Carbondale, IL, pp. 15–37.

Fox, R., and Harrell, K., 2008. An invitation to war: Constructing alliances and allegiances through Mycenean palatial feasts. In Baker, S., Allen, M., Middle, S., and Poole, K., (eds.), *Food and Drink in Archaeology I: University of Nottingham Postgraduate Conference 2007.* Prospect Books, Trowbridge, pp. 28–35.

Franklin, M., 2001. The archaeological and symbolic dimensions of soul food: Race, culture, and Afro-Virginian identity. In Orser, C. E., Jr., (ed.), *Race, Material Culture, and the Archaeology of Identity.* University of Utah Press, Salt Lake City, pp. 88–107.

Frazier, J., 2007. Sustainable use of wildlife: The view from archaeozoology. *Journal for Nature Conservation* 15, 163–173.

Friedel, D., and Reilly F. K., III, 2010. The flesh of God: Cosmology, food, and the origins of political power in ancient Southeastern Mesoamerica. In Staller, J. E., and Carrasco, M. D., (eds.), *Pre-Columbian Foodways: Interdisciplinary*

Approaches to Food, Culture, and Markets in Mesoamerica. Springer, New York, pp. 635–680.

Frison, G. C., 1968. A functional analysis of certain chipped stone tools. *American Antiquity* 33, 149–155.

Fritz, G. J., 2007. Pigweeds for the ancestors: Cultural identities and archaeobotanical identification methods. In Twiss, K. C., (ed.), *The Archaeology of Food and Identity.* Center for Archaeological Investigations, Southern Illinois University Carbondale, Occasional Paper no. 34. Center for Archaeological Investigations, Carbondale, IL, pp. 288–307.

Fullagar, R., Stephenson, B., and Hayes, E., 2017. Grinding grounds: Function and distribution of grinding stones from an open site in the Pilbara, Western Australia. *Quaternary International* 427, 175–183.

Fuller, D. Q., and Castillo, C., 2016. Diversification and cultural construction of a crop: The case of glutinous rice and waxy cereals in the food cultures of Eastern Asia. In Lee-Thorp, J., and Katzenberg, M. A., (eds.), *The Oxford Handbook of the Archaeology of Food and Diet.* Oxford University Press, Oxford. http://dx.doi.org/10.1093/oxfordhb/9780199694013.013.8

Gál, E., and Kunst, G. K., 2014. Offered to gods, eaten by people: Bird bones from the sanctuary of Jupiter Heliopolitanus in Carnuntum–Mühläcker (Austria). *International Journal of Osteoarchaeology* 24, 336–346.

Gamza, T., and Irish, J., 2012. A comparison of archaeological and dental evidence to determine diet at a predynastic Egyptian site. *International Journal of Osteoarchaeology* 22, 398–408.

Gat, J. R., 1996. Oxygen and hydrogen isotopes in the hydrologic cycle. *Annual Review of Earth and Planetary Sciences* 224, 225–262.

Gero, J. M., 1992. Feasts and females: Gender ideology and political meals in the Andes. *Norwegian Archaeological Review* 25, 1–16.

Gero, J. M., 2003. Feasting and the practice of stately manners. In Bray, T. L., (ed.), *The Archaeology and Politics of Food and Feasting in Early States and Empires.* Kluwer Academic/Plenum, New York, pp. 285–288.

Gifford-Gonzalez, D., 1993. Gaps in zooarchaeological analyses of butchery. Is gender an issue? In Hudson, J., (ed.), *Bones to Behavior: Ethnoarchaeological and Experimental Contributions to the Interpretation of Faunal Remains.* Southern Illinois University Press, Carbondale, pp. 181–199.

Gifford-Gonzalez, D., 2008. Thoughts on a method for zooarchaeological study of daily life. In Montón Subías, S., and Sánchez-Romero, M., (eds.), *Engendering Social Dynamics: The Archaeology of Maintenance Activities.* BAR International Series, Vol. 1862. BAR Publishing, Oxford, pp. 15–23.

Gijanto, L., and Walshaw, S., 2014. Ceramic production and dietary changes at Juffure, Gambia. *African Archaeological Review* 31, 265–297.

Gill, R. B., 2001. *The Great Maya Droughts: Water, Life, and Death.* University of New Mexico Press, Albuquerque.

Giovas, C. M., 2019. The beasts at large: Perennial questions and new paradigms for Caribbean translocation research. Part I: Ethnozoogeography of mammals. *Environmental Archaeology*, 24, 182–98.

Gokee, C. and Logan, A. L., 2014. Comparing craft and culinary practice in Africa: Themes and perspectives. *African Archaeological Review* 31, 87–104.

Golden, C. D., Wrangham, R. W., and Brashares, J. S., 2013. Assessing the accuracy of interviewed recall for rare, highly seasonal events: The case of wildlife consumption in Madagascar. *Animal Conservation* 16, 597–603.

Goldstein, D. J., and Hageman, J. B., 2010. Power plants: Paleobotanical evidence of rural feasting in Late Classic Belize In Staller, J. E., and Carrasco, M. D., (eds.), *Pre-Columbian Foodways: Interdisciplinary Approaches to Food, Culture, and Markets in Mesoamerica*. Springer, New York, pp. 421–440.

Goldstein, D. J., and Shimada, I., 2010. Feeding the fire: Food and craft production in the Middle Sicán period (AD 950–1050). In Klarich, E. A., (ed.), *Inside Ancient Kitchens: New Directions in the Study of Daily Meals and Feasts.* University Press of Colorado, Boulder, CO, pp. 161–189.

González Carretero, L., Wollstonecroft, M., and Fuller, D. Q., 2017. A methodological approach to the study of archaeological cereal meals: A case study at Çatalhöyük East (Turkey). *Vegetation History and Archaeobotany*, 26, 415–432.

Goody, J., 1982. *Cooking, Cuisine, and Class: A Study in Comparative Sociology.* Cambridge University Press, Cambridge.

Goring-Morris, N., and Horwitz, L. K., 2007. Funerals and feasts during the Pre-Pottery Neolithic B of the Near East. *Antiquity* 81, 902–919.

Gose, P., 2000. The state as a Chosen Woman: Brideservice and the feeding of tributaries in the Inka Empire. *American Anthropologist* 102, 84–97.

Goulder, J., 2015. Administrators' bread: An experiment-based re-assessment of the functional and cultural role of the Uruk bevel-rim bowl. *Antiquity* 84, 351–362.

Graff, S. R., 2018. Archaeological studies of cooking and food preparation. *Journal of Archaeological Research* 26, 305–351.

Graff, S. R., and Rodríguez-Alegría, E., (eds.), 2012. *The Menial Art of Cooking: Archaeological Studies of Cooking and Food Preparation.* University Press of Colorado, Boulder, CO.

Grau-Sologestoa, I., 2017. Socio-economic status and religious identity in medieval Iberia: The zooarchaeological evidence. *Environmental Archaeology* 24, 189–199.

Gray, A., 2008. "The Privilege of Civilisation": Cultural change at the Victorian table. In Baker, S., Allen, M., Middle, S., and Poole, K., (eds.), *Food and Drink in Archaeology I: University of Nottingham Postgraduate Conference 2007.* Prospect Books, Trowbridge, pp. 38–46.

Grayson, A. K., 1991. *Assyrian Rulers of the Early First Millenium I (1114–859 BC).* University of Toronto Press, Toronto.

Grayson, D. K., 2001. The archaeological record of human impacts on animal populations. *Journal of World Prehistory* 15, 1–68.

Greenfield, H., and Bouchnik, R., 2011. *Kashrut* and *shechita*: The relationship between dietary practices and ritual slaughtering of animals on Jewish identity. In Amundsen-Meyer, L., Engel, N., and Pickering, S., (eds.), *Identity Crisis: Archaeological Perspectives on Social Identity. Proceedings of the 42nd (2010) Annual Chacmool Archaeology Conference.* Chacmool Archaeological Association, University of Calgary, Calgary, pp. 106–120.

Gregoricka, L. A., and Sheridan, S. G., 2013. Ascetic or affluent? Byzantine diet at the monastic community of St. Stephen's, Jerusalem from stable carbon and nitrogen isotopes. *Journal of Anthropological Archaeology* 32, 63–73.

Gremillion, K. J., 2011. *Ancestral Appetites: Food in Prehistory*. Cambridge University Press, Cambridge

Gremillion, K. J., 2015. Human behavioral ecology and paleoethnobotany. In Marston, J. M., and D'Alpoim Guedes, J., (eds.), *Method and Theory in Paleoethnobotany*. University Press of Colorado, Boulder,CO, pp. 339–354.

Grieco, A. J., 1999. Food and social classes in Late Medieval and Renaissance Italy. In Flandrin, J.-L., and Montanari, M. (eds.), *Food: A Culinary History* (transl. A. Sonnenfeld). Columbia University Press, New York, pp. 302–312.

Grine, F. E., Sponheimer, M., Ungar, P. S., Lee-Thorp, J., and Teaford, M. F., 2012. Dental microwear and stable isotopes inform the paleoecology of extinct hominins. *American Journal of Physical Anthropology* 148, 285–317.

Groot, M., and Lentjes, D., 2013. Studying subsistence and surplus production. In Groot, M., Lentjes, D., and Zeiler, J., (eds.), *Barely Surviving or More Than Enough? The Environmental Archaeology of Subsistence, Specialisation and Surplus Food Production*. Sidestone Press, Leiden, pp. 7–28.

Guerra-Doce, E., 2015. Psychoactive substances in prehistoric times: examining the archaeological evidence. *Time and Mind* 8, 91–112.

Gumerman, G., IV, 1997. Food and complex societies. *Journal of Archaeological Method and Theory* 4, 105–139.

Gumerman, G., IV, 2002. Llama power and empowered fishermen: Food and power at Pacatnamu, Peru. In O'Donovan, M., (ed.), *The Dynamics of Power*. Occasional Paper No. 30. Center for Archaeological Investigations, Southern Illinois University, Carbondale, IL, pp. 238–256.

Gumerman, G., IV, 2010. Big hearths and big pots: Moche feasting on the north coast of Peru. In Klarich, E. A., (ed.), *Inside Ancient Kitchens: New Directions in the Study of Daily Meals and Feasts*. University Press of Colorado, Boulder, CO, pp. 111–131.

Gurven, M., Borgerhoff Mulder, M., Hooper, P. L., Kaplan, H., Quinlan, R., Sear, R. Schniter, E., Rueden, C.V., Bowles, S., Hertz, T., and Bell, A., 2010. Domestication alone does not lead to inequality: Intergenerational wealth transmission among horticulturalists. *Current Anthropology* 51, 49–64.

Hadjikoumis, A., 2016. Every dog has its day: Cynophagy, identity, and emerging complexity in Early Bronze Age Attica, Greece. In Marom, N., Yeshurun, R., Weissbrod, L., and Bar-Oz, G., (eds.), *Bones and Identity: Zooarchaeological Approaches to Reconstructing Social and Cultural Landscapes in Southwest Asia*. Oxbow, Oxford, pp. 225–245.

Halstead, P., 1987. Traditional and ancient rural economy in Mediterranean Europe: *plus ça change? Journal of Hellenic Studies* 107, 77–87.

Halstead, P., 1989. The economy has a normal surplus: Economic stability and social change among early farming communities of Thessaly, Greece. In Halstead, P., and O'Shea, J., (eds.), *Bad Year Economics: Cultural Responses to Risk and Uncertainty*. Cambridge University Press, Cambridge, pp. 68–80.

Halstead, P., 1996. Pastoralism or household herding? Problems of scale and specialization in early Greek animal husbandry. *World Archaeology* 28, 20–42.

Halstead, P., 2014. *Two Oxen Ahead: Pre-Mechanized Farming in the Mediterranean*. Wiley, Malden, MA.

Halstead, P., 2015. Feast, food, and fodder in Neolithic-Bronze Age Greece: Commensality and the construction of value. In Pollock, S., (ed.), *Between Feasts and Daily Meals: Toward an Archaeology of Commensal Spaces*. Topoi, Berlin, pp. 29–61.

Halstead, P., and Isaakidou, V., 2011. Political cuisine: Rituals of commensality in the Neolithic and Bronze Age Aegean. In Aranda Jiménez, G., Montón-Subías, S., and Sánchez-Romero, M., (eds.), *Guess Who's Coming to Dinner: Feasting Rituals in the Prehistoric Societies of Europe and the Near East*. Oxbow, Oxford, pp. 91–108.

Halstead, P., and O'Shea, J. M., eds., 1982. A friend in need is a friend indeed: Social storage and the origins of social ranking. In *Ranking, Resource, and Exchange*. Cambridge: Cambridge University Press, 1982, pp. 92–99.

Hamilakis, Y., 1999. Food technologies/technologies of the body: The social context of wine and oil production and consumption in Bronze Age Crete. *World Archaeology* 31, 38–54.

Hamilakis, Y., 2008. Time, performance, and the production of a mnemonic record: From feasting to an archaeology of eating and drinking. In Hitchcock, L., Laffineur, R., and Crowley, J., (eds.), *DAIS: The Aegean Feast*. Liège and Austin: University of Liege and University of Texas at Austin, pp. 3–19.

Hamilakis, Y., 2014. *Archaeology and the Senses: Human Experience, Memory, and Affect*. Cambridge University Press, Cambridge.

Hamilakis, Y., and Harris, K., 2011. The social zooarchaeology of feasting: The evidence from the "ritual" deposit at Nopigeia-Drapanias. 10th IntCretCongr (Khania 2006), A, 101–119.

Hamilakis, Y., and Konsolaki, E., 2004. Pigs for the gods: Burnt animal sacrifices as embodied rituals at a Mycenean sanctuary. *Oxford Journal of Archaeology* 23, 135–151.

Hamilakis, Y., and Sherratt, S., 2012. Feasting and the consuming body in Bronze Age Crete and Early Iron Age Cyprus. In Cadogan, G., Iakovou, M., Kopaka, K., and Whitley, J., (eds.), *Parallel Lives: Ancient Island Societies in Crete and Cyprus*. The British School at Athens (BSA Studies 20), London, pp. 187–207.

Harrison, J., 2012. William L. Rathje: 1945–2012. *UA News*, June 5, 2012. http://web.sbs.arizona.edu/college/news/william-l-rathje-1945-2012 (accessed January 8, 2018).

Hartman, G., Bar-Oz, G., Bouchnick, R., and Reich, R., 2013. The pilgrimage economy of Early Roman Jerusalem (1st century BCE–70 CE) reconstructed from the $\delta^{15}N$ and $\delta^{13}C$ values of goat and sheep remains. *Journal of Archaeological Science* 40, 4369–4376.

Hassig, R., 2016. Aztec logistics and the unanticipated consequences of empire. In VanDerwarker, A. M., and Wilson, G. D., (eds.), *The Archaeology of Food and Warfare: Food Insecurity in Prehistory*. Springer, New York, pp. 149–160

Hastorf, C. A., 1991. Gender, space, and food in prehistory. In Gero, J. M., and Conkey, M. W., (eds.), *Engendering Archaeology: Women and Prehistory*. Wiley-Blackwell, Cambridge, MA, pp. 132–159.

Hastorf, C. A., 2001. Agricultural production and consumption. In D'Altroy, T. N., and Hastorf, C. A., (eds.), *Empire and Domestic Economy*. Springer US, New York, pp. 155–178.

Hastorf, C. A., 2003. Andean luxury foods: Special food for the ancestors, deities and the elite. *Antiquity* 77, 545–554.

Hastorf, C. A., 2010. Sea changes in stable communities: What do small changes in practices at Çatalhöyük and Chiripa imply about community making? In Bandy, M., and Fox, J., (eds.), *Becoming Villagers: Comparing Early Village Societies*. University of Arizona Press, Tucson, pp. 140–161.

Hastorf, C. A., 2012. The *habitus* of cooking practices at Neolithic Çatalhöyük: What was the place of the cook? In Graff, S. R., and Rodríguez-Alegría, E., (eds.), *The Menial Art of Cooking: Archaeological Studies of Cooking and Food Preparation*. University Press of Colorado, Boulder, pp. 65–86.

Hastorf, C. A., 2015. Steamed or boiled: Identity and value in food preparation. In Pollock, S., (ed.), *Between Feasts and Daily Meals: Towards an Archaeology of Commensal Spaces*. Topoi, Berlin, pp. 243–276.

Hastorf, C. A., 2016. *The Social Archaeology of Food: Thinking about Eating from Prehistory to the Present*. Cambridge University Press, New York.

Hastorf, C. A., and Foxhall, L., 2017. The social and political aspects of food surplus. *World Archaeology*, 49, 26–39.

Hastorf, C. A., and Weismantel, M., 2007. Food: Where opposites meet. In Twiss, K. C., (ed.), *The Archaeology of Food and Identity*. Center for Archaeological Investigations, Southern Illinois University Carbondale, Occasional Paper no. 34. Center for Archaeological Investigations, Carbondale, IL, pp. 308–333.

Hayden, B., 1992. Models of domestication. In Price, T. D., and Gebauer, A. B., (eds.), *Transitions to Agriculture in Prehistory*. Monographs in World Archaeology 4. Prehistory Press, Madison, WI, pp. 11–19.

Hayden, B., 2001. Fabulous feasts: A prolegomenon to the importance of feasting. In Dietler, M., and Hayden, B., (eds.), *Feasts: Archaeological and Ethnographic Perspectives on Food, Politics, and Power*. Smithsonian Institution Press, Washington, DC, pp. 23–64.

Hayden, B., 2003. Were luxury foods the first domesticates? Ethnoarchaeological perspectives from Southeast Asia. *World Archaeology* 34, 458–469.

Hayden, B., 2014. *The Power of Feasts: From Prehistory to the Present*. Cambridge University Press, Cambridge.

Heiss, A. G., Antolín, F., Bleicher, N., Harb, C., Jacomet, S., Kühn, M., Marinova, E., Stika, H.-P., and Valamoti, S. M., 2017. State of the (t)art: Analytical approaches in the investigation of components and production traits of archaeological bread-like objects, applied to two finds from the Neolithic lakeshore settlement Parkhaus Opéra (Zürich, Switzerland). *PLOS ONE* 12, e0182401.

Hendon, J. A., 2000. Having and holding: Storage, memory, knowledge, and social relations. *American Anthropologist* 102, 42–53.

Hendy, J., Warinner, C., Bouwman, A., Collins, M. J., Fiddyment, S., Fischer, R., Hagan, R., Hofman, C. A., Holst, M., Chaves, E., Klaus, L., Larson, G., Mackie, M., McGrath, K., Mundorff, A. Z., Radini, A., Rao, H., Trachsel, C., Velsko, I. M., and Speller, C. F., 2018a. Proteomic evidence of dietary sources in ancient dental calculus. *Proceedings of the Royal Society B* 285, 20180977.

Hendy, J., Welker, F., Demarchi, B., Speller, C., Warinner, C., and Collins, M. J., 2018b. A guide to ancient protein studies. *Nature Ecology and Evolution* 2, 791–799.

Henry, A. G., Brooks, A. S., and Piperno, D. R., 2014. Plant foods and the dietary ecology of Neanderthals and early modern humans. *Journal of Human Evolution* 69, 44–54.

Henton, E., Martin, L., Garrard, A., Jourdan, A.-L., Thirlwall, M., and Boles, O., 2017. Gazelle seasonal mobility in the Jordanian steppe: The use of dental isotopes and microwear as environmental markers, applied to Epipalaeolithic Kharaneh IV. *Journal of Archaeological Science: Reports* 11, 147–158.

Henton, E., McCorriston, J., Martin, L., and Oches, E. A., 2014. Seasonal aggregation and ritual slaughter: Isotopic and dental microwear evidence for cattle herder mobility in the Arabian Neolithic. *Journal of Anthropological Archaeology* 33, 119–131.

Hesse, B., 1990. Pig lovers and pig haters: Patterns of Palestinian pork production. *Journal of Ethnobiology* 10, 195–225.

Hesse, B., and Wapnish, P., 1997. Can pig remains be used for ethnic diagnosis in the ancient Near East? In Silberman, N. A., and Small, D. B., (eds.), *The Archaeology of Israel: Constructing the Past, Interpreting the Present*. Sheffield Academic Press, Sheffield, pp. 238–270.

Hesse, B., and Wapnish, P., 1998. Pig use and abuse in the ancient Levant: Ethnoreligious boundary-building with swine. In Nelson, S., (ed.), *Ancestors for the Pigs: Pigs in Prehistory*. MASCA Research Papers in Science and Archaeology 15. University of Pennsylvania Museum of Archaeology and Anthropology, Philadelphia, pp. 123–135.

Hicks, D., 2010. Introduction. In Hicks, D., (ed.), *Ritual and Belief: Readings in the Anthropology of Religion*. Altamira, New York, pp. xiii–xxiii.

Hildebrand, E. A., 2003. *Enset, Yams, and Honey: Ethnoarchaeological Approaches to the Origins of Horticulture in Southwest Ethiopia*. Ph.D. thesis, Department of Anthropology, Washington University, St. Louis.

Hillson, S., 2005. *Teeth*, 2nd ed. Cambridge University Press, Cambridge.

Hofman, C. A., and Rick, T. C., 2018. Ancient biological invasions and island ecosystems: Tracking translocations of wild plants and animals. *Journal of Archaeological Research* 26, 65–115.

Hollimon, S., 2006. The archaeology of non-binary genders in Native North America. In Nelson, S. M., (ed.), *Handbook of Gender in Archaeology*. Altamira, Lanham, MD, pp. 435–450.

Horwitz, L. K., 2001. Animal offerings in the Middle Bronze Age: Food for the gods, food for thought. *Palestine Exploration Quarterly* 133, 78–90.

Howey, M. C. L., and Frederick, K., 2016. Immovable food storage facilities, knowledge, and landscape in non-sedentary societies: Perspectives from northern Michigan. *Journal of Anthropological Archaeology* 42, 37–55.

Humes, E., 2012. *Garbology: Our Dirty Love Affair With Trash*. Avery, New York.

Hunt, A. M. W., (ed.), 2016. *The Oxford Handbook of Archaeological Ceramic Analysis*. Oxford University Press, Oxford.

Hutchinson, W. F., Culling, M., Orton, D. C., Hänfling, B., Handley, L. L., Hamilton-Dyer, S., O'Connell, T. C., Richards, M. P., and Barrett, J. H., 2015. The globalization of naval provisioning: ancient DNA and stable isotope analyses of stored cod from the wreck of the Mary Rose, AD 1545. *Royal Society Open Science* 2, 150199.

Ibáñez, J. J., González-Urquijo, J. E., and Gibaja, J., 2014. Discriminating wild vs domestic cereal harvesting micropolish through laser confocal microscopy. *Journal of Archaeological Science* 48, 96–103.

Ijzereef, E. G., 1989. Social differentiation from animal bone studies. In Serjeant-son, D., and Waldron, T., (eds.), *Diet and Crafts in Towns*. British Archaeological Reports International Series 199. Oxbow, Oxford, pp. 41–53.

Ikram, S., 1995. *Choice Cuts: Meat Production in Ancient Egypt*. Peeters, Leuven.

Insoll, T., 1999. *The Archaeology of Islam*. Blackwell, Malden, MA.

Insoll, T., 2007. Introduction: Configuring identities in archaeology. In Insoll, T., (ed.), *The Archaeology of Identities: A Reader*. Routledge, London, pp. 1–18.

Insoll, T., 2011. Introduction: Ritual and religion in archaeological perspective. In Insoll, T., (ed.), *The Oxford Handbook of the Archaeology of Ritual and Religion*. Oxford University Press, Oxford, pp. 1–8.

Iriarte, J., Power, M. J., Rostain, S., Mayle, F. E., Jones, H., Watling, J., Whitney, B. S., and McKey, D. B., 2012. Fire-free land use in pre-1492 Amazonian savannas. *Proceedings of the National Academy of Sciences* 109, 6473–6478.

Isaakidou, V., 2007. Cooking in the Labyrinth: Exploring "cuisine" at Bronze Age Knossos. In Mee, C., and Renard, J., (eds.), *Cooking Up the Past: Food and Culinary Practices in the Neolithic and Bronze Age Aegean*. Oxbow, Oxford, pp. 5–24.

IUCN, 2017. The IUCN Red List of Threatened Species. Version 2017-3. International Union for Conservation of Nature. www.iucnredlist.org/

Jackson, H. E., 2015. Animals as symbols, animals as resources: The elite faunal record in the Mississippian world. In Arbuckle, B. S., and McCarty, S. A., (eds.), *Animals and Inequality in the Ancient World*. University Press of Colorado, Boulder, pp. 107–123.

Jackson, H. E., and Scott, S. L., 1995. The faunal record of the Southeastern elite: The implications of economy, social relations, and ideology. *Southeastern Archaeology* 14, 103–119.

Jackson, H. E., and Scott, S. L., 2003. Patterns of elite faunal utilization at Moundville, Alabama. *American Antiquity* 68, 552–572.

Jaffe, Y., Wei, Q., and Zhao, Y., 2017. Foodways and the archaeology of colonial contact: Rethinking the Western Zhou Expansion in Shandong. *American Anthropologist* 120, 55–71.

Jamieson, R. W., and Sayre, M. B., 2010. Barley and identity in the Spanish colonial Audiencia of Quito: Archaeobotany of the 18th century San Blas neighborhood in Riobamba. *Journal of Anthropological Archaeology* 29, 208–218.

Jaouen, K., and Pons, M.-L., 2016. Potential of non-traditional isotope studies for bioarchaeology. *Archaeological and Anthropological Sciences*, 1–16.

Jennings, J., and Chatfield, M., 2009. Pots, brewers, and hosts: Women's power and the limits of central Andean feasting. In Jennings, J., and Bowser, B., (eds.), *Drink, Power, and Society in the Andes*. University Press of Florida, Gainesville, pp. 200–231.

Jochim, M., 1976. *Hunter-Gatherer Subsistence and Settlement: A Predictive Model*. Academic Press, New York.

Johnson, A. W., and Earle, T., 2000. *The Evolution of Human Societies*. Stanford University Press, Stanford, CA.

Jones, G., 2005. Garden cultivation of staple crops and its implications for settlement location and permanence. *World Archaeology* 37, 164–176.

Jones, J. R., and Mulville, J. A., 2018. Norse animal husbandry in liminal environments: Stable isotope evidence from the Scottish North Atlantic Islands. *Environmental Archaeology*, 23, 338–351.

Jones, M., Hunt, H., Lightfoot, E., Lister, D., Liu, X., and Motuzaite-Matuzeviciute, G., 2011. Food globalization in prehistory. *World Archaeology* 43, 665–675.

Jones, M. K., 2007. *Feast: Why Humans Share Food*. Oxford University Press, Oxford.

Jones, O. R., 1993. Commercial foods, 1740–1820. *Historical Archaeology* 27, 25–41.

Jones, S., 2009. *Food and Gender in Fiji: Ethnoarchaeological Explorations*. Lexington, New York.

Jones, S. R., Walsh-Haney, H., and Quinn, R., 2015. Kana Tamata or feasts of men: An interdisciplinary approach for identifying cannibalism in prehistoric Fiji. *International Journal of Osteoarchaeology* 25, 127–145.

Joyce, R. A., 2008. *Ancient Bodies, Ancient Lives: Sex, Gender, and Archaeology*. Thames & Hudson, New York.

Joyce, R. A., and Henderson, J. S., 2007. From feasting to cuisine: Implications of archaeological research in an early Honduran village. *American Anthropologist* 109, 642–653.

Julien, M.-A., Bocherens, H., Burke, A., Drucker, D. G., Patou-Mathis, M., Krotova, O., and Péan, S., 2012. Were European steppe bison migratory? ^{18}O, ^{13}C, and Sr intra-tooth isotopic variations applied to a palaeoethological reconstruction. *Quaternary International* 271, 106–119.

Junker, L. L., 2001. The evolution of ritual feasting systems in prehispanic Philippine chiefdoms. In Dietler, M., and Hayden, B., (eds.), *Feasts: Archaeological and Ethnographic Perspectives on Food, Politics, and Power*. Smithsonian Institution Press, Washington, DC, pp. 267–310.

Junker, L. L., and Niziolek, L., 2010. Food preparation and feasting in the household and political economy of Pre-Hispanic Philippine chiefdoms. In Klarich, E. A., (ed.), *Inside Ancient Kitchens: New Directions in the Study of Daily Meals and Feasts*. University Press of Colorado, Boulder, pp. 17–53.

Keeley, L. H., 2016. Food for war, war for food, and war on food. In VanDerwarker, A. M., and Wilson, G. D., (eds.), *The Archaeology of Food and Warfare: Food Insecurity in Prehistory*. Springer, New York, pp. 291–302.

Keene, A. S., 1985. Nutrition and economy: Models for the study of prehistoric diet. In Gilbert, R. I., Jr., and Mileke, J. H., (eds.), *The Analysis of Prehistoric Diets*. Academic Press, Orlando, FL, pp. 155–190.

Kelly, L. S., 2001. A case of ritual feasting at the Cahokia site. In Dietler, M., and Hayden, B., (eds.), *Feasts: Archaeological and Ethnographic Perspectives on Food, Politics, and Power*. Smithsonian Institution Press, Washington, DC, pp. 334–367.

Kelly, L. S., and Kelly, J., 2007. Swans in the American Bottom during the Emergent Mississippian and Mississippian. *Illinois Archaeology* 15–16, 112–141.

Kennedy, J. R., 2015. Zooarchaeology, localization, and Chinese railroad workers in North America. *Historical Archaeology* 49, 122–133.

Killgrove, K., and Tykot, R. H., 2013. Food for Rome: A stable isotope investigation of diet in the Imperial period (1st–3rd centuries AD). *Journal of Anthropological Archaeology* 32, 28–38.

Kim, M., 2015. Rice in ancient Korea: Status symbol or community food? *Antiquity* 89, 838–853.

Kim, M., Shin, H.-N., Kim, J., Roh, K.-J., Ryu, A., Won, H., Kim, J., Oh, S., Noh, H., and Kim, S., 2016. The ins and the outs: Foodways, feasts, and social differentiation in the Baekje Kingdom, Korea. *Journal of Anthropological Archaeology* 43, 128–139.

Kim, N. C., and Kusimba, C. M., 2008. Pathways to social complexity and state formation in the Southern Zambezian region. *African Archaeological Review* 25, 131–152.

King, S. M., 2008. The spatial organization of food sharing in Early Postclassic households: An application of soil chemistry in Ancient Oaxaca, Mexico. *Journal of Archaeological Science* 35, 1224–1239.

Kirch, P. V., and O'Day, S. J., 2003. New archaeological insights into food and status: A case study from pre-contact Hawaii. *World Archaeology* 34, 484–497.

Klaus, H. D., 2015. Paleopathological rigor and differential diagnosis: Case studies involving terminology, description, and diagnostic frameworks for scurvy in skeletal remains. *International Journal of Paleopathology* 19, 96–110.

Koch, I., 2014. Goose keeping, elite emulation and Egyptianized feasting at Late Bronze Lachish. *Tel Aviv* 41, 161–179.

Koch, P., Akeret, O., Deschler-Erb, S., Huster-Plogmann, H., Pumpin, C., and Wick, L., 2018. Feasting in a sacred grove: A multidisciplinary study of the Gallo-Roman sanctuary of Kempraten, Switzerland. In Livarda, A., Madgwick, R., and Riera Mora, S., (eds.), *The Bioarchaeology of Ritual and Religion*. Oxbow, Oxford, pp. 69–85.

Koerper, H., and Kolls, A. L., 1999. The silphium motif adorning ancient Libyan coinage: Marketing a medicinal plant. *Economic Botany* 53, 133–143.

Kroeber, A. L., 1925. *Handbook of the Indians of California*. Bureau of American Ethnology Bulletin 78. Bureau of American Ethnology, Washington, DC.

Kuijt, I., 2015. The Neolithic refrigerator on a Friday night: How many people are coming to dinner and just what should I do with the slimy veggies in the back of the fridge? *Environmental Archaeology* 20, 321–336.

Kurin, D. S., 2016. Trauma, nutrition, and malnutrition in the Andean highlands during Peru's Dark Age (1000–1250 C.E.). In VanDerwarker, A. M., and Wilson, G. D., (eds.), *The Archaeology of Food and Warfare: Food Insecurity in Prehistory*. Springer, New York, pp. 229–258.

Lamb, A. L., Evans, J. E., Buckley, R., and Appleby, J., 2014. Multi-isotope analysis demonstrates significant lifestyle changes in King Richard III. *Journal of Archaeological Science* 50, 559–565.

Lambrides, A. B. J., and Weisler, M. I., 2016. Pacific Islands ichthyoarchaeology: Implications for the development of prehistoric fishing studies and global sustainability. *Journal of Archaeological Research* 24, 275–324.

Landon, D. B., 1996. Feeding Colonial Boston: A zooarchaeological study. *Historical Archaeology* 30, 1–153.

Langenwalter, P. E., II, 1980. The archaeology of 19th century Chinese subsistence at the Lower China store, Madera County, California. In Schuyler, R. E., (ed.), *Archaeological Perspectives on Ethnicity in America: Afro-American and Asian American Culture History*. Baywood, Farmingdale, NY, pp. 102–112.

Larsen, C. S., 2015. *Bioarchaeology: Interpreting Behavior from the Human Skeleton*, 2nd ed. Cambridge University Press, Cambridge.

Leach, H., 2003. Did East Polynesians have a concept of luxury foods? *World Archaeology* 34, 442–457.

LeCount, L. J., 2010. Maya palace kitchens: Suprahousehold food preparation at the Late and Terminal Classic site of Xunantunich, Belize. In Klarich, E. A., (ed.), *Inside Ancient Kitchens: New Directions in the Study of Daily Meals and Feasts*. University Press of Colorado, Boulder, pp. 133–159.

Lee, R. B., and DeVore, I., 1968. *Man the Hunter*. Aldine, Chicago.

Lehmann, L. V., 2015. The garbage project revisited: From a 20th century archaeology of food waste to a contemporary study of food packaging waste. *Sustainability* 7, 6994–7010.

Lentacker, A., Ervynck, A., and van Neer, W., 2004. Gastronomy or religion? The animal remains from the *mithraeum* at Tienen (Belgium). In O'Day, S. J., van Neer, W., and Ervynck, A., (eds.), *Behaviour Behind Bones: The Zooarchaeology of Religion, Ritual, Status, and Identity*. Oxbow, Oxford, pp. 77–94.

León-Portilla, M., 1963. *Aztec Thought and Culture: A Study of the Ancient Nahuatl Mind* (transl. J. E. Davis). University of Oklahoma Press, Norman.

Lepofsky, D., and Kahn, J., 2011. Cultivating an ecological and social balance: Elite demands and commoner knowledge in ancient Ma'ohi agriculture, Society Islands. *American Anthropologist* 113, 319–335.

Lev-Tov, J., 2004. Implications of risk theory for understanding nineteenth century slave diets in the southern United States. In O'Day, S. J., van Neer, W., and Ervynck, A., (eds.), *Behaviour Behind Bones: The Zooarchaeology of Religion, Ritual, Status, and Identity*. Oxbow, Oxford, pp. 304–317.

Levis, C., Costa, F. R. C., Bongers, F., Peña-Claros, M., Clement, C. R., Junqueira, A. B., Neves, E. G., Tamanaha, E. K., Figueiredo, F. O. G., Salomão, R. P., Castilho, C. V., Magnusson, W. E., Phillips, O. L., Guevara, J. E., Sabatier, D., Molino, J.-F., López, D. C., Mendoza, A. M., Pitman, N. C. A., Duque, A., Vargas, P. N., Zartman, C. E., Vasquez, R., Andrade, A., Camargo, J. L., Feldpausch, T. R., Laurance, S. G. W., Laurance, W. F., Killeen, T. J., Nascimento, H. E. M., Montero, J. C., Mostacedo, B., Amaral, I. L., Guimarães Vieira, I. C., Brienen, R., Castellanos, H., Terborgh, J., Carim, M. d. J. V., Guimarães, J. R. d. S., Coelho, L. d. S., Matos, F. D. d. A., Wittmann, F., Mogollón, H. F., Damasco, G., Dávila, N., García-Villacorta, R., Coronado, E. N. H., Emilio, T., Filho, D. d. A. L., Schietti, J., Souza, P., Targhetta, N., Comiskey, J. A., Marimon, B. S., Marimon, B.-H., Neill, D., Alonso, A., Arroyo, L., Carvalho, F. A., de Souza, F. C., Dallmeier, F., Pansonato, M. P., Duivenvoorden, J. F., Fine, P. V. A., Stevenson, P. R., Araujo-Murakami, A., Aymard C., G. A., Baraloto, C., do Amaral, D. D., Engel, J., Henkel, T. W., Maas, P., Petronelli, P., Revilla, J. D. C., Stropp, J., Daly, D., Gribel, R., Paredes, M. R., Silveira, M., Thomas-Caesar, R., Baker, T. R., da Silva, N. F., Ferreira, L. V., Peres, C. A., Silman, M. R., Cerón, C.,

Valverde, F. C., Di Fiore, A., Jimenez, E. M., Mora, M. C. P., Toledo, M.,
    Barbosa, E. M., Bonates, L. C. d. M., Arboleda, N. C., Farias, E. d. S.,
    Fuentes, A., Guillaumet, J.-L., Jørgensen, P. M., Malhi, Y., de Andrade
    Miranda, I. P., Phillips, J. F., Prieto, A., Rudas, A., Ruschel, A. R., Silva, N.,
    von Hildebrand, P., Vos, V. A., Zent, E. L., Zent, S., Cintra, B. B. L.,
    Nascimento, M. T., Oliveira, A. A., Ramirez-Angulo, H., Ramos, J. F., Rivas,
    G., Schöngart, J., Sierra, R., Tirado, M., van der Heijden, G., Torre, E. V.,
    Wang, O., Young, K. R., Baider, C., Cano, A., Farfan-Rios, W., Ferreira, C.,
    Hoffman, B., Mendoza, C., Mesones, I., Torres-Lezama, A., Medina, M.
    N. U., van Andel, T. R., Villarroel, D., Zagt, R., Alexiades, M. N., Balslev,
    H., Garcia-Cabrera, K., Gonzales, T., Hernandez, L., Huamantupa-Chuqui-
    maco, I., Manzatto, A. G., Milliken, W., Cuenca, W. P., Pansini, S., Pauletto,
    D., Arevalo, F. R., Reis, N. F. C., Sampaio, A. F., Giraldo, L. E. U., Sandoval,
    E. H. V., Gamarra, L. V., Vela, C. I. A., and ter Steege, H., 2017. Persistent
    effects of pre-Columbian plant domestication on Amazonian forest compos-
    ition. *Science* 355, 925–931.
Lewis, K., 2015. Trade routes. In Metheny, K. B., and Beaudry, M., (eds.), *Archae-
    ology of Food: An Encyclopedia*. Rowman & Littlefield, Lanham, MD,
    pp. 519–520.
Lewis, K. A., 2007. Fields and tables of Sheba: Food, identity, and politics in
    ancient southern Arabia. In Twiss, K. C., (ed.), *The Archaeology of Food and
    Identity*. Center for Archaeological Investigations, Southern Illinois University
    Carbondale, Occasional Paper no. 34. Center for Archaeological Investiga-
    tions, Carbondale, IL, pp. 192–217.
Librenti, M., Moine, C., and Sabbionesi, L., 2017. From table to identity: Under-
    standing social changes through tableware (a case study of San Paolo in
    Modena, Italy). In Vroom, J., Waksman, Y., and Oosten, R. v., (eds.), *Medieval
    MasterChef: Archaeological and Historical Perspectives on Eastern Cuisine and
    Western Foodways*. Brepols, Turnhout, Belgium, pp. 223–244.
Linduff, K. M., 2001. Women's lives memorialized in burial in Ancient China at
    Anyang. In Nelson, S. M., and Rosen-Ayalon, M., (eds.), *In Pursuit of Gender:
    Worldwide Archaeological Perspectives*. Altamira, Walnut Creek, CA,
    pp. 257–287.
Livarda, A., and Orengo, H. A., 2015. Reconstructing the Roman London flavours-
    cape: New insights into the exotic food plant trade using network and spatial
    analyses. *Journal of Archaeological Science* 55, 244–252.
Logan, A. L., and Cruz, M. D., 2014. Gendered taskscapes: Food, farming, and craft
    production in Banda, Ghana in the eighteenth to twenty-first centuries. *Afri-
    can Archaeological Review* 31, 203–231.
London, G., 2008. Why milk and meat don't mix: A new explanation for a puzzling
    kosher law. *Biblical Archaeology Review* 34, 66–69.
Luby, E. M., and Gruber, M. F., 2009. The dead must be fed: Symbolic meanings
    of the shellmounds of the San Francisco Bay Area. *Cambridge Archaeological
    Journal* 9, 95–108.
Luke, C., Roosevelt, C. H., and Scott, C. B., 2016. Yörük legacies: Space, scent, and
    sediment geochemistry. *International Journal of Historical Archaeology* 21,
    152–177.

Lupo, K. D., and Schmitt, D. N., 2016. When bigger is not better: The economics of hunting megafauna and its implications for Plio-Pleistocene hunter-gatherers. *Journal of Anthropological Archaeology* 44, 185–197.

Lutes, D., 1936. *The Country Kitchen*. Little, Brown, Boston, MA.

Lyman, R. L., 1987. On zooarchaeological measures of socioeconomic position and cost-efficient meat purchases. *Historical Archaeology* 21, 58–66.

Lyman, R. L., 1996. Applied zooarchaeology: The relevance of faunal analysis to wildlife management. *World Archaeology* 28, 110–125.

Lyman, R. L., and Cannon, K. P., (eds.), 2004. *Zooarchaeology and Conservation Biology*. University of Utah Press, Salt Lake City.

Lyons, D., 2014. Perceptions of consumption: Constituting potters, farmers, and blacksmiths in the culinary continuum in Eastern Tigray, Northern Highland Ethiopia. *African Archaeological Review* 31, 169–201.

MacClancy, J., 1993. *Consuming Culture: Why You Eat What You Eat*. Henry Holt & Co, New York.

MacLean, R., and Insoll, T., 2003. Archaeology, luxury, and the exotic: The examples of Islamic Gao (Mali) and Bahrain. *World Archaeology* 34, 558–570.

MacMahon, A., 2005. The taberna counters of Pompeii and Herculaneum. In Mac Mahon, A., and Price, J., (eds.), *Roman Working Lives and Urban Living*. Oxbow, Oxford, pp. 70–87.

Macmillan, D. C., and Phillip, S., 2008. Consumptive and non-consumptive values of wild mammals in Britain. *Mammal Review* 38, 189–204.

Madella, M., Jones, M. K., Goldberg, P., Goren, Y., and Hovers, E., 2002. The exploitation of plant resources by Neanderthals in Amud Cave (Israel): The evidence from phytolith studies. *Journal of Archaeological Science* 29, 703–719.

Madgwick, R., Lewis, J., Grimes, V., and Guest, P., 2019. On the hoof: Exploring the supply of animals to the Roman legionary fortress at Caerleon using strontium ($^{87}Sr/^{86}Sr$) isotope analysis. *Archaeological and Anthropological Sciences* 11, 223–235.

Madgwick, R., and Livarda, A., 2018. Ritual and religion: Bioarchaeological perspectives. In Madgwick, R., Livarda, A., and Riera Mora, S., (eds.), *The Bioarchaeology of Ritual and Religion*. Oxbow, Oxford, pp. 1–13.

Madsen, B. D., and Madsen, D. B., 1987. One man's meat is another man's poison: A revisionist view of the Seagull "Miracle". *Nevada Historical Society Quarterly* 30, 165–181.

Madsen, D. B., and Kirkman, J. E., 1988. Hunting hoppers. *American Antiquity* 53, 593–604.

Mahoney, P., Schmidt, C. W., Deter, C., Remy, A., Slavin, P., Johns, S. E., Miszkiewicz, J. J., and Nystrom, P., 2016. Deciduous enamel 3D microwear texture analysis as an indicator of childhood diet in medieval Canterbury, England. *Journal of Archaeological Science* 66, 128–136.

Mainland, I., 2006. Pastures lost? A dental microwear study of ovicaprine diet and management in Norse Greenland. *Journal of Archaeological Science* 33, 238–252.

Mainman, A., 2015. Tools/utensils, metal. In Metheny, K. B., and Beaudry, M., (eds.), *Archaeology of Food: An Encyclopedia*. Rowman & Littlefield, Lanham, MD, pp. 508–511.

Maixner, F., and Zink, A., 2015. Gut contents. In Metheny, K. B., and Beaudry, M., (eds.), *Archaeology of Food: An Encyclopedia*. Rowman & Littlefield, Lanham, MD, pp. 246.

Makarewicz, C. A., and Sealy, J., 2015. Dietary reconstruction, mobility, and the analysis of ancient skeletal tissues: Expanding the prospects of stable isotope research in archaeology. *Journal of Archaeological Science* 56, 146–158.

Marlar, R. A., Leonard, B. L., Billman, B. R., Lambert, P. M. and Marlar, J. E. 2000. Biochemical evidence of cannibalism at a prehistoric Puebloan site in southwestern Colorado. *Nature* 407, 74–78.

Marom, N., and Zuckerman, S., 2012. The zooarchaeology of exclusion and expropriation: Looking up from the lower city in Late Bronze Age Hazor. *Journal of Anthropological Archaeology* 31, 573–585.

Marshall, F., and Hildebrand, E., 2002. Cattle before crops: The beginnings of food production in Africa. *Journal of World Prehistory* 16, 99–143.

Mauss, M., 1990 [1925]. *The Gift: Forms and Function of Exchange In Archaic Societies*. Routledge, London.

McCann, J., 2001. Maize and grace: History, corn, and Africa's new landscapes, 1500–1999. *Comparative Studies in Society and History* 43, 246–272.

McCann, J. C., 2009. *Stirring the Pot: A History of African Cuisine*. Ohio University Press, Athens, OH.

McGovern, P. E., 2009. *Uncorking the Past: The Quest for Wine, Beer, and Other Alcoholic Beverages*. University of California Press, Berkeley.

McGovern, P. E., 2017. *Ancient Brews: Rediscovered and Recreated*. W. W. Norton, New York.

McGuire, D. C., 2016. A taste for mustard: An archaeological examination of a condiment and its bottles from a loyalist homestead in Upper Canada. *International Journal of Historical Archaeology* 20, 666–692.

McKee, L. W., 1999. Food supply and plantation social order: An archaeological perspective. In Singleton, T., (ed.), *I, Too, Am American: Studies in African-American Archaeology*. University Press of Virginia, Charlottesville, pp. 218–239.

McNeil, C. L., 2010. Death and chocolate: The significance of cacao offerings in ancient Maya tombs and caches at Copan, Honduras. In Staller, J. E., and Carrasco, M. D., (eds.), *Pre-Columbian Foodways: Interdisciplinary Approaches to Food, Culture, and Markets in Mesoamerica*. Springer, New York, pp. 293–314.

McNiven, I. J., 2013. Ritualized middening practices. *Journal of Archaeological Method and Theory* 20, 552–587.

McNiven, I. J., and Feldman, R., 2003. Ritually orchestrated seascapes: Hunting magic and dugong bone mounds in Torres Strait, NE Australia. *Cambridge Archaeological Journal* 13, 169–194.

Meigs, A., 1984. *Food, Sex, and Pollution: A New Guinea Religion*. Rutgers University Press, New Brunswick, NJ.

Mennell, S., 1996. *All Manners of Food: Eating and Taste in England and France from the Middle Ages to the Present*. University of Illinois Press, Chicago.

Merbs, C. F., 1980. The pathology of a La Jollan skeleton from Punta Minitas, Baja, California. *Pacific Coast Archaeological Society Quarterly* 16, 37–43.

Mercader, J., Abtosway, M., Baquedano, E., Bird, R. W., Díez-Martín, F., Domínguez-Rodrigo, M., Favreau, J., Itambu, M., Lee, P., Mabulla, A., Patalano, R., Pérez-González, A., Santonja, M., Tucker, L., and Walde, D., 2017. Starch contamination landscapes in field archaeology: Olduvai Gorge, Tanzania. *Boreas* 46, 918–934.

Meskell, L., 2002. The intersections of identity and politics in archaeology. *Annual Review of Anthropology* 31, 279–301.

Meulemans, L. G., 2015. *Vivaria in doliis*: A cultural and social marker of Romanised society? In Villing, A., and Spataro, M., (eds.), *Ceramics, Cuisine and Culture: The Archaeology and Science of Kitchen Pottery in the Ancient Mediterranean World*. Oxbow, Oxford, pp. 170–177.

Mills, B., 1999. Ceramics and the social contexts of food consumption in the northern Southwest. In Skibo, J. M., and Feinman, G. M., (eds.), *Pottery and People: Dynamic Interactions*. University of Utah Press, Salt Lake City, pp. 99–114.

Mills, B., 2007. Performing the feast: Visual display and suprahousehold commensalism in the Puebloan Southwest. *American Antiquity* 72, 210–239.

Mills, B., 2008. Colonialism and cuisine: Cultural transformation, agency, and history at Zuni Pueblo. In Horne, L., Bowser, B., and Stark, M., (eds.), *Cultural Transmission and Material Culture: Breaking Down Boundaries*. University of Arizona Press, Tucson, pp. 245–262.

Mills, B. J., 2004. Identity, feasting, and the archaeology of the Greater Southwest. In Mills, B. J., (ed.), *Identity, Feasting, and the Archaeology of the Greater Southwest*. University Press of Colorado, Boulder, pp. 1–23.

Mitchell, P. D., Yeh, H.-Y., Appleby, J., and Buckley, R., 2013. The intestinal parasites of King Richard III. *The Lancet* 382, 888.

Mobley-Tanaka, J. L., 1997. Gender and ritual space during the pithouse to pueblo transition: Subterranean mealing rooms in the North American Southwest. *American Antiquity* 62, 437–448.

Molleson, T. I., 1994. The eloquent bones of Abu Hureyra. *Scientific American* 271, 70–75.

Molleson, T. I., 2000. The people of Abu Hureyra. In Moore, A., Hillman, G., and Legge, A. J., (eds.), *Village on the Euphrates*. Oxford University Press, Oxford, pp. 301–324.

Monroe, J. C., and Janzen, A., 2014. The Dahomean feast: Royal women, private politics, and culinary practices in Atlantic West Africa. *African Archaeological Review* 31, 299–337.

Montgomery, J., Evans, J. A., Powlesland, D., and Roberts, C. A., 2005. Continuity or colonization in Anglo-Saxon England? Isotope evidence for mobility, subsistence practice, and status at West Heslerton. *American Journal of Physical Anthropology* 126, 123–138.

Montón Subías, S., 2002. Cooking in zooarchaeology: Is this issue still raw? In Miracle, P., and Milner, N., (eds.), *Consuming Passions and Patterns of Consumption*. McDonald Institute for Archaeological Research, Cambridge, pp. 7–15.

Morán, E., 2016. *Sacred Consumption: Food and Ritual in Aztec Art and Culture*. University of Texas Press, Austin.

Morehart, C., and de Lucia, K., 2015. Surplus: The politics of production and the strategies of everyday life – an introduction. In Morehart, C., and De Lucia, K., (eds.), *Surplus: The Politics of Production and the Strategies of Everyday Life*. University Press of Colorado, Boulder, pp. 3–43.

Morehart, C. T., and Morell-Hart, S., 2015. Beyond the ecofact: Toward a social paleoethnobotany in Mesoamerica. *Journal of Archaeological Method and Theory* 22, 483–511.

Moreno, A., 2007. *Feeding the Democracy: The Athenian Grain Supply in the Fifth and Fourth Centuries BC*. Oxford University Press, Oxford.

Morris, J., 2018. Animal biographies in the Iron Age of Wessex: Winnall Down, UK, revisited. In Livarda, A., Madgwick, R., and Riera Mora, S., (eds.), *The Bioarchaeology of Ritual and Religion*. Oxbow, Oxford, pp. 115–128.

Moss, M. L., 1993. Shellfish, gender, and status on the Northwest Coast: Reconciling archeological, ethnographic, and ethnohistorical records of the Tlingit. *American Anthropologist* 95, 631–652.

Mrozowski, S. A., Franklin, M., and Hunt, L., 2008. Archaeobotanical analysis and interpretations of enslaved Virginian plant use at Rich Neck Plantation (44wb52). *American Antiquity* 73, 699–728.

Mullins, P. R., 1999. Race and the genteel consumer: Class and African-American consumption, 1850–1930. *Historical Archaeology* 33, 22–38.

Munro, N. D., and Bar-Oz, G., 2005. Gazelle bone fat processing in the Levantine Epipalaeolithic. *Journal of Archaeological Science* 32, 223–239.

Murphy, B. P., and Bowman, D. M., 2007. The interdependence of fire, grass, kangaroos, and Australian Aborigines: A case study from central Arnhem Land, northern Australia. *Journal of Biogeography* 34, 237–250.

Mylona, D., 2008. *Fish-Eating in Greece from the Fifth Century B.C. to the Seventh Century A.D.: A Story of Impoverished Fishermen or Luxurious Fish Banquets?* BAR International Series S1754. BAR Publishing, Oxford.

Nash, D. J., 2010. Fine dining and fabulous atmosphere: Feasting facilities and political interaction in the Wari realm. In Klarich, E. A., (ed.), *Inside Ancient Kitchens: New Directions in the Study of Daily Meals and Feasts*. University Press of Colorado, Boulder, pp. 83–109.

Nehlich, O., 2015. The application of sulphur isotope analyses in archaeological research: A review. *Earth-Science Reviews* 142, 1–17.

Nehlich, O., Fuller, B. T., Jay, M., Mora, A., Nicholson, R. A., Smith, C. I., and Richards, M. P., 2011. Application of sulphur isotope ratios to examine weaning patterns and freshwater fish consumption in Roman Oxfordshire, UK. *Geochimica et Cosmochimica Acta* 75, 4963–4977.

Nelson, G. C., Lukacs, J. R., and Yule, P., 1999. Dates, caries, and early tooth loss during the Iron Age of Oman. *American Journal of Physical Anthropology* 108, 333–343.

Nelson, S. M., 2003. Feasting the ancestors in early China. In Bray, T., (ed.), *The Archaeology and Politics of Food and Feasting in Early States and Empires*. Kluwer Academic/Plenum, New York, pp. 65–89.

Nestle, M., 2012. Peevish about "protein". Food Politics blog. www.foodpolitics .com/2012/01/peevish-about-protein/ (accessed January 18, 2018).

Netting, R. M., 1971. *The Ecological Approach to Cultural Study*. Addison-Wesley Modular Publications, Reading, MA.

Newman, E. T., 2014. *Biography of a Hacienda: Work and Revolution in Rural Mexico*. University of Arizona Press, Tucson, AZ.

Nitsch, E., Andreou, S., Creuzieux, A., Gardeisen, A., Halstead, P., Isaakidou, V., Karathanou, A., Kotsachristou, D., Nikolaidou, D., Papanthimou, A., Petridou, C., Triantaphyllou, S., Valamoti, S. M., Vasileiadou, A., and Bogaard, A., 2017. A bottom-up view of food surplus: Using stable carbon and nitrogen isotope analysis to investigate agricultural strategies and diet at Bronze Age Archontiko and Thessaloniki Toumba, northern Greece. *World Archaeology* 49, 105–137.

Nitsch, E. K., Lamb, A., Heaton, T. H. E., Vaiglova, P., Fraser, R., Hartman, G., Moreno-Jiménez, E., López-Piñeiro, A., Peña-Abades, D., Fairbairn, A., Eriksen, J., and Bogaard, A., 2019. The preservation and interpretation of $\delta^{34}S$ values in charred archaeobotanical remains. *Archaeometry* 61, 161–178.

Nowell, A., Walker, C., Cordova, C. E., Ames, C. J. H., Pokines, J. T., Stueber, D., DeWitt, R., and al-Souliman, A. S. A., 2016. Middle Pleistocene subsistence in the Azraq Oasis, Jordan: Protein residue and other proxies. *Journal of Archaeological Science* 73, 36–44.

Nymann, H., 2015. Feasting on locusts and truffles in the second millennium BCE. In Kerner, S., Chou, C., and Warmind, M., (eds.), *Commensality: From Everyday Food to Feast*. Bloomsbury, New York, pp. 151–163.

O'Connell, J. F., and Allen, J., 2012. The restaurant at the end of the universe: Modelling the colonisation of Sahul. *Australian Archaeology*, 74, 5–17.

O'Connor, K., 2015. *The Never-Ending Feast: The Anthropology and Archaeology of Feasting*. Bloomsbury, London.

O'Shea, J., 1981. Coping with scarcity: Exchange and social storage. In Sheridan, A., and Bailey, G., (eds.), *Economic Archaeology*. British Archaeological Reports. BAR Publishing, Oxford, pp. 167–183.

Ohnuki-Tierney, E., 1993. *Rice as Self: Japanese Identities through Time*. Princeton University Press, Princeton, NJ.

Oliver, G. J., 2007. *War, Food, and Politics in Early Hellenistic Athens*. Oxford University Press, Oxford.

Olsen, S. J., 1964. Food animals of the Continental Army at Valley Forge and Morristown. *American Antiquity* 29(4), 506–509.

Olsen, S. L., 1995. Pleistocene horse-hunting at Solutré: Why bison jump analogies fail. In Johnson, E., (ed.), *Ancient Peoples and Landscapes*. Museum of Texas Tech University, Lubbock, TX, pp. 65–75.

Oppenheim, A. L., 1977. *Ancient Mesopotamia: Portrait of a Dead Civilization*. University of Chicago Press, Chicago.

Orengo, H. A., and Livarda, A., 2016. The seeds of commerce: A network analysis-based approach to the Romano-British transport system. *Journal of Archaeological Science* 66, 21–35.

Orser, C. E., Jr., 2007. *The Archaeology of Race and Racialization in Historic America*. University Press of Florida, Gainesville, FL.

Orton, C., and Hughes, M., 2013. *Pottery in Archaeology*, 2nd ed. Cambridge University Press, New York.

Orton, D. C., Morris, J., Locker, A., and Barrett, J. H., 2014. Fish for the city: Meta-analysis of archaeological cod remains and the growth of London's northern trade. *Antiquity* 88, 516–530.

Otto, A., 2015. Defining and transgressing the boundaries between ritual commensality and daily commensal practices: The case of Late Bronze Age Tall Bazi. In Pollock, S., (ed.), *Between Feasts and Daily Meals: Towards an Archaeology of Commensal Spaces*. Topoi, Berlin, pp. 205–223.

Panagiotakopulu, E., and Buckland, P. C., 2018. Early invaders: Farmers, the granary weevil, and other uninvited guests in the Neolithic. *Biological Invasions* 20, 219–233.

Parasecoli, F., 2005. Feeding hard bodies: Food and masculinites in men's fitness magazines. *Food and Foodways* 13, 17–38.

Parker Pearson, M., 2003. Food, identity, and culture: An introduction and overview. In Parker Pearson, M., (ed.), *Food, Culture, and Identity in the Neolithic and Early Bronze Age*. BAR International Series 1117. BAR Publishing, Oxford, pp. 1–30.

Parker Pearson, M., Cleal, R., Marshall, P., Needham, S., Pollard, J., Richards, C., Ruggles, C., Sheridan, A., Thomas, J., Tilley, C., Welham, K., Chamberlain, A., Chenery, C., Evans, J., Knusel, C., Linford, N., Martin, L., Montgomery, J., Payne, A., and Richards, M., 2007. The age of Stonehenge. *Antiquity* 81, 617–639.

Parker Pearson, M., Pollard, J., Richards, C., Thomas, J., Welham, K., Albarella, U., Chan, B., Marshall, P., and Viner, S., 2011. Feeding Stonehenge: Feasting in Late Neolithic Britain. In Aranda Jiménez, G., Montón-Subías, S., and Sánchez-Romero, M., (eds.), *Guess Who's Coming to Dinner: Feasting Rituals in the Prehistoric Societies of Europe and the Near East*. Oxbow, Oxford, pp. 73–90.

Pauketat, T. R., Kelly, L. S., Fritz, G. J., Lopinot, N. H., Elias, S., and Hargrave, E. A., 2002. The residues of feasting and public ritual at early Cahokia. *American Antiquity* 67, 257.

Pauketat, T. R., and Lopinot, N. H., 1997. Cahokian population dynamics. In Pauketat, T. R., and Emerson, T. E., (eds.), *Cahokia: Domination and Ideology in the Mississippian World*. University of Nebraska Press, Lincoln, pp. 103–123.

Paulette, T., 2016. Grain, storage, and state making in Mesopotamia (3200–2000 BCE). In Manzanilla, L. R., and Rothman, M., (eds.), *Storage in Ancient Complex Societies: Administration, Organization, and Control*. New York, Routledge, pp. 85–109.

Pavao-Zuckerman, B., and Loren, D. D., 2012. Presentation is everything: Food-ways, tablewares, and colonial identity at Presidio Los Adaes. *International Journal of Historical Archaeology* 16, 199–226.

Pearsall, D. M., 2015. *Paleoethnobotany: A Handbook of Procedures*, 3rd ed. Left Coast Press, Walnut Creek, CA.

Pearson, J., Grove, M., Özbek, M., and Hongo, H., 2013. Food and social complexity at Çayönü Tepesi, southeastern Anatolia: Stable isotope evidence of differentiation in diet according to burial practice and sex in the early Neolithic. *Journal of Anthropological Archaeology* 32, 180–189.

Pecci, A., Barba, L., and Ortiz, A., 2017. Chemical residues as anthropic activity markers: Ethnoarchaeology, experimental archaeology, and archaeology of food production and consumption. *Environmental Archaeology* 22, 343–353.

Peres, T. M., 2008. Foodways, economic status, and the antebellum Upland South in central Kentucky. *Historical Archaeology* 42, 88–104.

Peres, T. M., 2017. Foodways archaeology: A decade of research from the Southeastern United States. *Journal of Archaeological Research* 25, 421–460.

Perodie, J. R., 2001. Feasting for prosperity: A study of southern Northwest Coast feasting. In Dietler, M., and Hayden, B., (eds.), *Feasts: Archaeological and Ethnographic Perspectives on Food, Politics, and Power*. Smithsonian Institution Press, Washington, DC, pp. 185–214.

Petek, N., and Lane, P., 2017. Ethnogenesis and surplus food production: Communitas and identity building among nineteenth- and early twentieth-century Ilchamus, Lake Baringo, Kenya. *World Archaeology* 49, 40–60.

Peterson, J. D., 2006. Gender in early farming societies. In Nelson, S. M., (ed.), *Handbook of Gender in Archaeology*. Altamira, Lanham, MD, pp. 537–570.

Pezzarossi, G., Kennedy, R., and Law, H., 2012. "Hoe cake and pickerel": Cooking traditions, community, and agency at a nineteenth-century Nipmuc farmstead. In Graff, S. R., and Rodríguez-Alegría, E., (eds.), *The Menial Art of Cooking: Archaeological Studies of Cooking and Food Preparation*. University Press of Colorado, Boulder, pp. 201–229.

Phillips, D. A., Jr., and Sebastian, L., 2004. Large-scale feasting and politics: an essay on power in precontact Southwestern societies. In Mills, B., (ed.), *Identity, Feasting, and the Archaeology of the Greater Southwest*. University Press of Colorado, Boulder, pp. 233–258.

Picazo, M., 2008. Greek terracotta figurines: Images and representations of everyday life. In Montón Subías, S., and Sanchez-Romero, M., (eds.), *Engendering Social Dynamics: The Archaeology of Maintenance Activities*. BAR International Series 1862. BAR Publishing, Oxford, pp. 57–63.

Pilcher, J. M., 1998. *¡Que Vivan Los Tamales! Food and the Making of Mexican Identity*. University of New Mexico Press, Albuquerque, NM.

Pilcher, J. M., 2002. Industrial tortillas and folkloric Pepsi: The nutritional consequences of hybrid cuisines in Mexico. In Scranton, W. B. a. P., (ed.), *Food Nations: Selling Taste in Consumer Societies*. Routledge, New York, pp. 222–239.

Piperno, D. R., 2006. *Phytoliths: A Comprehensive Guide for Archaeologists and Paleoecologists*. Altamira, New York.

Pluckhahn, T., Compton, J., and Bonhage-Freund, M., 2006. Evidence of small-scale feasting from the Woodland Period site of Kolomoki, Georgia. *Journal of Field Archaeology* 31, 263–284.

Plutarch, 1914. *Plutarch's Lives*, with an English translation by Bernadotte Perrin. Harvard University Press, Cambridge, MA.

Pollock, S., 2003. Feasts, funerals, and fast food in early Mesopotamian states. In Bray, T., (ed.), *The Archaeology and Politics of Food and Feasting in Early States and Empires*. Kluwer Academic/Plenum, New York, pp. 17–38.

Pollock, S., 2015. Towards an archaeology of commensal spaces: An introduction. In Pollock, S., (ed.). *Between Feasts and Daily Meals: Toward an Archaeology of Commensal Spaces*. Topoi, Berlin, pp. 7–28.

Poole, K., 2013. Horses for courses? Religious change and dietary shifts in Anglo-Saxon England. *Oxford Journal of Archaeology* 32, 319–333.

Potter, B. 1902. *The Tale of Peter Rabbit*. Frederick Warne & Co, London.

Potter, J. M., 2010. Making meals (matter). In Klarich, E. A., (ed.), *Inside Ancient Kitchens: New Directions in the Study of Daily Meals and Feasts*. University Press of Colorado, Boulder, CO, pp. 241–251.

Potter, J. M., and Ortman, S. G., 2004. Community and cuisine in the prehispanic American Southwest. In Mills, B. J., (ed.), *Identity, Feasting, and the Archaeology of the Greater Southwest*. University Press of Colorado, Boulder, CO, pp. 173–191.

Pumpelly, R., 1908. *Explorations in Turkmenistan*, Vol. I. Carnegie Institution, Washington DC.

Pyle, H., 1883. *The Merry Adventures of Robin Hood*. Project Gutenberg, www.gutenberg.org.

Rathje, W. L., and McCarthy, M., 1977. Regularity and variability in contemporary garbage. In South, S., (ed.), *Research Strategies in Historical Archaeology*. Academic Press, New York, pp. 261–286.

Rathje, W. L., and Murphy, C., 1992. *Rubbish! The Archaeology of Garbage*. Harper Perennial, New York.

Razafimanahaka, J. H., Jenkins, R. K. B., Andriafidison, D., Randrianandrianina, F., Rakotomboavonjy, V., Keane, A., and Jones, J. P. G., 2012. Novel approach for quantifying illegal bushmeat consumption reveals high consumption of protected species in Madagascar. *Oryx* 46, 584–592.

Reddy, S. N., 2015. Feeding family and ancestors: Persistence of traditional Native American lifeways during the Mission Period in coastal Southern California. *Journal of Anthropological Archaeology* 37, 48–66.

Redzepi, R., 2018. Rene Radzepi's description of a menu item at Noma (posted on Facebook, Instagram, and Twitter). https://twitter.com/reneredzepinoma/status/974000935939837954; www.instagram.com/p/BgUIG4mgTW2/

Reents-Budet, D., 1998. Elite Maya pottery and artisans as social indicators. *Archaeological Papers of the American Anthropological Association* 8, 71–89.

Reinhart, K., 2015. Ritual feasting and empowerment at Yanshi Shangcheng. *Journal of Anthropological Archaeology* 39, 76–109.

Reinhard, K. J., Ambler, J. R., and Szuter, C. R., 2007. Hunter-gatherer use of small animal food resources: Coprolite evidence. *International Journal of Osteoarchaeology* 17, 416–428.

Reinhard, K. J., and Araujo, A., 2016. Parasitological analysis. In Metheny, K. B., and Beaudry, M., (eds.), *Archaeology of Food: An Encyclopedia*. Rowman & Littlefield, Lanham, MD, pp. 400–402.

Reinhard, K. J., Ferreira, L. F., Bouchet, F., Sianto, L., Dutra, J. M. F., Iniguez, A., Leles, D., Le Bailly, M., Fugassa, M., Pucu, E., and Araújo, A., 2013. Food, parasites, and epidemiological transitions: A broad perspective. *International Journal of Paleopathology* 3, 150–157.

Reitz, E. J., Ruff, B. L., and Zierden, M. A., 2006. Pigs in Charleston, South Carolina: Using specimen counts to consider status. *Historical Archaeology* 40, 102–124.

Reitz, E. J., and Wing, E. S., 2008. *Zooarchaeology*, 2nd ed. Cambridge University Press, New York.

Reynard, L. M., and Hedges, R. E. M., 2008. Stable hydrogen isotopes of bone collagen in palaeodietary and palaeoenvironmental reconstruction. *Journal of Archaeological Science* 35, 1934–1942.

Reynard, L. M., Pearson, J. A., Henderson, G. M., and Hedges, R. E. M., 2013. Calcium isotopes in juvenile milk-consumers. *Archaeometry* 55, 946–957.

Rice, P. M., 2015. *Pottery Analysis: A Sourcebook*, 2nd ed. University of Chicago Press.

Richards, M. P., Fuller, B. T., Sponheimer, M., Robinson, T., and Ayliffe, L., 2003. Sulphur isotopes in palaeodietary studies: A review and results from a controlled feeding experiment. *International Journal of Osteoarchaeology* 13, 37–45.

Rick, T. C., and Erlandson, J., (eds.), 2008. *Human Impacts on Ancient Marine Ecosystems: A Global Perspective*. University of California Press, Berkeley, CA.

Rick, T. C., and Lockwood, R., 2013. Integrating paleobiology, archeology, and history to inform biological conservation. *Conservation Biology* 27, 45–54.

Riehl, S., 2015. Archaeobotany. In Metheny, K. B., and Beaudry, M., (eds.), *Archaeology of Food: An Encyclopedia*. Rowman & Littlefield, New York, pp. 29–31.

Robb, J., 2007. *The Early Mediterranean Village*. Cambridge University Press, Cambridge.

Roberts, B. W., and Thornton, C., (eds.), 2014. *Archaeometallurgy in Global Perspective: Methods and Syntheses*. Springer, New York.

Roberts, P., Weston, S., Wild, B., Boston, C., Ditchfield, P., Shortland, A. J., and Pollard, A. M., 2012. The men of Nelson's navy: A comparative stable isotope dietary study of late 18th century and early 19th century servicemen from Royal Naval Hospital burial grounds at Plymouth and Gosport, England. *American Journal of Physical Anthropology* 148, 1–10.

Rodríguez-Alegría, E., 2005. Eating like an Indian: Negotiating social relations in the Spanish Colonies. *Current Anthropology* 46, 551–573.

Rodríguez-Alegría, E., 2012. From grinding corn to dishing out money: A long-term history of cooking in Zaltocan, Mexico. In Graff, S. R., and Rodríguez-Alegría, E., (eds.), *The Menial Art of Cooking: Archaeological Studies of Cooking and Food Preparation*. University Press of Colorado, Boulder, pp. 99–117.

Rofes, J., 2004. Prehispanic guinea pig sacrifices in southern Peru; The case of El Yaral. In O'Day, S. J., van Neer, W., and Ervynck, A., (eds.), *Behaviour Behind Bones: The Zooarchaeology of Religion, Ritual, Status, and Identity*. Oxbow, Oxford, pp. 95–100.

Roffet-Salque, M., Dunne, J., Altoft, D. T., Casanova, E., Cramp, L. J. E., Smyth, J., Whelton, H., and Evershed, R. P., 2017. From the inside out: Upscaling organic residue analyses of archaeological ceramics. *Journal of Archaeological Science: Reports* 16, 627–640.

Rogers, J., and Waldron, T., 2001. DISH and the monastic way of life. *International Journal of Osteoarchaeology* 11, 357–365.

Roselló Izquierdo, E., and Morales Muñiz, A., 1991. Calatrava la Vieja: Primer informe sobre la fauna de vertebrados recuperada en ele yacimiento almohade. Tercera parte: peces. *Boletín de Arqueología Medieval* 5, 113–133.

Rosenberg, D., Garfinkel, Y., and Klimscha, F., 2017. Large-scale storage and storage symbolism in the ancient Near East: A clay silo model from Tel Tsaf. *Antiquity* 91, 885–900.

Rowley-Conwy, P., 2018. Zooarchaeology and the elusive feast: From performance to aftermath. *World Archaeology* 50, 221–241.

Russell, K. W., 1988. *After Eden: Behavioral Ecology of Early Food Production in the Near East and North Africa*. British Archaeological Reports, International Series 391. Oxbow, Oxford.

Russell, J., 2009. For children today, table manners still trump talent. *The Guardian*, July 28, 2008.

Russell, N., 2012. *Social Zooarchaeology*. Cambridge University Press, New York.

Russell, N., and Bogaard, A., 2010. Subsistence actions at Çatalhöyük. In Steadman, S. R., and Ross, J. C., (eds.), *Agency and Identity in the Ancient Near East: New Paths Forward*. Equinox, London, pp. 63–79.

Russell, N., Martin, L., and Buitenhuis, H., 2005. Cattle domestication at Çatalhöyük revisited. *Current Anthropology* 46, S101–S108.

Ryan, P., 2014. Phytolith studies in archaeology. In Smith, C., (ed.), *Encyclopedia of Global Archaeology*. Springer, New York, pp. 5920–5931.

Sahlins, M., 1972. *Stone Age Economics*. Aldine de Gruyter, New York.

Sallaberger, W., 2015. Home-made bread, municipal mutton, royal wine: Establishing social relations during the preparation and consumption of food in religious festivals at Late Bronze Age Emar. In Pollock, S., (ed.), *Between Feasts and Daily Meals. Toward an Archaeology of Commensal Spaces*. Editions Topoi, Berlin, pp. 181–204.

Salque, M., Bogucki, P. I., Pyzel, J., Sobkowiak-Tabaka, I., Grygiel, R., Szmyt, M., and Evershed, R. P., 2013. Earliest evidence for cheese making in the sixth millennium BC in northern Europe. *Nature* 493, 522–525.

Samuel, D., 2010. Experimental grinding and ancient Egyptian flour production. In Ikram, S., and Dodson, A., (eds.), *Beyond the Horizon: Studies in Egyptian Art, Archaeology, and History in Honor of Barry J. Kemp*. American University in Cairo Press, Cairo, pp. 456–477.

Scarborough, V. L., and Valdez, F., 2014. The alternative economy: Resilience in the face of complexity from the Eastern Lowlands. *Archeological Papers of the American Anthropological Association* 24, 124–141.

Schiffer, M. B., 2017. *Archaeology's Footprints in the Modern World*. University of Utah Press, Salt Lake City.

Schmitt, D. N., and Lupo, K. D., 2008. Do faunal remains reflect socioeconomic status? An ethnoarchaeological study among Central African farmers in the northern Congo Basin. *Journal of Anthropological Archaeology* 27, 315–325.

Schulz, P., and Gust, S. M., 1983. Faunal remains and social status in 19th century Sacramento. *Historical Archaeology* 17, 44–53.

Scott, E. M., 1996. Who ate what? Archaeological food remains and cultural diversity. In Reitz, E., Newsom, L. A., and Scudder, S. J., (eds.), *Case Studies in Environmental Archaeology*. Plenum, New York, pp. 339–356.

Scott, E. M., 2001a. Food and social relations at Nina Plantation. *American Anthropologist* 103, 671–691.

Scott, E. M., 2001b. "An Indolent Slothfull Set of Vagabonds": Ethnicity and race in a colonial fur-trading community. In Orser, C. E., (ed.), *Race and the Archaeology of Identity*. University of Utah Press, Salt Lake City, pp. 14–35.

Scott, E. M., 2007. "Pigeon soup . . . and plover in pyramids": French foodways in New France and the Illinois Country. In Twiss, K. C., (ed.), *The Archaeology of Food and Identity*. Center for Archaeological Investigations, Southern Illinois University Carbondale, Occasional Paper no. 34. Center for Archaeological Investigations, Carbondale, IL, pp. 243–259.

Scott, J. C., 2017. *Against the Grain: A Deep History of the Earliest States*. Yale University Press, New Haven, CT.

Selbitschka, A., 2018. Sacrifice vs. sustenance: Food as a burial good in late pre-imperial and early imperial Chinese tombs and its relation to funerary rites. *Early China* 41, 179–243.

Seo, M., Oh, C. S., Chai, J.-Y., Jeong, M. S., Hong, S. W., Seo, Y.-M., and Shin, D. H., 2014. The changing pattern of parasitic infection among Korean populations by paleoparasitological study of Joseon Dynasty mummies. *Journal of Parasitology* 100, 147–150.

Shanahan, M., 2015. Food and capitalism. In Metheny, K. B., and Beaudry, M., (eds.), *Archaeology of Food: An Encyclopedia*. Rowman & Littlefield, Lanham, MD, pp. 175–180.

Shea, J. J., 2013. *Stone Tools in the Paleolithic and Neolithic Near East*. Cambridge University Press, New York.

Sheets, P. D., 2017. Abundance in the ancient Maya village of Ceren? In Smith, M. L., (ed.), *Abundance: The Archaeology of Plenitude*. University Press of Colorado, Boulder, pp. 95–116.

Shillito, L.-M., 2013. Grains of truth or transparent blindfolds? A review of current debates in archaeological phytolith analysis. *Vegetation History and Archaeobotany* 22, 71–82.

Sianto, L., Teixeira-Santos, I., Chame, M., Chaves, S. M., Souza, S. M., Ferreira, L. F., Reinhard, K., and Araujo, A., 2012. Eating lizards: A millenary habit evidenced by paleoparasitology. *BMC Research Notes* 5, 586.

Simoons, F. J., and Simoons, E. S., 1968. *A Ceremonial Ox of India: The Mithan in Nature, Culture, and History*. University of Wisconsin Press, Madison.

Skibo, J., 1999. *Ants for Breakfast: Archaeological Adventures among the Kalinga*. University of Utah Press, Salt Lake City.

Skibo, J. M., 1992. *Pottery Function: A Use-Alteration Perspective*. Plenum, New York.

Skibo, J. M., 2013. *Understanding Pottery Function*. Springer, New York.

Smith, F., 2008. *The Archaeology of Alcohol and Drinking*. University Press of Florida, Gainesville, FL.

Smith, M. L., 2015. Feasts and their failures. *Journal of Archaeological Method and Theory* 22, 1215–1237.

Smith, M. L., 2017. The archaeology of abundance. In Smith, M. L., (ed.), *Abundance: The Archaeology of Plenitude*. University Press of Colorado, Boulder, pp. 1–22.

Smith, S. T., 2003. Pharaohs, feasts, and foreigners: Cooking, foodways, and agency on ancient Egypt's southern frontier. In Bray, T., (ed.), *The Archaeology and Politics of Food and Feasting in Early States and Empires*. Kluwer Academic/Plenum, New York, pp. 39–64.

Snead, J. E., 2016. Burning the corn: Subsistence and destruction in Ancestral Pueblo conflict. In VanDerwarker, A. M., and Wilson, G. D., (eds.), *The Archaeology of Food and Warfare: Food Insecurity in Prehistory*. Springer, New York, pp. 133–148.

Snoeck, C., Pouncett, J., Claeys, P., Goderis, S., Mattielli, N., Parker Pearson, M., Willis, C., Zazzo, A., Lee-Thorp, J. A., and Schulting, R. J., 2018. Strontium isotope analysis on cremated human remains from Stonehenge support links with west Wales. *Scientific Reports* 8, 10790.

Sobolik, K., 2000. Dietary reconstruction as seen in coprolites. In Kiple, K. F., and Ornelas, K. C., (eds.), *The Cambridge World History of Food*. Cambridge University Press, Cambridge, pp. 44–51.

Somerville, A. D., Martin, M. A., Hayes, L. P., Hayward, D., Walker, P. L., and Schoeninger, M. J., 2017. Exploring patterns and pathways of dietary change: Preferred foods, oral health, and stable isotope analysis of hair from the Dani of Mulia, Papua, Indonesia. *Current Anthropology* 58, 31–56.

Spataro, M., and Villing, A., (eds.), 2015. *Ceramics, Cuisine and Culture: The Archaeology and Science of Kitchen Pottery in the Ancient Mediterranean World*. Oxbow, Oxford.

Spielmann, K. A., 2002. Feasting, craft specialization, and the ritual mode of production in small-scale societies. *American Anthropologist* 104, 195–207.

Stahl, A. B., 2014. Intersections of craft and cuisine: Implications for what and how we study. *African Archaeological Review* 31, 383–393.

Staller, J. E., 2010. Ethnohistoric sources on foodways, feasts, and festivals in Mesoamerica. In Staller, J. E., and Carrasco, M. D., (eds.), *Pre-Columbian Foodways: Interdisciplinary Approaches to Food, Culture, and Markets in Mesoamerica*. Springer, New York, pp. 23–69.

Stallibrass, S., and Thomas, R., (eds.), 2008a. *Feeding the Roman Army: The Archaeology of Production and Supply in NW Europe*. Oxbow, Oxford.

Stallibrass, S., and Thomas, R., 2008b. Food for thought: What's next on the menu? In Stallibrass, S., and Thomas, R., (eds.), *Feeding the Roman Army: The Archaeology of Production and Supply in NW Europe*. Oxbow, Oxford, pp. 146–169.

Stark, R. J., 2014. A proposed framework for the study of paleopathological cases of subadult scurvy. *International Journal of Paleopathology* 5, 18–26.

Stein, G., 2012. Food preparation, social context, and ethnicity in a prehistoric Mesopotamian colony. In Graff, S. R., and Rodríguez-Alegría, E., (eds.), *The Menial Art of Cooking: Archaeological Studies of Cooking and Food Preparation*. University Press of Colorado, Boulder, CO, pp. 47–63.

Stevens, N. E., and McElreath, R., 2015. When are two tools better than one? Mortars, millingslabs, and the California acorn economy. *Journal of Anthropological Archaeology* 37, 100–111.

Stiner, M. C., and Munro, N. D., 2002. Approaches to prehistoric diet breadth, demography, and prey ranking systems in time and space. *Journal of Archaeological Method and Theory* 9, 175–208.

Storey, A., 2015. Pacific Oceanic exchange. In Metheny, K. B., and Beaudry, M., (eds.), *Archaeology of Food: An Encyclopedia*. Rowman & Littlefield, Lanham, MD, pp. 365–369.

Storey, A. A., Ramírez, J. M., Quiroz, D., Burley, D. V., Addison, D. J., Walter, R., Anderson, A. J., Hunt, T. L., Athens, J. S., Huynen, L., and Matisoo-Smith, E. A., 2007. Radiocarbon and DNA evidence for a pre-Columbian introduction of Polynesian chickens to Chile. *Proceedings of the National Academy of Sciences of the United States of America* 104, 10335–10339.

Styring, A. K., Ater, M., Hmimsa, Y., Fraser, R., Miller, H., Neef, R., Pearson, J. A., and Bogaard, A., 2016. Disentangling the effect of farming practice from aridity on crop stable isotope values: A present-day model from Morocco and its application to early farming sites in the eastern Mediterranean. *The Anthropocene Review* 3, 2–22.

Styring, A. K., Charles, M., Fantone, F., Hald, M. M., McMahon, A., Meadow, R. H., Nicholls, G. K., Patel, A. K., Pitre, M. C., Smith, A., Sołtysiak, A., Stein, G., Weber, J. A., Weiss, H., and Bogaard, A., 2017. Isotope evidence for agricultural extensification reveals how the world's first cities were fed. *Nature Plants* 3, 17076. doi: 10.1038/nplants.2017.76.

Sunseri, C. K., 2014. Pelts and provisions: Faunal remains and the emergence of social inequality in Central Coastal California. In Arbuckle, B. S., and McCarty, S. A., (eds.), *Animals and Inequality in the Ancient World*. University Press of Colorado, Boulder, CO, pp. 167–186.

Sunseri, C. K., 2015. Food politics of alliance in a California frontier Chinatown. *International Journal of Historical Archaeology* 19, 416–431.

Sutton, A. F., and Hammond, R. W., 1984. *The Coronation of Richard III: The Extant Documents*. St. Martin's Press, New York.

Sutton, D. E., 2001. *Remembrance of Repasts: An Anthropology of Food and Memory*. Berg, New York.

Sutton, D. E., 2010. Food and the senses. *Annual Review of Anthropology* 39, 209–223.

Sutton, D. E., 2011. Memory as a sense: A gustemelogical approach. *Food, Culture and Society* 14, 468–475.

Sutton, M., 1995. Archaeological aspects of insect use. *Journal of Archaeological Method and Theory* 2, 253–298.

Swenson, E., 2015. The archaeology of ritual. *Annual Review of Anthropology* 44, 329–345.

Sykes, N., 2005. Hunting for the Anglo-Normans: zooarchaeological evidence for medieval identity. In Pluskowski, A., (ed.), *Just Skin and Bones? New Perspectives on Animal–Human Relations in the Historic Past*. BAR British Series 1410. BAR Publishing, Oxford, pp. 73–80.

Sykes, N. J., 2006. The impact of the Normans on hunting practices in England. In Woolgar, C., Serjeantson, D., and Waldron, T., (eds.), *Food in Medieval England: History and Archaeology*. Oxford University Press, Oxford, pp. 162–175.

Sykes, N. J., 2007. Taking sides: The social life of venison in medieval England. In Pluskowski, A., (ed.), *Breaking and Shaping Beastly Bodies: Animals as Material Culture in the Middle Ages*. Oxbow, Oxford, pp. 149–160.

Sykes, N., 2014a. *Beastly Questions: Animal Answers to Archaeological Issues.* Bloomsbury Academic, New York.

Sykes, N. J., 2014b. The rhetoric of meat apportionment: Evidence for exclusion, inclusion, and social position in Medieval England. In Arbuckle, B. S., and McCarty, S. A., (eds.), *Animals and Inequality in the Ancient World.* University Press of Colorado, Boulder, pp. 353–373.

Sykes, N., 2017. Fair game: Exploring the dynamics, perception, and environmental impact of "surplus" wild foods in England 10kya–present. *World Archaeology* 49, 61–72.

Sykes, N., Ayton, G., Bowen, F., Baker, K., Baker, P., Carden, R. F., Dicken, C., Evans, J., Hoelzel, A. R., Higham, T. F. G., Jones, R., Lamb, A., Liddiard, R., Madgwick, R., Miller, H., Rainsford, C., Sawyer, P., Thomas, R., Ward, C., and Worley, F., 2016. Wild to domestic and back again: The dynamics of fallow deer management in medieval England (c. 11th–16th century AD). *STAR: Science and Technology of Archaeological Research* 2, 113–126.

Sykes, N., and Curl, J., 2010. The rabbit. In Sykes, N., (ed.), *Extinctions and Invasions: A Social History of British Fauna.* Oxbow, Oxford, pp. 116–126.

Tacail, T., Thivichon-Prince, B., Martin, J. E., Charles, C., Viriot, L., and Balter, V., 2017. Assessing human weaning practices with calcium isotopes in tooth enamel. *Proceedings of the National Academy of Sciences* 114, 6268–6273.

Tate, C. E., 2010. The axolotl as food and symbol in the Basin of Mexico, from 1200 BC to today. In Staller, J. E., and Carrasco, M. D., (eds.), *Pre-Columbian Foodways: Interdisciplinary Approaches to Food, Culture, and Markets in Mesoamerica.* Springer, New York, pp. 511–533.

Taylor, T., 2011. Death. In Insoll, T., (ed.), *The Oxford Handbook of the Archaeology of Ritual and Religion.* Oxford University Press, New York, pp. 89–104.

Thomas, G., McDonnell, G., Merkel, J., and Marshall, P., 2016. Technology, ritual, and Anglo-Saxon agriculture: The biography of a plough coulter from Lyminge, Kent. *Antiquity* 90, 742–758.

Thomas, R., 2007a. Chasing the ideal? Ritualism, pragmatism and the Later Medieval hunt. In Pluskowski, A., (ed.), *Breaking and Shaping Beastly Bodies: Animals as Material Culture in the Middle Ages.* Oxbow, Oxford, pp. 125–148.

Thomas, R., 2007b. They were what they ate: Maintaining social boundaries through the consumption of food in Medieval England. In Twiss, K. C., (ed.), *The Archaeology of Food and Identity Center for Archaeological Investigations.* Southern Illinois University Carbondale Occasional Paper no 34. Southern Illinois University, Carbondale, pp. 130–151.

Thompson, V. D., Marquardt, W. H., Cherkinsky, A., Roberts Thompson, A. D., Walker, K. J., Newsom, L. A., and Savarese, M., 2016. From shell midden to midden-mound: The geoarchaeology of Mound Key, an anthropogenic island in southwest Florida, USA. *PLOS ONE* 11, e0154611.

Thomson, V. A., Lebrasseur, O., Austin, J. J., Hunt, T. L., Burney, D. A., Denham, T., Rawlence, N. J., Wood, J. R., Gongora, J., Girdland Flink, L., Linderholm, A., Dobney, K., Larson, G., and Cooper, A., 2014. Using ancient DNA to study the origins and dispersal of ancestral Polynesian chickens across the Pacific. *Proceedings of the National Academy of Sciences* 111, 4826–4831.

Tremayne, A. H., and Winterhalder, B., 2017. Large mammal biomass predicts the changing distribution of hunter-gatherer settlements in mid-late Holocene Alaska. *Journal of Anthropological Archaeology* 45, 81–97.

Turchin, P., 2009. A theory for formation of large empires. *Journal of Global History* 4, 191–217.

Turkon, P., 2004. Food and status in the prehispanic Malpaso Valley, Zacatecas, Mexico. *Journal of Anthropological Archaeology* 23, 225–251.

Turkon, P., 2007. Variation in food preparation and status in Mesoamerica. In Twiss, K. C., (ed.), *The Archaeology of Food and Identity*. Center for Archaeological Investigations, Southern Illinois University Carbondale, Occasional Paper no. 34. Center for Archaeological Investigations, Carbondale, IL.

Tuross, N., Reynard, L. M., Harvey, E., Coppa, A., and McCormick, M., 2017. Human skeletal development and feeding behavior: The impact on oxygen isotopes. *Archaeological and Anthropological Sciences* 9, 1453–1459.

Twiss, K. C., 2007. Home is where the hearth is: Food and identity in the Neolithic Levant. In Twiss, K. C., (ed.), *The Archaeology of Food and Identity*. Center for Archaeological Investigations, Southern Illinois University Carbondale Occasional Paper no 34. Center for Archaeological Investigations, Carbondale, IL, pp. 50–68.

Twiss, K. C., 2008. Transformations in an early agricultural society: Feasting in the southern Levantine Pre-Pottery Neolithic. *Journal of Anthropological Archaeology* 27, 418–442.

Twiss, K. C., 2012. The complexities of home cooking: Public feasts and private meals inside the Çatalhöyük house. *eTopoi*. Special vol 2. http://journal.topoi.org/index.php/etopoi/article/view/23

Twiss, K. C., 2015. Methodological and definitional issues in the archaeology of food. In Kerner, S., Chou, C., and Warmind, M., (eds.), *Commensality: From Everyday Food to Feast*. Bloomsbury Academic, New York, pp. 89–98.

Twiss, K. C., and Bogaard, A., 2017. Coping with abundance: The challenges of a good thing. In Smith, M. L., (ed.), *Abundance: The Archaeology of Plenitude*. University Press of Colorado, Boulder, pp. 165–179.

United Nations Office on Drugs and Crime. 2011. Transnational Organized Crime in the Fishing Industry. Vienna. www.unodc.org/documents/human-trafficking/Issue_Paper_-_TOC_in_the_Fishing_Industry.pdf.

Ur, J. A., and Colantoni, C., 2010. The cycle of production, preparation, and consumption in a northern Mesopotamian city. In Klarich, E. A., (ed.), *Inside Ancient Kitchens: New Directions in the Study of Daily Meals and Feasts*. University Press of Colorado, Boulder, pp. 55–81.

US Department of Health and Human Services and US Department of Agriculture. *2015–2020 Dietary Guidelines for Americans* [Internet]. 8th ed. 2015 Dec. http://health.gov/dietaryguidelines/2015/

Valamoti, S. M., 2017. Culinary landscapes and identity in prehistoric Greece: An archaeobotanical exploration. In Gori, M., and Ivanova, M., (eds.), *Balkan Dialogues: Negotiating Identity between Prehistory and the Present*. Routledge, New York, pp. 169–194.

Valamoti, S., and Charles, M., 2005. Distinguishing food from fodder through the study of charred plant remains: An experimental approach to dung-derived chaff. *Vegetation History and Archaeobotany* 14, 528–533.

Valamoti, S., Moniaki, A., and Karathanou, A., 2011. An investigation of processing and consumption of pulses among prehistoric societies: Archaeobotanical, experimental and ethnographic evidence from Greece. *Vegetation History and Archaeobotany* 20, 381–396.

Valenzuela-Lamas, S., Valenzuela-Suau, L., Saula, O., Colet, A., Mercadal, O., Subiranas, C., and Nadal, J., 2014. *Shechita* and *Kashrut*: Identifying Jewish populations through zooarchaeology and taphonomy. Two examples from Medieval Catalonia (North-Eastern Spain). *Quaternary International* 330, 109–117.

van der Sluis, L. G., Hollund, H. I., Kars, H., Sandvik, P. U., and Denham, S. D., 2016. A palaeodietary investigation of a multi-period churchyard in Stavanger, Norway, using stable isotope analysis (C, N, H, S) on bone collagen. *Journal of Archaeological Science: Reports* 9, 120–133.

van der Veen, M., (ed.), 2003a. *Luxury foods. World Archaeology* 34(3).

van der Veen, M., 2003b. When is food a luxury? *World Archaeology* 34, 405–427.

van der Veen, M., 2007. Food as an instrument of social change: Feasting in Iron Age and Early Roman southern Britain. In Twiss, K. C., (ed.), *The Archaeology of Food and Identity*. Center for Archaeological Investigations, Southern Illinois University, Carbondale, IL, pp. 112–129.

van der Veen, M., 2008. Food as embodied material culture; diversity and change in plant food consumption in Roman Britain. *Journal of Roman Archaeology* 21, 83–110.

van der Veen, M., 2014. The materiality of plants: plant–people entanglements. *World Archaeology* 46, 799–812.

van der Veen, M., and Livarda, A., 2008. New food plants in Roman Britain; Dispersal and social access. *Environmental Archaeology* 13, 11–36.

van der Werff, J. H., 2003. The third and second lives of amphoras in Alphen aan den Rijn, The Netherlands. *Journal of Roman Pottery Studies* 10, 109–116.

van Gijn, A. L., 2014. Science and interpretation in microwear studies. *Journal of Archaeological Science* 48, 166–169.

van Huis, A., and Oonincx, D. G. A. B., 2017. The environmental sustainability of insects as food and feed. A review. *Agronomy for Sustainable Development* 37, 43.

Van Keuren, S., 2004. Crafting feasts in the prehispanic Southwest. In Mills, B. J., (ed.), *Identity, Feasting, and the Archaeology of the Greater Southwest*. University Press of Colorado, Boulder, pp. 192–209.

van Neer, W., and Ervynck, A., 2004. Remains of traded fish in archaeological sites: Indicators of status, or bulk food? In O'Day, S. J., van Neer, W., and Ervynck, A., (eds.), *Behaviour Behind Bones: The Zooarchaeology of Religion, Ritual, Status, and Identity*. Oxbow Books, Oxford, pp. 203–214.

VanDerwarker, A. M., Bardolph, D. N., Hoppa, K. M., Thakar, H. B., Martin, L. S., Jaqua, A. L., Biwer, M. E., and Gill, K. M., 2016. New World paleoethnobotany in the New Millennium (2000–2013). *Journal of Archaeological Research* 24, 125–177.

VanDerwarker, A., Scarry, C. M., and Eastman, 2007. Menus for families and feasts: Household and community consumption of plants at Upper Saratown, North Carolina. In Twiss, K. C., (ed.), *The Archaeology of Food and Identity*.

Center for Archaeological Investigations, Southern Illinois University Carbondale, Occasional Paper no. 34. Center for Archaeological Investigations, Carbondale, IL.

VanDerwarker, A. M., and Wilson, G. D., 2016. War, food, and structural violence in the Mississippian Central Illinois Valley. In VanDerwarker, A. M., and Wilson, G. D., (eds.), *The Archaeology of Food and Warfare*. Springer, New York, pp. 75–105.

Vanpoucke, S., Mainland, I., De Cupere, B., and Waelkens, M., 2009. Dental microwear study of pigs from the classical site of Sagalassos (SW Turkey) as an aid for the reconstruction of husbandry practices in ancient times. *Environmental Archaeology* 14, 137–154.

Verhoeven, M., 2011. The many dimensions of ritual. In Insoll, T., (ed.), *The Oxford Handbook of the Archaeology of Ritual and Religion*. Oxford University Press, Oxford, pp. 115–132.

Verlaan, J. J., Oner, F. C., and Maat, G. J. R., 2007. Diffuse idiopathic skeletal hyperostosis in ancient clergymen. *European Spine Journal* 16, 1129–1135.

Vigne, J. D., Daujat, J., and Monchot, H., 2016. First introduction and early exploitation of the Persian fallow deer on Cyprus (8,000–6,000 cal. BC). *International Journal of Osteoarchaeology*, 26, 853–866.

Vigne, J.-D., Zazzo, A., Cucchi, T., Carrère, I., Briois, F., and Guilaine, J., 2014. The transportation of mammals to Cyprus sheds light on early voyaging and boats in the Mediterranean Sea. *Eurasian Prehistory* 10, 157–176.

Vika, E., and Theodoropoulou, T., 2012. Re-investigating fish consumption in Greek antiquity: Results from $\delta^{13}C$ and $\delta^{15}N$ analysis from fish bone collagen. *Journal of Archaeological Science* 39, 1618–1627.

Villing, A., and Spataro, M., 2015. Investigating ceramics, cuisine, and culture – past, present and future. In Spataro, M., and Villing, A., (eds.), *Ceramics, Cuisine, and Culture: The Archaeology and Science of Kitchen Pottery in the Ancient Mediterranean World*. Oxbow, Oxford, pp. 1–25.

Viner, S., Evans, J., Albarella, U., and Parker Pearson, M., 2010. Cattle mobility in prehistoric Britain: Strontium isotope analysis of cattle teeth from Durrington Walls (Wiltshire, Britain). *Journal of Archaeological Science* 37, 2812–2820.

Voss, B. L., 2005. From *Casta* to *Californio*: Social identity and the archaeology of culture contact. *American Anthropologist* 107, 461–474.

Voss, B. L., 2008a. *The Archaeology of Ethnogenesis: Race and Sexuality in Colonial San Francisco*. University of California Press, Berkeley.

Voss, B. L., 2008b. Gender, race, and labor in the archaeology of the Spanish Colonial Americas. *Current Anthropology* 49, 861–893.

Voss, B. L., Kennedy, J. R., Tan, J., and Ng, L. W., 2018. The archaeology of home: *Qiaoxiang* and nonstate actors in the archaeology of the Chinese diaspora. *American Antiquity* 83, 407–426.

Waldron, T., 2006. Nutrition and the skeleton. In Woolgar, C., Serjeantson, D., and Waldron, T., (eds.), *Food in Medieval England: History and Archaeology*. Oxbow, Oxford, pp. 254–266.

Walker, A., Zimmerman, M. R., and Leakey, R. E. F., 1982. A possible case of hypervitaminosis A in *Homo erectus*. *Nature* 296, 248.

Walker, P. L., Bathurst, R. R., Richman, R., Gjerdrum, T., and Andrushko, V. A., 2009. The causes of porotic hyperostosis and cribra orbitalia: A reappraisal of the iron-deficiency-anemia hypothesis. *American Journal of Physical Anthropology* 139, 109–125.

Wallace, B., 2009. L'Anse aux Meadows, Leif Eriksson's home in Vinland. *Journal of the North Atlantic* 2, 114–125.

Wallis, N. J., and Blessing, M. E., 2015. Ritualized deposition and feasting pits: Bundling of animal remains in Mississippi Period Florida. *Cambridge Archaeological Journal* 25, 79–98.

Ward, C., 2003. Pomegranates in eastern Mediterranean contexts during the Late Bronze Age. *World Archaeology* 34, 529–541.

Warinner, C., Hendy, J., Speller, C., Cappellini, E., Fischer, R., Trachsel, C., Arneborg, J., Lynnerup, N., Craig, O. E., Swallow, D. M., Fotakis, A., Christensen, R. J., Olsen, J. V., Liebert, A., Montalva, N., Fiddyment, S., Charlton, S., Mackie, M., Canci, A., Bouwman, A., Rühli, F., Gilbert, M. T. P., and Collins, M. J., 2014. Direct evidence of milk consumption from ancient human dental calculus. *Scientific Reports* 4, 7104.

Warinner, C., Speller, C., Collins, M. J., and Lewis, C. M., Jr., 2015. Ancient human microbiomes. *Journal of Human Evolution* 79, 125–136.

Warner, M., 2015. *Eating in the Side Room: Food, Archaeology, and African American Identity*. University Press of Florida, Gainesville, FL.

Washburn, S., and Lancaster, C. S., 1968. The evolution of hunting. In Lee, R. B., and DeVore, I., (eds.), *Man the Hunter*. Aldine, Chicago, pp. 293–303.

Watson, J. L., 2000. China's Big Mac attack. *Foreign Affairs* 79, 120–134.

Weismantel, M., 1988. *Food, Gender, and Poverty in the Ecuadorian Andes*. University of Pennsylvania Press, Philadelphia.

Weiss, H., Courty, M.-A., Wetterstrom, W., Guichard, F., Senior, L., Meadow, R., and Curnow, A., 1993. The genesis and collapse of third millennium North Mesopotamian civilization. *Science* 261, 995–1004.

Wells, P., 2018. The new Noma: Frequently asked questions. *The New York Times*, April 24 2008.

Wesson, C. B., 1999. Chiefly power and food storage in southeastern North America. *World Archaeology* 31, 145–164.

Whitaker, A. R., and Hildebrandt, W. R., 2011. Why were Northern fur seals spared in Northern California? A cultural and archaeological explanation. In Braje, T. J., and Rick, T. C., (eds.), *Human Impacts on Seals, Sea Lions, and Otters: Integrating Archaeology and Ecology in the Northeast Pacific*. University of California Press, Berkeley, pp. 197–219.

White, C. D., 2005. Gendered food behaviour among the Maya. *Journal of Social Archaeology* 5, 356–382.

White, C. D., Nelson, A. J., Longstaffe, F. J., Grupe, G., and Jung, A., 2009. Landscape bioarchaeology at Pacatnamu, Peru: Inferring mobility from $\delta^{13}C$ and $\delta^{15}N$ values of hair. *Journal of Archaeological Science* 36, 1527–1537.

White, C. D., Pohl, M. E. D., Schwarcz, H. P., and Longstaffe, F. J., 2001. Isotopic evidence for Maya patterns of deer and dog use at Preclassic Colha. *Journal of Archaeological Science* 28, 89–107.

Wiessner, P., 2001. Of feasting and value: Enga feasts in a historical perspective (Papua New Guinea). In Dietler, M., and Hayden, B., (eds.), *Feasts: Archaeological and Ethnographic Perspectives on Food, Politics, and Power.* Smithsonian Institution Press, Washington, DC, pp. 115–143.

Wiessner, P., and Schiefenhovel, W., (eds.), 1996. *Food and the Status Quest: An Interdisciplinary Perspective.* Berghahn, Providence, RI.

Williams, E., 2010. Salt production and trade in ancient Mesoamerica. In Staller, J. E., and Carrasco, M. D., (eds.), *Pre-Columbian Foodways: Interdisciplinary Approaches to Food, Culture, and Markets in Mesoamerica.* Springer, New York, pp. 175–190.

Wills, W. H., and Crown, P. L., 2004. Commensal politics in the prehispanic Southwest: An introductory review. In Mills, B. J., (ed.), *Identity, Feasting, and the Archaeology of the Greater Southwest.* University Press of Colorado, Boulder, pp. 153–172.

Wilson, D. C., and Rathje, W. L., 2001. Garbage and the modern American feast. In Dietler, M., and Hayden, B., (eds.), *Feasts: Archaeological and Ethnographic Perspectives on Food, Politics, and Power.* Smithsonian Institution Press, Washington, DC, pp. 404–421.

Wilson, G. D., and VanDerwarker, A. M., 2016. Toward an archaeology of food and warfare. In VanDerwarker, A. M., and Wilson, G. D., (eds.), *The Archaeology of Food and Warfare: Food Insecurity in Prehistory.* Springer, New York, pp. 1–12.

Wing, E. S., 1978. Use of dogs for food: An adaptation to the coastal environment. In Stark, B. L., and Voorhies, B., (eds.), *Prehistoric Coastal Adaptations: The Economy and Ecology of Maritime Middle America.* Academic Press, New York, pp. 29–41.

Wing, E. S., and Brown, A. B., 1979. *Paleonutrition: Method and Theory in Prehistoric Foodways.* Academic Press, New York.

Winter, I. J., 2007. Representing abundance: The visual dimension of the agrarian state. In Stone, E. C., (ed.), *Settlement and Society: Essays Dedicated to Robert McCormick Adams.* Cotsen Institute of Archaeology, Los Angeles, pp. 117–138.

Winterhalder, B., Puleston, C., and Ross, C., 2015. Production risk, inter-annual food storage by households and population-level consequences in seasonal prehistoric agrarian societies. *Environmental Archaeology* 20, 337–348.

Wiseman, D. J., 1952. A new stela of Aššur-naṣir-pal II. *Iraq* 14, 24–44.

Wolverton, S., and Lyman, R. L., (eds.), 2012. *Conservation Biology and Applied Zooarchaeology.* University of Arizona Press, Tucson.

Wright, C. C., 2014. *Calcium Isotopes in Sheep Dental Enamel: A New Approach to Studying Weaning and Dairying in the Archaeological Record.* Ph.D. thesis, Oxford University, Oxford.

Wright, E., Viner-Daniels, S., Parker Pearson, M., and Albarella, U., 2014. Age and season of pig slaughter at Late Neolithic Durrington Walls (Wiltshire, UK) as detected through a new system for recording tooth wear. *Journal of Archaeological Science* 52, 497–514.

Wright, J. C., 2004. A survey of evidence for feasting in Mycenaean society. In Wright, J. C. (ed.), *The Mycenaean Feast.* American School of Classical Studies at Athens, Princeton, NJ, pp. 13–58.

Wright, K. I., 2000. The social origins of cooking and dining in early villages of Western Asia. *Proceedings of the Prehistoric Society* 2, 89–122.

Zedeño, M. N., 2017. Rethinking the impact of abundance on the rhythm of bison hunter societies. In Smith, M. L., (ed.), *Abundance: The Archaeology of Plenitude*. University Press of Colorado, Boulder, pp. 23–44.

Zeder, M. A., 1991. *Feeding Cities: Specialized Animal Economy in the Ancient Near East*. Smithsonian Institution Press, Washington, DC.

Zeder, M. A., 1998. Pigs and emergent complexity in the ancient Near East. In Nelson, S., (ed.), *Ancestors for the Pigs: Pigs in Prehistory*. MASCA Research Papers in Science and Archaeology 15. University of Pennsylvania Museum of Archaeology and Anthropology, Philadelphia, pp. 109–122.

Zeder, M. A., 2016. Domestication as a model system for niche construction theory. *Evolutionary Ecology* 30, 325–348.

Zeder, M. A., Bar-Oz, G., Rufolo, S. J., and Hole, F., 2013. New perspectives on the use of kites in mass-kills of Levantine gazelle: A view from northeastern Syria. *Quaternary International* 297, 110–125.

Zimring, C. A., 2015. The happiest of finds: William L. Rathje's influence on the field of discard studies. *Ethnoarchaeology* 7, 173–178.

Zimring, C. A., and Rathje, W. L., (eds.), 2012. *Encyclopedia of Consumption and Waste: The Social Science of Garbage*. SAGE, Los Angeles.

Zori, D., Byock, J., Erlendsson, E., Martin, S., Wake, T., and Edwards, K. J., 2013. Feasting in Viking Age Iceland: Sustaining a chiefly political economy in a marginal environment. *Antiquity* 87, 150–165.

Index